ROUTLEDGE LIBRARY EDITIONS:
THE LABOUR MOVEMENT

Volume 24

LIBERALISM AND THE RISE OF LABOUR 1890–1918

LIBERALISM AND THE RISE OF LABOUR 1890–1918

KEITH LAYBOURN AND
JACK REYNOLDS

LONDON AND NEW YORK

First published in 1984 by Croom Helm Ltd

This edition first published in 2019
by Routledge
2 Park Square, Milton Park, Abingdon, Oxon OX14 4RN

and by Routledge
711 Third Avenue, New York, NY 10017

Routledge is an imprint of the Taylor & Francis Group, an informa business

© 1984 K. Laybourn and J. Reynolds

All rights reserved. No part of this book may be reprinted or reproduced or utilised in any form or by any electronic, mechanical, or other means, now known or hereafter invented, including photocopying and recording, or in any information storage or retrieval system, without permission in writing from the publishers.

Trademark notice: Product or corporate names may be trademarks or registered trademarks, and are used only for identification and explanation without intent to infringe.

British Library Cataloguing in Publication Data
A catalogue record for this book is available from the British Library

ISBN: 978-1-138-32435-0 (Set)
ISBN: 978-0-429-43443-3 (Set) (ebk)
ISBN: 978-1-138-34070-1 (Volume 24) (hbk)
ISBN: 978-1-138-34073-2 (Volume 24) (pbk)
ISBN: 978-0-429-44050-2 (Volume 24) (ebk)

Publisher's Note
The publisher has gone to great lengths to ensure the quality of this reprint but points out that some imperfections in the original copies may be apparent.

Disclaimer
The publisher has made every effort to trace copyright holders and would welcome correspondence from those they have been unable to trace.

Liberalism and the Rise of Labour 1890-1918

KEITH LAYBOURN & JACK REYNOLDS

CROOM HELM
London & Sydney

ST. MARTIN'S PRESS
New York

©1984 K. Laybourn and J. Reynolds
Croom Helm Ltd, Provident House, Burrell Row,
Beckenham, Kent BR3 1AT
Croom Helm Australia Pty Ltd, First Floor, 139 King Street,
Sydney, NSW 2001, Australia

British Library Cataloguing in Publication Data

Laybourn, Keith
   Liberalism & the rise of Labour 1890-1918.
   1. Labour Party – Great Britain – History
   2. West Yorkshire – Politics and government
   I. Title   II. Reynolds, Jack
   324.24107'09428'1   JN1129.L3
   ISBN 0-7099-1651-5

All rights reserved, For information write:
St. Martin's Press, Inc., 175 Fifth Avenue, New York, NY 10010
First Published in the United States of America in 1984

Library of Congress Card Catalog Number: 83-40700
ISBN 0-312-48342-2

Printed and bound in Great Britain

CONTENTS

List of Tables and Figures
Dedication
Preface
Acknowledgements
Abbreviations

1. THE RISE OF LABOUR AND THE DECLINE OF LIBERALISM: THE GENERAL PROBLEM AND WEST YORKSHIRE   1

2. THE ORIGINS OF SOCIALISM AND INDEPENDENT LABOUR   15

3. TRADE UNIONS AND THE INDEPENDENT LABOUR PARTY: THE GENESIS OF THE ILP IN WEST YORKSHIRE   40

4. LIBERAL RESPONSES AND LABOUR DIFFICULTIES IN THE 1890s   76

5. LABOUR RESURGENCE 1900-6   103

6. LIBERAL DECLINE AND LABOUR GROWTH 1906-14   142

7. THE FIRST WORLD WAR   178

8. CONCLUSION   203

Epilogue   207

Bibliography   211

Index   218

TABLES AND FIGURES

Figures

1.1　Map of the West Yorkshire Constituencies
　　　1885-1918　　　　　　　　　　　　　　　　　　　5

Tables

2.1　The Membership of Engineering Unions in
　　　Yorkshire between the 1860s and the
　　　1890s　　　　　　　　　　　　　　　　　　　　 26
3.1　Labour Unions/ILP branches in West
　　　Yorkshire, 1891-5　　　　　　　　　　　　　 43
3.2　Trades Councils in the West Yorkshire
　　　Textile District up to 1895　　　　　　　　 45
3.3　The Membership of the West Yorkshire ILP
　　　organisations in the 1890s　　　　　　　　 62
3.4　The Municipal Successes of the ILP in
　　　Four West Yorkshire textile towns,
　　　1891-1900　　　　　　　　　　　　　　　　　　65
3.5　The Number of ILP Representatives in
　　　West Yorkshire, 1891-1900　　　　　　　　　 65
3.6　West Yorkshire Parliamentary Contests
　　　fought by the ILP, 1892-5　　　　　　　　　 69
4.1　The Parliamentary Representatives of
　　　West Yorkshire, 1891-1900　　　　　　　　　 77
4.2　West Yorkshire Parliamentary Contests
　　　fought by the ILP, 1892-5　　　　　　　　　 77
5.1　West Yorkshire Trades Council affili-
　　　ated to the Labour Representation
　　　Committee　　　　　　　　　　　　　　　　　106
5.2　Local Labour Representation Committee
　　　in West Yorkshire　　　　　　　　　　　　　107
5.3　The Number of Votes and the Proportion
　　　of Votes received by the leading pol-
　　　itical parties of West Yorkshire at

Tables and Figures

	general elections, 1885-1910	108
5.4	The Number of Municipal Representatives returned for Labour in Four West Yorkshire Towns and Cities, 1900-6	109
5.5	The Number of Labour Representatives on Local Political Bodies in West Yorkshire, 1900-6	109
5.6	The Municipal Balance of Power in Bradford, Leeds and Huddersfield, 1900-6	115
6.1	Municipal Representatives in Four West Yorkshire Municipalities, 1906-14	149
6.2	The Number of Local Representatives on Local Political Bodies in West Yorkshire, 1906-14	149
6.3	The Liberal-Conservative Pact in Bradford, 1906-13	151
6.4	The Municipal Balance of Power in Bradford, Leeds and Huddersfield, 1906-13	152
6.5	Parliamentary By-Elections in West Yorkshire at which Labour candidates were involved	153

TO JULIA AND EVELYN

PREFACE

We have two main purposes in writing this book. The first is to explain why West Yorkshire should have produced a flourishing Labour movement in the late nineteenth and early twentieth centuries. The second is to question the view that the Labour Party simply emerged as a viable party during the First World War by stepping into the political vacuum created by the split within Liberal ranks. We feel that the evidence of Labour's growth before 1914 – particularly in securing trade-union support from the 1890s onwards and in rapidly increasing its local political successes after 1909 suggests that the First World War was less significant to Labour's political rise in West Yorkshire than it might have been nationally, or in other regions of the country.

It is amazing, given the importance of the West Yorkshire textile area in the embryonic growth of the Independent Labour Party and the Labour Party, that there has not, until now, been a detailed published account of the West Yorkshire Labour movement. Most accounts have, hitherto, concentrated upon the famous national events which occurred in West Yorkshire – the Inaugural Conference of the National ILP at Bradford in 1893 being the most famous – and not attempted to explain the complexity of a region in which the ILP caught on in some areas, such as Bradford and Halifax, but failed to sustain much of an impact in other areas, such as Huddersfield and Keighley. Only recently has detailed research been undertaken to examine the political record of Labour and Liberalism in the various industrial constituencies of West Yorkshire and much of this remains to be published. Therefore, this book is an attempt to fill the gap. Of course, in a book of a couple of hundred pages it is

Preface

impossible to offer a detailed study of all the 22
constituencies and 23 seats which we take as the
West Yorkshire area. Indeed in a good proportion of
these constituencies there is comparatively little
to report, and the evidence of pre-war Labour
growth is sketchy. For this reason, whilst we have
attempted to do justice to the whole West Yorkshire
area we have inevitably had to concentrate upon the
areas of greatest Labour activity, such as Bradford,
Halifax, Leeds, Keighley and Huddersfield, whilst
recognising the significant developments which were
occurring in the surrounding districts.

As research into the early Labour Party and
the Liberal Party continues so new evidence and
perspectives will appear. In the meantime we offer
our assessment of the main features of Labour history in West Yorkshire. Whilst future research
may qualify our findings, we hope to have provided
a suggestive guide through the quagmire of early
Labour politics in West Yorkshire.

Pudsey and Bradford   Keith Laybourn
                                        Jack Reynolds

ACKNOWLEDGEMENTS

This book could not have been written without the help of many individuals and institutions. We owe a particular debt to the staff of many West Yorkshire libraries who have been generous in their advice and help. Whilst our thanks extend to all those library staff who have helped us in our research we would particularly like to thank David James, the Bradford Archivist, Elvira Willmott, the Local Studies Adviser for Bradford Libraries Division, Dr. Alan Betteridge, the Archivist for Calderdale, and their respective staffs for their unstinting support of our research.
 This research has, of course, been sustained and illuminated by discussions with many individuals over many years. The enthusiasm and critical advice of Dr. David Clark MP, Martin Crick, John Halstead, Bill Lancaster, Cyril Pearce, Robert Perks and Dr. David Wright has been invaluable to our work. Tony Jowett deserves particular mention, having helped to shape some of our ideas for chapter seven.
 Our thanks must also go to David James and the Bradford Archives Department for permission to use the Keir Hardie election card for the 1896 East Bradford By-Election on the front cover. Elizabeth Dawson patiently typed the camera-ready copy for this book and David Lawford was responsible for the artwork.
 The years of research and long hours spent in writing this book have placed a considerable burden upon our wives and it is to them - Julia and Evelyn - that this book is dedicated.

ABBREVIATIONS

ASE	Amalgamated Society of Engineers
BSP	British Socialist Party
BWL	British Workers' League
COS	Charity Organisation Society
CVLL	Colne Valley Labour League
CVLU	Colne Valley Labour Union
CVSL	Colne Valley Socialist League
ILP	Independent Labour Party
ISEL	Industrial Syndicalist Education League
LEA	Labour Electoral Association (Bradford)
LRC	Labour Representation Committee
NAC	National Administrative Council (of the ILP)
NEC	National Executive Committee (of the LRC and Labour Party)
SDF	Social Democratic Federation
SDP	Social Democratic Party
UDC	Union of Democratic Control
WMF	Workers' Municipal Federation (Bradford)

Chapter One

THE RISE OF LABOUR AND THE DECLINE OF LIBERALISM:
THE GENERAL PROBLEM AND WEST YORKSHIRE

The rise of the Labour Party between 1890 and 1924 and the decline of the Liberal Party in the same period are political events of more than usual significance for our own times. From a peak of 400 members of parliament in the 1906 General Election the Liberal Party crashed down to 40 in the general election of 1924. The Labour Party had made comparable gains, rising from a mere handful of members at the beginning of the century to 191 in 1923 - enough to form a minority government. Even in the general election of 1924, the defeated Labour Party had 151 parliamentary representatives and was clearly the alternative party of government to the Conservatives. It was little more than 30 years since the Independent Labour Party, the progenitor of the Labour Party, had held its first annual conference in Bradford in 1893.

The primary cause of the Liberal decline was obvious. Voters had abandoned the Liberal Party in favour of Labour or Conservatism. The problem of the historian was to analyse the timing of this change. Was the shift in political support before 1914 - the expression in politics of class division in society - decisive? Or did the Liberal Party lose a hold on public opinion, which it had recaptured after an apparant decline at the beginning of the century, as a result of the internal battles between Asquith and Lloyd George during the war and in the immediate post-war years? In other words, had the Liberal Party faced the challenge offered by the 'emergence of the masses' into politics, and become the natural party of the working classes before 1914 only to be destroyed in the 1920s by the conflicting political ambitions of their principal men. In our view, the evidence of the West Yorkshire textile area overwhelmingly suggests that

The Rise of Labour

decline of the Liberal Party was a continuous process from the late nineteenth century onwards and that this reflected the fundamental change in the structure and organisation of society. The Liberal Party was losing its supporters from the 1880s onwards. Despite the radicalism of the great governments dominated by Asquith and Lloyd George before 1914, the intransigence of hardcore Liberalism, as expressed for instance in the Liberal clubs of the West Yorkshire textile district, guaranteed that it did not offer itself as an effective party of social reform at the local level. Far less would its programme take on that element of crusading passion needed to arouse the working class into something like concerted political action. There was a long history of working-class support for Liberalism but few middle-class Liberals were unaware of class distinctions within the party or could bring themselves to ignore the assumptions of working-class deference this implied. In West Yorkshire, the Liberal Party never became, for working-class men and women, 'our party' in the comprehensive sense the Labour Party achieved.

The strength of nineteenth century Liberalism lay in its economic philosophy – its faith in the impersonality of economic forces; its view of the needs and obligation of the religious life - equality between the sects and hostility therefore to the special position of the Anglican church; the central principle of individualism which gave Liberals their deep-rooted suspicion of the executive power of the bureaucratic state. By the last twenty years of the nineteenth century, the value of these ideas was being challenged. A good many West Yorkshire woolmen were abandoning the economic liberalism which had been the corner stone of Victorian political consensus. In 1882, Samuel Cunliffe Lister, one of Bradford's most influential manufacturers, began a nationwide campaign for what he called 'Fair Trade', the introduction of British tariffs against those who hampered the movement of British goods.[1] By 1904, in the Bradford and District Chamber of Commerce there was a majority in favour of the controlled introduction of tariffs. In religion also the position was weakening. The strength of the Liberal Party lay in its connection with Nonconformity but well-to-do Liberals were drifting into the Anglican church. As for the working class, while there was perhaps a significant increase in their numbers amongst Primitive Methodists, they as a whole remained indifferent to the claims of religion. And, of course, the importance of the connection generally diminished as society became increasingly secular. There were adjustments also required in the unifying principle of individualism and personal independence. Liberals themselves had contributed to the growth of the power of the state when they fought to transfer local power from the hands of self-elected oligarchies to the democracy of borough and county councils, working under the supervision of central authority. By the end of the century demarcation lines between individual and state responsibility were being redefined in ways which many Liberals found difficult to accommodate.

Some Liberals did however respond to the new circumstances. Recognising the importance of the spirit of collectivism developing in English society, men like J.A. Hobson, L.T. Hobhouse, C.F.C. Masterman and Herbert Samuel tried to remould Liberalism in such a way as to reconcile individualism with the need for social reform which allowed greater state intervention.[2] Some writers have in fact argued that their efforts were rewarded and that the fortunes of the Liberal Party picked up as the programme developed.[3] There can be little doubt that in terms purely and simply of parliamentary elections the Liberal Party benefited enormously from the gratitude felt by working people for the great advances of the period 1906 to 1910. Indeed one writer goes so far as to maintain that the Liberal Party was benefiting from the development of class politics and was well on the way to countering the ILP/Labour Party claims to be the party of the working class.[4]

But this view, in our opinion, is based on a narrow view of the evidence for it concentrates too exclusively on the evidence of parliamentary elections. It ignores the physical difficulties of organising a completely new working-class party and the obstacles in the operation of the franchise which still hampered the expression of working-class political opinion. It has been estimated that about six million adult males could not vote under the provision of the two franchise acts of 1867 and 1884. Some were disenfranchised under the householder and lodger provisions, some through the difficulty of operating the seven different franchises and some simply because they could not fulfill the twelve-month residential qualification - a not unusual problem given the high level of residential mobility of working men. It is not enough to say that this was a question of random inequality which affected the Liberal Party as much as Labour.[5] An election agent was essential if any local party was to poll its full strength and clearly the Liberals were far better placed in this regard than Labour before the First World War. The working class did not begin to register its true vote until after the introduction of a new franchise act in 1918.[6]

Much of the discussion in favour of the post-1914 decline of the Liberal Party centres upon the work of P.F. Clarke in his book <u>Lancashire and the New Liberalism</u>. As the title implies the evidence is drawn almost exclusively from Lancashire and its politics are not necessarily typical of the country as a whole. In fact we think that the textile district of the West Riding of Yorkshire, West Yorkshire, probably offers a better insight into the process by which the Labour Party emerged. Apparently the Liberal Party in Lancashire was in great difficulty by the end of the century and compelled to look for new policies in the hope of surviving. In the West Riding the Liberal Party was much more powerful, returning either 19 or 20 of the 23 MPs who represented West Yorkshire between 1906 and 1914.[7] Perhaps inevitably the challenge to Liberalism in West Yorkshire was keener. Bradford was the birthplace of the Independent Labour Party, and the textile district of the West Riding the main initial centre of the movement which produced the Labour Party.[8]

A number of the central themes of Liberal and Labour history are well illustrated in a study of West Yorkshire. The importance of examining the results of local municipal and other elections is established for these show a steady, though not entirely continuous, rise in Labour fortunes before 1914.[9] Thus in Bradford, working-class candidates standing independently of the two major parties took 22.4 per cent of the municipal vote in 1893, 18.8 per cent in 1900 and 43.1 per cent in 1913.[10] Labour was in fact the most rapidly rising political party on Bradford City Council, though the organisation of the municipal political system meant that it was not yet in a position to take over the administration of the city.

A study of West Yorkshire also provides a useful insight into the real strength of the new Liberalism at the grass roots of politics. The new Liberalism was not well represented in West

The Rise of Labour

Figure 1.1: Map of West Yorkshire Parliamentary Constituencies 1885 – 1918

Yorkshire. Its most notable and politically active exponent was William Pollard Byles, sometime editor and owner of the <u>Bradford Observer</u>. His advocacy of social reform and his support of the working classes was sustained from the 1880s onwards. Yet working-class opinion never found him entirely convincing and local Liberals as a whole were at least upset by his activities. After a tempestuous career in Bradford, Shipley and Leeds he was obliged to leave Bradford to pursue his political career in Salford. One critical observer commented: 'It is a hard fate, but it is necessary if Mr Byles should fulfill the political role to which he is irresistably drawn'.[11] There were others: E.J. Smith for instance, a friend of Fred Jowett, a passionate advocate of housing reform whose work produced a blue print on which the development of Bradford's post-war municipal housing plan was based; Jacob Moser and his wife Rebecca, who directed the transformation of Bradford's charitable organisations in the years immediately before the First World War.[12] But their political following was slight. A more typical representative of the new Liberalism in the eyes of Bradford's working class was H.H. Bentham, Chairman of the Board of Guardians, a member of the Royal Commission on the Poor Law and a signatory of the Majority report of that inquiry, but best recalled in Bradford for his stern opposition to the introduction of school meals.[13] On the whole it was the 'Alfred Illingworth' figure which still represented Liberalism in the textile area. Free trade, voluntaryism and personal independence remained, for such men, at the heart of their political creed. Illingworth had died in 1907, but his opposition to the Eight-Hour Movement, his reluctance to accept schemes for old-age pensions or health insurance, his refusal to look for the possibility of abolishing half-time working for young children, his bad-tempered intervention against Fred Jowett, the ILP candidate in the West Bradford parliamentary election of 1906 were not forgotten and there were men like George Garnett, the Greengates mill owner, to step into his shoes.[14] Old Liberalism based upon the leadership of a few Non-conformist business families sustained places like Keighley and Huddersfield as Liberal strongholds up to and even beyond the First World War.[15] In the circumstances it is not surprising that time and time again we come across examples of Liberal intransigence - expressed usually by Liberal executive committees refusing to consider working men as candidates for local election.

The West Yorkshire region also demonstrated clearly one of the central features of the situation. Perhaps for the first time in British history the structure of working-class society showed real possibilities of unity in political action. The Labour-Capital relationship was clarifed and effectively polarised, and the class-based division of opinion which accompanied the Manningham Mills strike of 1891 – the catalyst of events which led to the founding of the ILP – confirmed it.[16] The paternalism which as a managerial device had masked the division between Labour and Capital, persisted in some parts of the West Riding. In the smaller towns and villages there was a good deal still, for one or two firms could generally control most of the facilities of such areas. J.C. Horsfall exercised in Glusburn near Keighley the sort of authority that Sir Titus Salt had exercised in Saltaire. Bairstow and Harley held between them much the same position in nearby Sutton. The Fosters of Black Dyke Mills dominated the village of Queensbury and the proprietors of the Low Moor Iron Works the district of Wibsey Low Moor.[17] But in the larger towns there is plenty of evidence of the diminution of such influences. Some of the oldest and largest established firms – the founders of West Yorkshire's industrial greatness – had disappeared. In Bradford, the Rands went out of business in 1873 for lack of heirs.[18] The Bowling Iron Company went into liquidation in 1897.[19] In 1892 the Salt family sold the whole of the Saltaire complex to a local consortium.[20] One or two large firms emerged to take their places, but generally they were replaced by smaller units whose resources could not provide the sort of quid pro quo on which such relationships depended. Generally the relationship of Labour to Capital was reaching a more modern polarisation. In printing, the Federation of Master Printers confronted the local branch of the National Typographical Association, and in the Dyeing trade, the Bradford Dyers' Association battled with the Amalgamated Society of Dyers, and almost everywhere the trade union – though met with great hostility – was (however reluctantly) accepted as the bargaining agent of workingmen.[21]

There were also more general social indicators of the position. The social geography of the

large towns had responded to the development of the
class-divided society and the building speculators
were isolating one class from another. The new
working-class district in Bradford which stretched
across the eastern slopes of the bowl of hills was
a good example of these developments. It was built
between 1870 and 1890 and owned by small owners of
property who held blocks of four or eight houses
each. As an area, it offered few facilities except
those available on the long-existing thoroughfares
it overran. Yet it was not as homogeneous as it
appeared on the surface. The regimental files of
dark-grey-slate roofed houses masked a number of
minor social diversities. These separated those
who lived in the terrace houses on the periphery,
those who lived in the back-to-back houses and
those who lived in the larger side-scullery houses.
All nevertheless shared the same facilities, the
chapels, the churches, the schools, shops and public
houses along Otley Road, Barkerend Road and Leeds
Road. The area never developed into a community in
the way that a place like Saltaire or other earlier
building developments based upon old townships
could. But it drew together a sizeable portion of
Bradford's working class. About a half of the en-
rolled trade unionists of Bradford lived there.
A number of leading members of the Bradford ILP had
their homes within a few minutes walk of each other
in the area.[22]

By the 1890s much of the antagonism which the
Irish immigration brought into West Yorkshire was
disappearing. The Irish were never to be entirely
assimilated or their culture submerged but within
the framework of their own institutions they were
being effectively integrated into the fabric of
society. They had their own schools, subject, like
other schools, to the control of the school boards.
In school board elections they voted Conservative,
on other matters with the Liberals until the turn
of the century when increasingly the Irish vote
came to the Labour Party.

By 1890 also a whole generation of working-
class children had shared the common experience of
school board elementary education. The tendency,
noted in J.S. Winder's report on education in
Bradford in 1861, for craftsmen and others of the
better paid to send their children to small and in-
adequate private schools diminished rapidly.[23]
Almost all working-class children savoured the
facilities which the board schools provided; young
working-class adults formed an element in society

linked by the newly-shared experience of education.

We are not of course arguing that the inexorable pressures of sociological change made the rise of the ILP inevitable. We are saying that the material conditions for such a development existed. Why it actually occurred and the manner in which it emerged depended on the way men acted in the complex juxtaposition of old and new in social life. The work of recent historians has demonstrated that the condition of the Liberal Party and its response to the Labour challenge varied from region to region, and in an earlier article we provided what we consider to be a useful framework for the analysis of the problem. A number of questions have to be asked. How strong was the Socialist tradition in the area? How powerful and well-organised was the trade union movement and how firmly was it linked with the local Liberal Party? To what extent did the local Liberal Party respond to the demands of the working class? To what extent could the new Independent movement absorb a wide range of differing opinions, providing a platform for the far-reaching aspirations of Socialism and social reformism of many working-class radicals?

    We found that in Bradford, the birthplace of the ILP, there was a small Socialist movement active in the 1880s, largely composed of trade unionists, who gradually won the support of the Bradford Trades Council at a time when the Liberal Party appeared to be blatantly disregarding the interests of the organised working classes. Bradford trade unionists, hitherto prepared to accept the leadership of the well-to-do, became increasingly disillusioned with the effectiveness of the political representation they enjoyed at the municipal and national level and supported the ILP as the vehicle for their political aspirations. Trade unionism was thus the vital factor in the growth of the Bradford Labour movement.[24] Jeff Hill, writing about Manchester, had come to a similar conclusion.[25] Yet research into Rochdale and Bolton has suggested that where the local Liberal Party was able to hang on to trades-council support it was able to blight the growth of the Labour Party.[26] Still further research, into Keighley and Huddersfield, has suggested that if the local trades council was weak then its capture by the Labour Party would not necessarily produce a significant political breakthrough for Labour.[27]
    David Howell's recent book on <u>British</u>

Workers and the Independent Labour Party summarises much of the research and tends to support our contention that the key factor in the growth of Labour was trade-union, or trades council, support.[28] Yet there appears to be at least one exception to this rule. David Clark's book Colne Valley: Radicalism to Socialism reflects that the success of Victor Grayson in the 1907 Colne Valley parliamentary by-election was inspired by an individualistic, ethical branch of Socialism which was alien to trade unionism and its emphasis upon collective action.[29] But even in Colne Valley the importance of trade unionism cannot be fully ignored, for many of the early leaders of the Colne Valley Labour Union/League were in fact trade unionists.

Like most major debates the one which was focused on the rise of Labour and the decline of Liberalism has led to a good deal of academic pettiness and belligerence which is anathama to compromise. Yet sober opinion would, even at this interim stage, reflect that several main conclusions have emerged. In the first place, no one can be categorical about the timing of the Liberal decline or Labour growth because of the immense regional and local variations which have been observed. Secondly, advocacy of new Liberalism as the redeemer of Liberalism is no longer tenable; too much research has indicated the absence of its influence in many regions of the country.[30] Thirdly, although the impact of unequal franchise remains unclear, municipal and parliamentary by-election results suggest that Labour's electoral strength was rising rapidly between 1910 and 1914.[31] But if there is one lesson to learn from this debate it must be that an attempt to apply a general theory to the whole country will not work.[32] It is imperative that more research should be undertaken into constituency politics if a satisfactory conclusion to this debate is to be reached.

This study of the West Yorkshire textile region is an attempt to deal with one major regional gap in our knowledge. Apart from a few brief articles comparatively little has been published on constituency politics in West Yorkshire.[33] David Clark's study of Colne Valley is in fact the only fully detailed study to have been published for a West Yorkshire constituency.[34] The first purpose of this book will be to present the political picture that was emerging in the Yorkshire textile constituencies between the 1890s and the First World War. The main thrust of this book will be directed at answering the questions raised by the recent and current debate. It will be suggested that the Labour movement had broken the traditional two-party political system in some constituencies but that the Liberal Party still held on well in many constituencies. It will also be argued that Liberal resilience was very largely based upon the old, rather than the new, Liberalism and that wealthy Nonconformist families, often rooted in the woollen textile industry, still held sway within the Liberal Party. Trade-union support was also vital in sustaining a growing Labour Party and where it was not a preponderant force the growth of Labour was likely to be fitful. Yet gains were made even in the most unlikely areas. The Labour movement made significant inroads into the position of both the Liberal and Conservative parties in the Yorkshire textile industry, particularly in the early 1890s, between 1901 and 1906 and from 1910 to the First World War. With its political successes it brought hope of an improvement in the conditions of life endured by the working classes, though its real effect upon the lives of most was minimal. Yet at least the Liberal heartland was under threat and the way had been paved for a political takeover by the Labour Party. Labour gains from an obdurate and trenchant old, rather than new, Liberalism was the picture of politics in West Yorkshire before August 1914.

NOTES

1. Bradford Observer, 3, 7 Feb. 1880; B.H. Brown, The Tariff Movement in Great Britain 1881-1893 (Columbia University Press, Columbia and London, 1943); K. Laybourn, 'The Attitude of Yorkshire Trade Unions to the Economic and Social Problems of the Great Depression, 1873-1896', unpublished PhD thesis, University of Lancaster, 1973, pp. 94-6.
2. P. Clarke, Liberals and Social Democrats (Cambridge University Press, Cambridge, 1978 and 1981).
3. P.F. Clarke, Lancashire and the New Liberalism (Cambridge University Press, Cambridge, 1971; H.V. Emy, Liberals, Radicals and Social Politics 1892-1914 (Cambridge University Press, London, 1973); M. Freeden, The New Liberalism: An Ideology of Social Reform (Clarendon, Oxford, 1978).
4. Clarke, Lancashire and the New Liberalism.
5. P.F. Clarke, 'Liberals, Labour and the

Franchise', English Historical Review, 1977, pp. 582-9.

6. R. McKibbin, The Evolution of the Labour Party 1910-1924 (Oxford University Press, London, 1974), pp. xv.

7. The West Yorkshire area is taken to include the following constituencies: Bradford Central, Bradford East, Bradford West, Dewsbury, Halifax (two seats), Huddersfield, Leeds Central, Leeds East, Leeds North, Leeds South, Leeds West, Wakefield, Colne Valley, Elland, Holmfirth, Keighley, Morley, Pudsey, Otley, Shipley, Sowerby and Spen Valley.

8. J. Reynolds and K. Laybourn, 'The Emergence of the Independent Labour Party in Bradford', International Review of Social History, Vol. XX (1975), Part 3, pp. 313-46.

9. M.G. Sheppard and J.L. Halstead, 'Labour's Municipal Election Performances in Provincial England and Wales 1901-1913', Bulletin of the Society for the Study of Labour History, 39, Autumn 1979, pp. 39-62.

10. Bradford Trades and Labour Council, Year Books for 1912, 1913 and 1914 (Bradford Trades Council, Bradford, 1912, 1913 and 1914).

11. Bradford Daily Telegraph, 31 Mar. 1903.

12. F. Brockway, Socialism over Sixty Years: The Life of Jowett of Bradford (Allen and Unwin, London, 1946), pp. 58.

13. K. Laybourn, 'The Issue of School Feeding in Bradford, 1904-1907', Journal of Educational Administration and History, Vol. XIV, No. 2, Jul. 1982, p. 31.

14. Yorkshire Daily Observer, 2 Jan. 1907.

15. The Brigg Family, for instance, exercised some paternal powers in Keighley and John Brigg, later Sir John Brigg, was MP for Keighley from 1895 until his death in 1911.

16. E.P. Thompson, 'Homage to Tom Maguire' in A. Briggs and J. Saville, Essays in Labour History (Macmillan, London, 1960), pp. 306-8; C. Pearce, The Manningham Mills Strike, Bradford, December 1890-April 1891 (University of Hull Occasional Papers in Economic and Social History, Hull, 1975); K. Laybourn, 'The Manningham Mills Strike: its importance in Bradford history', Bradford Antiquary, 1976, pp. 7-35.

17. E. Sigsworth, Black Dyke Mills (Liverpool University Press, Liverpool, 1958).

18. Bradford Observer, 10 Jun. 1873.

19. H. Long, 'The Bowling Ironworks',

Industrial Archaeology Vol. 5, no. 2, May 1968, pp. 171-7.
20. Saltaire and Shipley Times, 5 Aug. 1893.
21. Bradford Typographical Society, Minutes, Deposited in the J.B. Priestley Library, University of Bradford.
22. Reynolds and Laybourn, 'The Emergence of the Independent Labour Party in Bradford', p. 320.
23. Parliamentary Papers, 1861, Vol. XXL, Part II, pp. 175-242: Report of the Assistant Commissioner J.S. Winder Esqu., on the State of Popular Education in Rochdale and Bradford.
24. Reynolds and Laybourn, 'Emergence of the Independent Labour Party in Bradford', p. 313.
25. J. Hill, 'Manchester and Salford Politics and the Early Development of the Independent Labour Party', International Review of Social History, Vol. XXVI (1981), Part 2, pp. 171-201.
26. M. Coneys, 'The Labour Movement and the Liberal Party in Rochdale 1890-1906', unpublished MA dissertation, Huddersfield Polytechnic, 1982; P. Howarth, 'The Development of the Bolton Independent Labour Party, 1885-1895', unpublished MA dissertation, Huddersfield Polytechnic, 1982.
27. D. James, 'The Keighley ILP 1892-1900 "Realising the Kingdom of Heaven"' in J.A. Jowitt and R.K.S. Taylor (eds.) Bradford 1890-1914: The Cradle of the Independent Labour Party (Bradford Occasional Papers No 2, Extra-Mural Department, Leeds University, Bradford, 1980); R. Perks is concluding his research on Huddersfield for a PhD at Huddersfield Polytechnic. A.W. Purdue, 'The Liberal and Labour Parties in North-East Politics, 1900-1914: The Struggle for Supremacy', International Review of Social History, XXVI (1981), Part 1, pp. 1-24 has made a similar point about the Liberal Party's control of trade unionism in the North East.
28. D. Howell, British Workers and the Independent Labour Party 1888-1906 (Manchester University Press, Manchester, 1983).
29. D. Clark, Colne Valley: Radicalism to Socialism. The Portrait of a Northern constituency in the formative years of the Labour Party 1890-1910 (Longman, London, 1981).
30. K.O. Morgan, 'The New Liberalism and the Challenge of Labour: The Welsh Experience', in K.D. Brown (ed.) Essays in Anti-Labour History (Macmillan, London, 1974), pp. 159-82; A. Howkins, 'Edwardian Liberalism and Industrial Unrest: a class view of the decline of Liberalism', History Workshop Journal, 4 (Autumn, 1977).

31. Sheppard and Halstead, 'Labour's Municipal Election Performance'; K.D. Wald, 'Class and the Vote before the First World War', <u>British Journal of Political Science</u>, Vol. 8 (1978), pp. 441-57.

32. Clarke, <u>Lancashire and the New Liberalism</u>, particularly the introductory remarks.

33. Apart from the articles already cited there have also been the following publications: M. Pugh, 'Yorkshire and the New Liberalism', <u>Journal of Modern History</u>, vol. 50, part 3 (1978), D1139-D1155; A. Roberts, 'Leeds Liberalism and late Victorian Politics', <u>Northern History</u>, V, (1970), pp. 131-56.

34. Clark, <u>Colne Valley: Radicalism to Socialism</u>.

Chapter Two

THE ORIGINS OF SOCIALISM AND INDEPENDENT LABOUR

Most students of modern history acknowledge the significance of the revolutionary changes which took place in the structure of European industrial society towards the end of the nineteenth century. These were bound up with the growing impersonality of the business unit, increases in the size and scope of international markets and the deeper involvements of political authorities in many aspects of economic life. In the evolution of social activity, the element with which this study is concerned, the emergence of the masses into politics, is fundamental. Universal manhood suffrage came before 1870 in France and in Germany but in both countries the most significant developments in working-class politics came after that date, in France under the Third Republic and in Germany after the repeal of anti-Socialist legislation in 1890. Spain, Belgium, the Netherlands, and Norway all passed manhood suffrage legislation between 1890 and 1898 and in the last quarter of the century Socialist parties sprang up in all Western European countries. The Second International of the European Socialist parties was established in 1889.

In the United Kingdom - as elsewhere - the struggle for a democratic society was long and painful, though, generally, after 1850, less violent than elsewhere. Its success was embodied in a series of enactments which broke down some of the authority held previously by a property-owning oligarchy of middle and upper classes. The act of 1867 conceded the franchise to male householers living in the parliamentary boroughs and another in 1884 extended the privilege to male householders in the county constituencies. The Secret Ballot Act of 1872 and the Corrupt Practices Act of 1883 cleared the way for the introduction of proper democratic procedures. In 1918, all males over 21 and women over 30 were allowed to vote and all women were finally included in the franchise in 1928. Meanwhile the act of 1882 had opened up municipal government to working men by its abolition of the property qualification for local councillors and aldermen.[1]

Between the Reform Act of 1832 and that of 1867, however, the structure of politics was little changed. By and large membership of the political nation was confined to males of the upper and middle classes. A small number of working men throughout the country had the vote. In the parliamentary borough of Bradford, for instance, only about seven per cent of the electors were working men. There were about 1,500, however, who had a vote in the county elections as freeholders. Occasionally, Chartist candidates appeared at the hustings - Ernest Jones had stood for Halifax in 1848 - but generally, like Julian Harney in Bradford in 1852, they withdrew from the contest after a vote had been taken by a show of hands and before the ballot proper.[2] The prevailing mood of the political nation after 1848 was one of consensus based on a belief in free trade and an ill-defined concept of progress. The core of its support in West Yorkshire was found in the votes of non-dogmatic Tories and Moderate Liberals. Radicalism was powerful and vocal there for there was a wealthy dissenting community led by some of the richest industrialists in the district but it had no automatic majority over the combined forces of Tory and Moderate Liberal until after 1867. Perhaps the best evidence of the prevailing harmony was to be found in Bradford. Between 1850 and 1867 there were six parliamentary elections but only two of them were contested in this borough.[3] Of the two seats, one was held by H.W. Wickham, a director of the great Low Moor Iron Works, and a convert from Toryism to moderate Liberalism in 1852.[4] The other was held at different times by Robert Milligan, the first mayor of Bradford and head of the great mercantile enterprise of Milligan and Forbes, Titus Salt, second mayor of Bradford and the founder of Saltaire, and W.E. Forster, a prosperous manufacturer in the neighbouring village of Burley and one of the country's leading politicians.[5] All were classed as Radicals, though the degree of their commitment was questioned from time to time. By the 1860s, both Milligan and Forster had abandoned any belief in manhood suffrage they may have had, and there were

The Origins of Socialism

those who suspected that Salt might even be moving into the Tory camp. The only permanent political organisations were the Electoral Registration associations; elections were run by the <u>ad hoc</u> committees of what were known as 'friends of the candidates'.6

The working-class vote, such as it was, and the support of organised non-electors tended to go to Radical candidates. There was already in existence an understanding between working men and middle-class Radicals that one of the main objectives of politics was the extension of the franchise in some way to at least some sections of the working classes. But an eventual move in that direction formed part of the consensus idea of progress. There was more agreement within the consensus on the need for 'cautious gradualism' than there was on the form such progress had to take. The act of 1867 was the product of this 'cautious gradualism' - it ensured that (as Tawney commented) the British working man would enter the ballot box with cap in hand.7 The universal manhood suffrage demanded by the Chartists had not been conceded. The vote went to men with established residential qualification, either lodger or household tenure, and other proofs of Victorian responsibility. It reflected the old constitutional principle that the vote was a privilege attaching to men who had some interest in the maintenance of property; it contained elements of that Victorian view, held by some working men as well as others, that only a minority of working men could be considered intelligent and rational human beings capable of serious thought and judgement. Large numbers of working men, even in the urban constituencies, did not vote under the act. It demanded a year's residential qualification; men defined as lodgers had to register themselves, unlike other voters who were registered automatically; men who had accepted poor relief in the previous year were excluded along with criminals and bankrupts. In 1871, there were about 39,000 adult males in Bradford; in 1874 the electorate numbered 24,331.8

A fundamental change of course had taken place. In Bradford, the electorate grew from just short of 6,000 in 1866 to 27,000 by 1880 and it became largely working class in the process. The parties responded promptly to the new system. Machinery was quickly created almost everywhere to maintain control of the vastly augmented vote, (or, as its creators might have said, to allow democracy to function effectively). The mechanism of the modern party system was created. At the social level, Liberal and Conservative clubs appeared, and at the formal political level permanent associations were established. Bradford provided an early model. In 1866, the Conservatives started the Conservative Working Men's Association and in the following year the Bradford Conservative Association.9 The Liberals drew together into a single organisation almost all their supporters in the town - the moderate Registration Society, the Radical middle-class Reform Union and almost all the members of the Radical working-class Reform League. The new Liberal Electoral Association provided a new base in which Moderate and Radical were united in a pledge to support the same programme and the same candidates.10 It was organised by wards and so provided plenty of opportunity of minor office for its ordinary members. Its principal committee was an executive of 24 members. Only four of them were members of the working class.

Working-class activity was certainly stimulated. A number of working men stood as parliamentary candidates in different parts of the country and one or two of them were elected. But this did not introduce a new element into politics for such men and their supporters remained no more than a section of the Liberal Party with special interests in trade union and working conditions. It was in fact little more than a formal strengthening of arrangements which had existed in a looser form since the 1850s. Sir Titus Salt, commenting on the parliamentary by-election of 1869, gave the situation a good Liberal gloss.11 Bradford working men had rallied to the support of Edward Miall, the chief propagandist of the Liberation Society and a very orthodox 'laissez-faire' Liberal. It is not easy to see just what working men got out of supporting him. He was perhaps the best available candidate though his opponent, M.W. Thompson, claimed to be as good a democrat and not a kill-joy into the bargain.12 Miall, however, offered them the dignity of committed Radicalism; he also had the reputation of being a friend to the working man, though he failed to justify it when he had an opportunity to vote on trade-union matters. Salt's comment was revealing. Bradford's working men, he said, had done their duty, as he had always known they would and he was proud of them.13

The situation was exposed more starkly in the Bradford election of 1874. James Hardaker, a stone mason and a very prominent member of Bradford's so-called 'aristocracy of labour', stood for election with the backing of the local Trades Council. He was the secretary of the local branch of the Operative Stonemasons' Union, a Sunday School teacher and a leading member of the working men's teetotal organisation. His father ran a small building firm, which he eventually inherited. Although he had declared his intention to remain independent of other political organisations, he quickly threw in his lot with the official Liberal-Radicals once the election became imminent. He had made little progress in getting together the funds needed to fight the election. When Alfred Illingworth, Bradford's Radical leader, offered to finance his campaign and made promises to cover a parliamentary salary if Hardaker were to be elected, Hardaker had no hesitation in agreeing to stand as a Radical candidate in tandem with J.V. Godwin, wealthy wool merchant and another ex-mayor of Bradford. The election was dominated by the education issue for the principal opponent of official Liberal-Radicalism was W.E. Forster, author of the 1870 Education Act which for the time being had shattered the unity of the Liberals. Nevertheless, it seems at least odd that Hardaker should have placed the issue of trade union legislation last in his list of legislative priorities.[14] The 'people's' government, led by the 'people's' William, which Bradford working men, earning Salt's praise, had helped to elect, and which Hardaker now supported, had passed the notorious Criminal Law Amendment Act in 1872. It had aroused great anger among the local unions who organised one of the most impressive demonstrations in the country against it and in consequence helped to re-establish the Bradford and District Trades Council - the body which had first sponsored Hardaker. We can best suppose that Hardaker was subject to irresistable pressure on the issue for, middle-class Radicals had never displayed much affection for trade unions. It is clear, however, that working-class representation of this sort had not raised the enthusiasm of Bradford's working men to a level at which they would face the financial sacrifices of expenditure on a parliamentary candidate.

Working men were capable of expressing independent views and taking independent action. Even during the quiet fifties, old Bradford Chartists like George White, William Angus, Abraham Sharp, James Wilkinson and George Fletcher hammered away at the manhood suffrage theme, though most speakers conceded the need for middle-class support.[15] In

The Origins of Socialism

the sixties there was more aggression. In 1864, for instance, a working men's committee engineered a demonstration against the Prime Minister, in protest at his well-known opposition to franchise reform, when he came to Bradford to lay the foundation stone of the new Wool Exchange. It was an unhappy experience for the old man; he was reported as preferring to recall his visit to Saltaire as the most impressive episode of his visit to Bradford.[16] During the agitations for the Act of 1867, the Bradford branch of the National Reform League became one of the two or three most influential in the country, organising along with the Leeds men, the two great West Riding demonstrations on Woodhouse Moor in favour of the Act.[17]

There was always a basic element of collaboration with the middle classes and if anything the spirit of political independence diminished in the seventies. But there were always elements of uneasy dischord in the situation. The democratic implications of the 1867 Act led to a number of defections from the Liberal Party; among those in Bradford were S.C. Lister, M.W. Thompson, H.W. Ripley and several of the most respected members of the German community. These elements also underlay the running dispute between W.E. Forster and his Radical constituents which went on until his death in 1886. The trade union issue also was always likely to provoke controversy and this was particularly the case when trade-union activity began tentatively to penetrate branches of the textile industry untouched by such activities for many years. Some of Bradford's senior employers were among the most generous supporters of the National Federation of Associated Employers formed in 1873 specifically to combat what they called 'the growing menace of trade unionism'.[18]

The fragile and uneasy relationship between the organised working class and the Liberal Party of Bradford was not so evident elsewhere. It emerges that by the mid-1850s the Chartists were operating as the Advanced Liberal Party in Leeds. The Labour movement had become absorbed within the political world of Liberalism. When J. Hales and S. Brighty visited Leeds in the late 1860s to assess the state of the Liberal organisation they reported:

> The increase ... in Leeds is enormous. The old register was only, 8,480, whilst the new one will be little over 38,000. This extra-

> ordinary addition is principally composed of
> mechanics and factory workers, or as they are
> termed here 'mill hands'. There has been no
> guage taken of their opinion, but they are
> believed to be liberal ... The Trade Societies
> are both numerous and strong, and will be
> useful for working ...[19]

This situation appears to have persisted well into the 1880s when James Kitson, a large engineering employer, suggested that Herbert Gladstone, the son of the Liberal Prime Minister, should stand for Leeds West, where he had his works and where there was a strong Co-operative tradition.[20]

Most other areas of West Yorkshire record a similar situation to that of Leeds. Liberalism was preponderant amongst the working classes of Keighley, Halifax and the vast majority of West Yorkshire communities where the efforts of organised labour were slight and fitful.

By the 1880s, the way was being prepared for a more determined assault on the structure of establishment politics. Trade unions took up the political issues much more strongly and the matter of Labour representation became a regular theme of TUC debates. The working-class ethic of democracy evolved more positively with the spread of Socialism and Socialist thought; though its development owed much to the values of a working-class subculture which had always defied the norms of middle-class hegemony. For many, John Ruskin confirmed an opinion that 'a dedication to the great art of getting on' was not necessarily the best of virtues.[21] Henry George's work provided fresh ammunition for the renewed assault on the sources of exploitation and deprivation and for forty years the work of Marx and Engels had been building up a definition of contemporary Socialism.[22] The formal organisation of opinion along socialist and independent labour lines began in 1884 with the establishment of H.M. Hyndman's Social Democratic Federation, William Morris's Socialist League and the Fabian Society of Sydney Webb, Bernard Shaw and Graham Wallas.[23] Both the SDF and the Socialist League drew their inspiration from the work of Marx and Engels. All were committed to the replacement of nineteenth century Liberal-Capitalism by more humane forms of social organisation than had hitherto emerged. And in addition to their understanding of Socialism, working men and women brought their practical experience of life in industrial society to the development of their democratic institutions - the ILP founded in 1893, the Labour Representation Committee founded in 1900 and the Labour Party which for practical purposes may be dated from 1906 though given formal constitutional basis in 1918.

In West Yorkshire also a new group of working-class leaders was assembling. In Bradford, Samuel Shaftoe, a skep basket maker, one of the founders of the Bradford Trades Council and for many years its leading member had arrived in 1865.[24] Charles Leonard Robinson, a cabinet maker and Bradford's first Independent Labour town councillor, was active in Bradford republican circles by the early 1870s.[25] James Bartley, an Ulsterman from Newry, typographer and journalist, seen by many as the true originator of the Bradford ILP had come in 1872 and W.H. Drew, one of his close associates, was there by the late 1880s.[26] To this emergent Labour leadership may be added many Bradford-born leaders, including Frederick William Jowett, born in 1865, Bradford's first Labour MP, Paul Bland, Jesse Mitchell and George Minty, whom Jowett regarded as Bradford's first Socialists and Joseph Hayhurst, a dyer and Bradford's first Labour Mayor.[27] In Leeds, there was Tom Maguire, Socialism's most passionate advocate in the 1880s, John Lincoln Mahon, a prominent national figure in Morris's Socialist League, and Alfred Mattison, a Leeds engineer.[28] Angus George and Jacob Sanctuary were emerging as Labour leaders in Saltaire, George Garside in the Colne Valley, Ben Turner in Batley, James Beever in Halifax and Allan Gee in Huddersfield.[29] Not all were Socialists and not all were clearly independent Labour men. Some of them maintained a Liberal allegiance all their lives and were engaged in bitter quarrels with Socialists and ILPers. But all contributed to the development of a more aggressive temper in the Labour movement both in the industrial and political field.

The social environment of their activities offered particular advantages. It seems that by the 1880s the working classes were less fragmented than they had ever been. For one thing, the activities of building speculators in the latter part of the century simplified the social geography of the towns and tended to isolate the various classes much more effectively. As we have already suggested, the working-class district of East Bradford was being developed between 1870 and 1890. As it

The Origins of Socialism

emerged it nurtured the solidarity of working-class people. It was a fruitful base of recruitment for the early Bradford ILP, and many of the leading ILP activists had their homes in the district, often within ten minutes' walk of each other. Growing social and geographical unity amongst the working-classes also began to reduce the social distinctions between the working classes in other West Yorkshire towns as well.

The general weakening of paternalism, as we have already observed, also tended to weaken the identification of the working classes with the employers and provided the opportunity for Socialists and those committed to Independent Labour politics to press forward their gospel. In addition, the onset of trade depressions from the mid-1870s tended to loosen the unquestioning commitment of many working men to the Liberal and Conservative parties.

Some of the disillusionment of working men was given expression after the publication of the evidence given by Bradford businessmen to the Royal Commission on the Depression in Trade and Industry of 1886. Neither Henry Mitchell, the senior Bradford Conservative, nor Jacob Behrens, a prominent Liberal Unionist, had made much of the high levels of unemployment with which the woollen and worsted textile trade was afflicted, though they were clear that there had been a squeeze on profits and prices.[30] Bradford working men were enraged at the one-sided nature of this evidence and complaints both at the monthly meetings of the Trades Council and in the local press were vociferous.[31]

But the most obvious proof came from the spread of trade unionism for the trade union was the most obvious challenge to the paternalistic relationship between master and men. Whatever the accommodation which may have been made with the powerful cotton unions in Lancashire, there can be little doubt that in West Yorkshire many employers saw the trade unions as the enemy. H.W. Ripley, who had dismissed one of his oldest employees in 1869 for voting against him and had long regarded West Bowling as a sort of feudal fief, expressed a fairly general concern when he refused to recognise a dyers' union during the dyers' strike of 1880.[32] Addressing his workpeople he said

> Many of you, grandfathers, fathers, and sons, have worked at Bowling all your lives and this is the first occasion on which you have, during

the long series of years, ever assumed a
hostile attitude. I appeal to you not to
listen to the advances of men who really care
nothing about you, and have not your real
interests at heart.33

During the last quarter of the century, trade
unionism, taking on a new lease of life, spread
more deeply into the semi-skilled and unskilled
trades and practically in Bradford for the first
time since the great strike of 1825, the lower
grades of the textile industry responded. Skilled
men - overlookers, the most highly trained of the
woolsorters, stuffpressers, makers-up and packers -
had been organised for many years though they preferred to think of themselves as friendly societies
rather than trade unions. Their motto, the president of one of these unions said, was 'united to
help, not combined to injure' and continued that
'they had no connection with strikes or trade
unions. They were a class of men whose object was
the benefit of each other in employment and to as-
sist each other in sickness and death'.34 However,
the Bradford-based National Union of Woolsorters,
an organisation of semi-skilled workers ineligible
to join the very exclusive society of highly-skilled
artisans, was started in 1873. It spread quite
rapidly in the textile area and was able in fact to
absorb the exclusive woolsorters' society in 1892.35
The Amalgamated Society of Dyers, refounded in 1878
after a false start in 1872, had 700 members in 1888
and 2,000 in 1892.36 The machine woolcombers, also
failing to establish an organisation in 1872, started the Bradford and District Woolcombers' Society
in 1892 and by 1894 had some 1,200 members.37 The
West Riding Power Loom Weavers' Association, initially formed out of the combination of weavers
unions in Huddersfield and Dewsbury in 1885, opened
its ranks to spinners in 1892, ultimately changing
its name to the General Union of Textile Workers.38

But despite this flourish and the dedication
it implied, the West Yorkshire textile industry
remained weak trade union country. Ben Turner, in
his autobiography, described Bradford 'as the most
heartbreaking district' he could remember, and
Halifax as 'hopeless'.39 Few of the weavers and
spinners, the largest section of the factory workforce, joined the weavers' association in these
towns, although there was more success in Huddersfield, Dewsbury and Batley, as Turner acknowledged.
In Bradford and Halifax the majority of them were

The Origins of Socialism

women and young people, not easily organised, and their proportion of the total workforce had increased as the trade depression had intensified. In Bradford in the 1850s about half the weavers were women; by the 1880s the proportion had increased to two-thirds. In addition, and perhaps more significant than the presence of large numbers of women in the trades, was the fact that with the collapse of textile unionism in the Bradford and Leeds area in 1825, no tradition of union organisation had been able to grow. Equally important, although there were a number of large firms in existence, a very large proportion of the textile workers were employed in small businesses. All had their own trade practices and price lists, and the fixing of piece rates was a very difficult operation. Indeed, it was not until 1913 and 1914, respectively, that the woollen and worsted trades established basic wage rates, both piece and time, for the district.[40] Even then, many firms did not pay standard rates to weavers and spinners. Throughout the late nineteenth and early twentieth centuries small firms continued to 'fine' their workers for alleged poor work, isolated and discharged 'trouble-makers' and at the same time offered a sort of 'face-to-face relationship' which generated a sense of loyalty to the 'boss'. It was also in the small firms that hostility to trade unions was greatest, for it was here that pressure to keep wages as low as possible was at its highest due to their inability to take advantage of the economies of scale.

Trade unionism was naturally more effective amongst the crafts and in the male-dominated industries. The engineering industry was well unionised in Leeds, Halifax and Keighley. Engineering was almost as diversified in West Yorkshire as was textiles. In Keighley the production centred upon textile machinery while in Halifax and Leeds the main line of production was in boilers and railway engines. The common bond between these districts was the power and guidance of the large national craft amalgamations, and particularly the Amalgamated Society of Engineers and the Friendly Society of Ironfounders. Table 2.1 indicates how successful these two organisations were in Yorkshire as a whole. Yet it must not be supposed that craft unions were exceptionally powerful and successful organisations. Local industrial disputes often disabused engineers of the view that their position was invulnerable. As we will indicate, the 1889 engineering dispute in Keighley shook the confidence

Table 2.1: The Membership of Engineering Unions in Yorkshire between the 1860s and the 1890s

	ASE		FSI	
	1868	1892	1873	1896
Yorkshire Branches	25	53	18	20
Yorkshire Membership	4,400	9,100	3,700	4,300
National Membership	34,000	71,000	12,000	16,000

Source: Details from <u>Parliamentary Papers</u>, Cmnd. 4123, XXXI, 1868-9, <u>Eleventh and Final Report of the Trade Union Commission</u>, Appendix J; <u>Annual Report</u> of the ASE, 1892; Annual Reports of the Friendly Society of Ironfounders.

of engineers in the mastery of their own trade. It is not without good reason that many of the early Labour leaders in West Yorkshire were members of the ASE.[41]

Elsewhere, craft unionism was not as secure as it first appeared. Bradford plasterers in 1870 were reported as being able to enforce the rules vigorously; the master, it was said, was 'not permitted to accept the aid of his nearest relative' if he was not in the union.[42] One of the by-laws of the Bradford Bricklayers' Labourers' union was said to read: 'You are strictly cautioned not to overstep good rules by doing double work and causing others to do the same in order to gain a smile from the master. Such foolhardy and doubtful actions leave a good portion of good members out of employment'.[43] But what was important was the extent to which a union could really enforce its rules and here we have as direct evidence only the records of the Bradford printers which date from the mid 1860s. These speak of a constant struggle to establish their rules rather than of their automatic and successful employment in the face of every infringement. Printers, even with their long-established traditions of chapel organisation, high premiums on trained skills and superior levels of education did not control their labour market. In Bradford, as late as 1892, one-sixth of the printers were not members of the local branch of the Typographical Association, and in the villages of the West Riding there was practically no recruitment at all.[44] The labour market was always over stocked. Young men just out of apprenticeship and old men unable to

maintain the speed of work could only find the
casual work available at the busy time of the week
when the weekly publications were going to press and
in the busy time of the year when Bradford firms
were producing Christmas cards.[45] A number of employers including the <u>Bradford Daily Telegraph</u> did
not recognise the union as yet. The impression that
these circumstances were not unique to the printers
is confirmed by William Cudworth whose work on the
conditions of the industrial working classes of
Bradford suggests that few trades had adequate control of such matters as apprenticeship.[46]

But in these unions a good deal of progress
was being made by the end of the century, and the
printers were among the most notably pugnacious.
They had been threatened by technical change at
last. In 1889, the Thorne Composing machine was
introduced into the offices of the <u>Bradford Observ-
er</u> and its appearance started a series of acrimonious disputes which were not satisfactorily resolved until 1896.[47] By this time all the Bradford men
were members of the union and the non-union firms
had surrendered. Chapels in the rural districts
from Wharfedale to Spen Valley had joined the union.
Its policy became extremely aggresive. It complained and threatened when public bodies employed non-
union men and started the Fair Contracts movement
throughout its area of recruitment. Altogether it
was a long way from the occasion in 1867 when the
printers, trying to negotiate the first wage increase they had requested in thirty years, assured
their masters that they 'did not intend to press
their claims arrogently, nor ... use anything but
moral suasion to attain their object'.[48]

The diffusion of trade unionism throughout
working-class society in West Yorkshire - even if
not a powerful movement - expressed very clearly a
growing unity of working-class life. Its particular development created fields of activity for
Socialists and independent Labour men to cultivate,
for these men saw industrial and political organisation not as separate elements but as two sides of
an homogeneous Labour movement. The situation in
the textile area was very different from that in the
mining areas in South Yorkshire and in the cotton
areas of Lancashire. In West Yorkshire there were
no large unions able to deliver, <u>en bloc</u>, a working-
class vote which would ensure a political majority
for the party and candidate they favoured. They
could therefore be ignored when they demanded political concessions from the other parties; but the way

lay open for the creation of an independent working-class party. In the non-unionised trades the 'Independent' men could (and did) contribute to the beginning of new unions and infiltration of other unions was easier for the fact that there were no powerful and successful organisations dominated by men dedicated to the other parties.

Thus it seems that the time was ripe for the evolution of a comprehensive Labour movement for much of the fragmentation of the past was being eliminated. Nevertheless, the struggle for an independent Labour party was not merely a struggle with the upper classes. It was also a fight between men who supported the existing parties, particularly the 'old-fashioned' Liberals, on the one hand, and the new Socialist-Independent men on the other.

The first public statements of the new spirit abroad did not appear to arouse much general enthusiasm. In February 1884, William Morris came to Bradford to lecture on behalf of the Democratic Federation, soon to become the SDF. He had been invited by a small committee of local Radicals who had just started a programme of Sunday lectures for working men. The committee included such veteran Radicals as James Hanson and T.T. Empsall, the younger W.P. Byles, part-owner of the Bradford Observer, as well as Angus George, the manager of the Tailors shop at Saltaire Co-operative Stores. The title of Morris's lecture was 'Useful Work v Useless Toil'. In it, he made a fierce attack on the supremacy of the middle classes:

> The idea of bettering the existing condition of things had taken the form of philanthropy, the preaching of thrift, and perhaps in a way compelling an economic and social revolution. All those plans for the reform of the abuses of society were useless because they were all founded on the supremacy that was founded on the system of Capitalism ... from whence sprang the class of victims which formed the foundationstone of our social edifice of luxury and well-being. It was that supremacy, on the contrary, that Socialism attacked.[49]

Morris's lecture attracted a large audience but apparently received only a lukewarm reception. The Bradford Observer commented that 'the audience, which filled the Temperance Hall, was amused, if not converted', and Morris himself was disappointed at the impact he had made: for he referred to Bradford's working men later as a 'sad set of Philistines' content to let their wives and children supplement the household income with wages from the spinning and weaving departments of the mills.[50] The second lecture given by a local person, the Rev. J. Cockson, on 'English Socialism, or the Poor Man's Politics' was received more willingly. Cockson accepted much of Morris's denunciation of extremes of poverty and wealth, but his solution was more to the taste of an audience composed principally of the 'aristocrats of labour'. If only men were good! The revolution was needed rather in men's hearts than in the institutions of society.

Parliamentary reform in 1884 and 1885 caused some activity. The Act of 1884, extending the principle of the 1867 Act to male householders outside the parliamentary boroughs, gave the vote to the majority of working men living in the West Riding rural areas of the Calder, Spen, Colne and Aire Valleys. Well attended meetings were held throughout the area and by early 1885 the Liberals and the Tories had set up political organisations to take over from the county associations.[51] In the parliamentary boroughs there were more positive signs of political interest amongst the working classes. Samuel Shaftoe stood as a trade union candidate at a municipal election at East Bowling in Bradford. He was defeated by 672 votes to 513 to the regret of the Bradford Observer, a Liberal paper, which was actively supporting the workingman's cause.[52]

The re-distribution of seats also strengthened the cry for working-class representation. In place of the two members, both elected by a poll of the whole vote, Bradford was to have three constituencies, each with its own MP. Given the social geography of the town this meant that in one constituency at least, East Bradford, the working-class vote would easily predominate. Working-class leaders thought that this should naturally be a working-class seat and started, in February 1885, the process of securing a Labour candidate. At the beginning of March the Bradford Observer published an article from S. Neil, of the Northumberland Miners' Union, in which the point was made that so far working men had been little more than voting machines manipulated by the party organisations. They needed to be represented by men who spoke for them, like them and with them as did their companions in the pits. The same issue contained a letter from a

Bradford working man making the same plea: 'What advantage will it be to the working men of Bradford when we have three instead of two members if the interests of all three clash with those who elect them'. He went on to suggest that with men like Abraham Sharp to call on - men who had devoted their lives to the political battle and had held their own with the greatest in the land - Bradford need not fear that intelligent and forceful representation might not be found.[53]

The committee, set up to explore the situation in the new East division, were much more concerned that the 'fiasco of 1874' (Hardaker's contest) should not be repeated and emphasised in their public statements that their candidate would keep clear of all party connections. They had thus to find out to what extent working men were prepared to support a candidate financially, and circulated trade unionists for information. The answers were disappointing. The reply of the printers was typical. The Typographical Society replied that the question of a Labour candidate for Bradford 'was inopportune' and reluctantly the committee stood down.[54] In other parts of West Yorkshire similar events were taking place. The Leeds Trades Council proposed to ask Henry Broadhurst to stand as their candidate but nothing came of it and in the Colne Valley discussion went no further than the question of financial obligation.[55]

Later in the year the Bradford Trades Council tried a less-ambitious project. It asked the Liberal Executive Council to nominate one working man in their list for the forthcoming School Board elections. Although the proposed candidate was John Hollings, president of the Trades Council and a much respected life-long Liberal, the idea was rejected with some contempt.[56]

Other sources of inspiration and activity were however developing. By 1886 there were two small branches of Morris's Socialist League in existence in Bradford and Leeds; a good many of their members were among the founders of the National ILP in 1893. In Leeds they included Tom Maguire, E. Connell, J. Flinn, Tom Paylor and Alfred Mattison; in Bradford, Fred Pickles, Paul Bland and Fred Jowett and a number about whom we have little more than tantalising hints - among them Karl Heuze and Karl Burlauf, German political refugees and G.A. Gaskell a local artist.[57] By 1887 both groups were pursuing policies which had been given the stamp of approval by H.H. Champion and the heirs of Marx - Engels,

The Origins of Socialism

Aveling and Eleanor Marx – and which led them away from the anti-parliamentarianism of the Socialist League and led them directly into the working-class struggle. Their efforts were to be aimed at winning the trade unions and to the formation of a united Labour movement with its own political party and its trade union movement.

In Leeds the prominent figures in this political movement were Tom Maguire and John Lincoln Mahon. Maguire, who has been the subject of some detailed study, was a Leeds-Irish photographic assistant who appears to have turned towards Socialism in about 1883.[58] By 1885, after some determined propaganda work in Leeds, he had mustered sufficient supporters to form the Leeds branch of the Socialist League, a body of about 15 to 20 members, many of them of Irish and East European descent, which provided the pioneering spirit of Socialism not only in Leeds but throughout West Yorkshire.[59] From the early days, Maguire and the Leeds Socialist League became increasingly characterised by their commitment to winning support from within the working class, and particularly amongst trade unions. In this endeavour they were helped by John Lincoln Mahon, a national figure in the Socialist League who became a close personal friend of Maguire. Mahon came to Leeds, as National Secretary of the Socialist League, in 1885 to help establish the branch in Leeds and was a frequent visitor to Leeds before settling there between 1890 and 1894.[60]

Mahon had been prominent within Socialist League ranks in trying to get the national leadership to drop its disdain of working with working-class organisations, a move which eventually took him, Maguire and others from the anti-parliamentary attitude of Morris to the pro-parliamentary attitude of the ILP. In 1887, Mahon put forward a resolution to the annual conference of the Socialist League demanding that

> every effort be made to penetrate the existing political organisations with Socialism; that all possible help be given to such movements as trades-unionism, co-operation, national and international labour federations, etc. by which the working classes are trying to better their condition; that Parliament, municipal and other local-government bodies, and the contests for the election of members to them, be taken advantage of for spreading the principle of Socialism and organising the people into

> a Socialist Labour Party ... tho' complete
> emancipation can only be achieved by the tran-
> sformation of society into a co-op common-
> wealth.61

The anti-parliamentarians defeated the resolution; nevertheless, it embodied the sort of policy which the Leeds and Bradford branches of the Socialist League were to pursue as they, and their members, embraced the challenge of winning political support which was to lead their main activists into the ILP.

Maguire and Mahon shared their views with other Socialist and independent Labour men throughout West Yorkshire. In July 1887, James Bartley had a series of letters published in the <u>Bradford Observer</u>. He pointed to the injustices of a system organised to ensure that Labour always played second fiddle to Capital and called for a 'practical means of giving expression to working-class needs'. Something beyond simple trade union organisation was needed, for except in very rare circumstances he could not see how pure-and-simple trade unionism could exert direct political influence.62 Certainly the few trade union MPs there were had made little impact upon the House of Commons. Bartley called for a new party freed from all other political influences, avoiding the extremes of theorising Socialism and the errors of capitalistic Liberalism, for 'Socialist propaganda was not sufficiently belligerent to make much headway and no true help could be expected from the Liberals in their existing organisations'. He offered the new party a tentative programme - mildly Socialist, though much of it was simple radicalism - adult suffrage, reform of local government, disestablishment of the Anglican Church, abolition of the House of Lords, land law reform, nationalisation of railways and payment of MPs. This had to be a working-class party, supporting its activities from its own financial resources and represented at every level by working men who thought like them.

> And the party must not be composed of men who
> are ashamed to wear as their headgear the
> billycock of their class. There must be no
> chimney pots in the new party. Its members
> must be men who are sufficiently courageous to
> defy caste and all that caste means. They
> must be the sworn enemies of that feeling
> which has done so much to keep the workers
> enslaved - the feeling of artificial respect

for class power.[63]

He had recently attended a conference in London of like-minded men and he had returned convinced of the need for a big national conference supported by immediate local initiative.

Fred Jowett and G.A. Gaskell joined Bartley in the discussion. There was nothing to expect from the parties, said Jowett, for their concern was merely to protect the 'sacred rights of capitalism. If we ask the Tories for social change, they answer confiscation. If Liberal leaders be approached the times are said to be inopportune for such change'.[64] Gaskell said it was obvious that a new party was coming into existence. It would, he said, represent men and not 'hands'. It would discard the 'servility of the present slave-labour representatives' - and he was particularly scathing about the activities of the trade-union MP Thomas Burt who, he said, offered no challenge to anybody. Meanwhile wages were low and unemployment high - working men would have to be much more militant if they were to get anywhere.

The Socialism of these men is not easy to define. Bartley, in particular, gives the impression that he was basically an Independent Labour man. All of them would have defined Socialism as a way of approaching the problem of fundamental social reform, of fulfilling Labour's aspirations, rather than of a scientific analysis of the nature of society. But all understood the implications of the class struggle and were prepared to fight it. The Bradford 'independents' differed from the Leeds Socialists in that they were not much concerned with the need for a missionary campaign to make converts to Socialism. The emphasis of their programme was placed on the need for a separate party through which they could act - the party's activities would make Socialists for them.

Another stimulus to activity was provided by the trade union Liberals. At the beginning of 1887, trade unionists met in Bradford to discuss the creation of a wider Labour interest on the political field. It was attended by most of the leaders of the Bradford Trades Council. As a result of its deliberations a Bradford branch of the Labour Electoral Association was established, to fight parliamentary and local elections.[65] They were as committed as the Independent-Socialists to the need for working-class representation for the working class. Shaftoe had declared angrily after the Liberals had rejected John Holling's request to be nominated for election to the School Board that 'If the political parties ignore the cause of labour as they have done in the past, then Labour must run its own men, whatever political party may suffer or political chieftain be disappointed'.66

The fundamental lack of agreement between the Liberal trade unionists and the Independent-Socialist group was quickly revealed. The Liberal trade unionists really demanded little more than Hardaker in the Bradford parliamentary election of 1874 - a separate labour interest within the embrace of the existing Liberal organisation. They held firm to the Liberal creed of individualism and a minimum of state activity in the economic and social concerns of the people. This was understandable; men like Shaftoe had spent a political lifetime in the Liberal Party and had achieved a measure of success and some local prestige.67 Since they were the most important members of the existing trade unions, it was inevitable that the 'independent' men should regard them as the principal barrier to the creation of an homogeneous Labour movement with its own political party.

Yet it should not be assumed that even at this early stage the embryonic Independent-Socialist movement in West Yorkshire was exclusively working-class in its orientation. It is clear that in West Yorkshire, as well as in the country at large, there were many middle-class people who were being drawn to Socialism. In Bradford there were, amongst those who were to become prominent later, E.R. Hartley, a butcher; Willie Leach, a textile merchant and manufacturer; Arthur Priestman, a Quaker textile businessman of some substance, and many Congregational ministers, such as the Rev. T. Rhondda Williams and the Rev. R. Roberts. In Leeds, there were the Ford sisters, particularly Isabella and Bessie, members of a well-established Quaker family. In addition there were Congregationalists, such as the Rev. Westrope, and A.R. Orage, a school teacher who later moved from the ILP to Guild Socialism while editing in London the literary and political paper the New Age. In Halifax there was John Lister, a well-to-do landowner who later became the first Treasurer of the National ILP; Montague Blatchford, the brother of Robert Blatchford; and the Rev. Bryan Dale, a Congregational minister. In Colne Valley there were a number of small manufacturers emerging into early Labour movement, most particularly France Littlewood who also, like John Lister, became the Treasurer of the National ILP.68

Although these people, and many of their type, were drawn to the Independent-Socialist movement for a variety of reasons- the Ford sisters were involved by virtue of their work in trying to improve the conditions of tailoresses in the Leeds tailoresses strike of late 1889 and Willie Leach was drawn in through his friendship with Fred Jowett - it is clear that many were won to the movement by the flood of Fabian literature which emerged during the late 1880s and by the book *Fabian Essays*. By the end of 1892 there were Fabian societies at Batley, Bradford, Copley (near Halifax), Halifax, Huddersfield, Leeds and Sowerby Bridge. A branch was also formed at Dewsbury before May 1893.69 There may not have been the overwhelming middle-class presence in these branches which characterised the Fabian organisation in London, but it is clear that there was a strong middle-class presence in some of these provincial branches and that Fabian 'gradualism' helped ease many members of the middle class into the ILP.

Although the records of West Yorkshire Fabian activities are sketchy the middle-class nature of much of their support is provided by the surviving details of the Halifax Fabian Society. It was formed by John Lister, the Rev. Bryan Dale and a number of small manufacturers and businessmen, although there were some prominent trade unionists, such as James Beever, who figured prominently in the early history of the Halifax ILP and was Halifax's first Labour agent, who were prominent in the branch activities. John Lister's account of the early days of the Labour movement make it clear that the Halifax Fabian Society was formed by middle-class people such as himself and that, with the Halifax Trades Council, it was responsible for the formation of the Halifax Labour Union, the forerunner of the Halifax ILP. Lister also makes clear that the Fabian Society did much propaganda work in West Yorkshire in the late 1880s and early 1890s.70

This middle-class presence within the early West Yorkshire Labour movement offered both advantages and disadvantages. The main advantages were that it provided the emergent ILP with financial and propaganda help. The Halifax ILP did not manage to clear the financial debt it had built up with Lister, though he wrote much of it off, until 1900. Also by the mid 1890s most of the West Yorkshire Fabian societies had become submerged within the local ILP branches. The main disadvantages, however, related to the suspicion in which middle-class support was often held by the working-class representatives. This did not always break the surface of equanimity which the early ILP built up but was all too evident in the Mahon-Lister conflict of 1893, when Mahon, objecting to the radical-democratic demands of Lister in the Halifax parliamentary by-election of 1893, advised the Halifax working men not to vote for Lister. The rumpus which this created is examined in more detail in chapter three and it is evident that Mahon's views were shared by others. Tom Maguire felt that if the Leeds ILP was to avoid the mistakes of the past it must 'fall more closely into touch with the humbler wants of the people ... It must relinquish the delight of manipulating Fabian statistics and come a little nearer to the unfamiliar weekly wage question ...'71

It would be wrong to underestimate the influence of the work of Marx in the formulation of individual ideas. But on the whole the Socialism of the movement was not one based on a scientific analysis of society. Socialism for most was the fulfilment of a Labour dream, the completion of a homogeneous movement - in which the trade unions organised men and women for industry, the co-operative movement organised them for the provision of their daily needs and the Labour Union organised them for democratic political action. Socialism was the expression of working class need in politics. As such, a programme of fundamental social reform could be presented which took a great deal from the Liberal radicalism which most of them had left behind - a programme which left available a bridge for others of the Liberal Party. Thus the name itself was significant. Many of the most important pioneers of the movement had been members of the Socialist League, most of the members were proud to call themselves Socialists. Nevertheless the movement started as a movement of <u>Labour Unions</u>.

NOTES

1. George Lichtheim, <u>The Origins of Socialism</u> (Weidenfeld and Nicolson, London, 1968).
2. <u>Bradford Observer</u>, 8 Jun. 1852, 19 Apr. 1865, 15 Mar. 1868; J. James, <u>Continuation and Additions to the History of Bradford</u> (Longman Green, Bradford 18-6), p. 117; <u>Parliamentary Papers</u>, 1866,

lvii, p. 747.
    3. J. Reynold, The Great Paternalist, Titus Salt and the Growth of Nineteenth Century Bradford (Temple Smith, London, 1983), chapter four.
    4. Ibid., p. 202.
    5. Ibid., p. 206.
    6. Ibid., p. 39.
    7. Ross Terrill, R.H. Tawney and His Times: Socialism and Fellowship (Andre Deutsch, London, 1973), p. 173.
    8. Parliamentary Papers, Census of England and Wales, 1871.
    9. Bradford Observer, 4, 6 Oct, 22 Nov. 1866.
    10. Ibid., 16 Jan. 1868.
    11. Ibid., 12 Feb. to 12 Mar. 1869.
    12. Ibid.
    13. Ibid.
    14. D.G. Wright, 'The Bradford Election of 1874' in J.A. Jowitt and R.K.S. Taylor (eds.) Nineteenth Century Bradford Elections (Bradford Centre Occasional Papers No. 1, University of Leeds, Department of Adult Education, Leeds, 1979); pp. 62, 64, 66; Bradford Observer Budget, 7 Sep. 1889.
    15. Bradford Observer, 22 Apr. 1852, 21, 28 Jan. 1858.
    16. Ibid., 21 Jul., 4, 14 Aug. 1864; Reynold's Newspaper, 14 Aug. 1964.
    17. Ibid., 16 Jan. 1868, Feb. 1874, passim.
    18. Capital and Labour, 31 Dec. 1873.
    19. T. Woodhouse, 'The working class' in D. Fraser (ed.), A History of Modern Leeds (Manchester University Press, Manchester, 1980), p. 356.
    20. Ibid., p. 357.
    21. J. Ruskin, The Crown of Wild Olives (George Allen, London, 1886, 1906 ed.) pp. 105-6.
    22. D. McLellan, Karl Marx: His Life and Thought (Macmillan, London, 1978).
    23. A.M. McBriar, Fabian Socialism and English Politics, 1884-1918 (Cambridge University Press, London, 1966).
    24. Mary Ashraf, Bradford Trades Council, 1872-1972 (Bradford Trades Council, Bradford, 1972).
    25. K. Laybourn and J. Saville, 'Charles Leonard Robinson 1845-1911' in J. Bellamy and J. Saville, Dictionary of Labour Biography, vol. 3 (Macmillan, London, 1976), Vol. 3, pp. 155-6.
    26. K. Laybourn and J. Saville, 'W.H. Drew 1854-1933', in J. Bellamy and J. Saville, Dictionary of Labour Biography, Vol. 4 (Macmillan, London, 1977), pp. 75-7.
    27. Brockway, Socialism over Sixty Years,

pp. 29-30.
28. E.P. Thompson, 'Homage to Tom Maguire', in A. Briggs and J. Saville, Essays in Labour History (Macmillan, London, 1960, 1967), pp. 276-316.
29. K. Laybourn, 'The Attitude of Yorkshire Trade Unions to the Economic and Social Problems of the Great Depression, 1873-1896', unpublished PhD thesis, University of Lancaster, 1973, biographical sketches, pp. 478-85.
30. Reynolds and Laybourn, 'The Emergence of the Independent Labour Party in Bradford', p. 322.
31. Ibid.
32. S.C. Kell, 'The Political Attitude of our Law-Making Classes to the Unenfranchised', Bradford Review, also issued as a pamphlet in Bradford, 1861; Bradford Observer, 28 Mar. 1870.
33. Bradford Observer, 7 Feb. 1880.
34. Ibid., 6 Feb. 1868, 31 Jan. 1870.
35. Laybourn, 'The Attitude of Yorkshire Trade Unions', chapter three; Reynolds and Laybourn, 'The Emergence of the Independent Labour Party in Bradford', p. 321.
36. Reynolds and Laybourn, 'The Emergence of the Independent Labour Party in Bradford', p. 321.
37. Bradford Observer, 8 Mar. 1872.
38. Laybourn, 'Yorkshire Trade Unions', chapter three.
39. B. Turner, About Myself (Toulmin, London, 1930); B. Turner, A Short History of the General Union of Textile Workers (Yorkshire Factory Times, Heckmondwyke, 1920), pp. 124, 153-6.
40. J.A. Jowitt and K. Laybourn, 'The Wool Textile Dispute of 1925', Journal of Local Studies, Vol. 2, No. 1 (Spring, 1982), p. 11. The details are presented in an article by Ben Turner entitled 'Textile Workers at Bay', Yorkshire Factory Times, 6 Aug. 1925.
41. Laybourn, 'The Attitude of Yorkshire Trade Unions', chapter three.
42. W.T. Thornton, On Labour, Its Wrongful Claims and Rightful Dues: Its Actual, Present and Possible Future (London, 1869, 1870 edition), pp. 206-7.
43. Ibid.
44. J. Reynolds, The Letter Press Printers of Bradford (Bradford Graphical Society, Bradford, 1972), pp. 19-26.
45. Ibid., p. 6.
46. W. Cudworth, The Condition of the Industrial Working Classes of Bradford and District (Byles, Bradford, 1887).

47. Reynolds, Letter Press Printers.
48. Letter of Bradford Letter Press Printers to employers, 23 Nov. 1867, at front of Minutes of Letter Press Printers now deposited in the J.B. Priestley Library, University of Bradford.
49. Bradford Oberserver Budget, 23 Feb. 1884.
50. Philip Henderson (ed.) The Letters of William Morris to his Family and Friends (Longmans, Green & Co., London, 1950). letter dated 25 Feb. 1885.
51. Bradford Observer Budget, 6, 20 Mar. 1885.
52. Ibid., 6 Mar. 1885.
53. Ibid.
54. Ibid., 27 Feb, 17 Mar., 2 Apr. 1885; Bradford Typographical Society, Minutes, Mar. 1885.
55. Bradford Observer Budget, 3 Apr. 1885.
56. Reynolds and Laybourn, 'The Emergence of the Independent Labour Party in Bradford', p. 314.
57. Brockway, Socialism over Sixty Years, p. 30.
58. Thompson, 'Homage to Tom Maguire', pp. 292-3.
59. Ibid., pp. 292-302.
60. Ibid., passim.
61. E.P. Thompson, William Morris: Romantic to Revolutionary (Merlin Press, London, 1955, 1977 edition), p. 452.
62. Bradford Observer, 12, 20, 27 Jul. 1887.
63. Ibid., 2 Aug. 1887.
64. Ibid., 18 Aug. 1887.
65. Reynolds and Laybourn, 'The Emergence of the Independent Labour Party in Bradford', p. 322.
66. Bradford Observer, 25 Sep. 1885.
67. K. Laybourn and J. Saville, 'Samuel Shaftoe 1841-1911', in J. Bellamy and J. Saville (eds.), Dictionary of Labour Biography, Vol. 3, pp. 158-60.
68. H.J.O. Drake, 'John Lister of Shibden Hall, 1847-1933', unpublished Ph.D thesis, University of Bradford, 1973.
69. Thompson, 'Homage to Tom Maguire', p. 302.
70. Drake, 'John Lister of Shibden Hall', passim.
71. Quoted by T. Woodhouse, 'Trade Unions and Independent Labour Politics in Leeds 1885-1894', unpublished paper, p. 33.

Chapter Three

TRADE UNIONS AND THE INDEPENDENT LABOUR PARTY: THE GENESIS OF THE ILP IN WEST YORKSHIRE

Even as late as 1890 the Labour movement in West Yorkshire was a weak vehicle for the political aspirations of the working class. Trade unionism was patchy, Labour's political organisation was fitful, flimsy and embryonic, and the trades councils of the West Riding were only just beginning to emerge and become effective in protecting the economic interests of working men. In truth, the Liberal Party had little to worry about and was confident in its estimation that at least two-thirds of the working-class voters would continue to vote Liberal in future. It was this almost endemic weakness of Labour organisations which deluded the Liberal Party into thinking that it could stand still in the face of the 'little breezes' of discontent that occasionally emerged.[1] What local Liberal parties failed to appreciate was the seething discontent which had erupted amongst trade unionists as a result of the Manningham Mills strike of 1890 and 1891. This neglect combined with working-class anger and frustration to produce an Independent Labour movement which eventually made significant inroads into the existing two-party political system. Between 1890 and 1895 the genesis of a viable ILP occurred in West Yorkshire.

What transformed the small Socialist societies of the 1880s into a burgeoning Labour movement was the support which came from trade unions and trades councils. For a variety of reasons an increasing proportion of trade unionists became frustrated at the obduracy of Liberalism in the face of rising working-class expectations. The fact that many leading Liberals were prominent employers in the engineering and textile industries and also formed the local political oligarchy meant that economic issues could be readily translated into political ones. A Socialist presence in a climate of industrial conflict helped to unite the frustrations of trade unionists and channel their rising energies towards Socialist and Independent Labour activities. This was most readily apparent in Keighley and Bradford.

In Keighley, normally the most sedate of towns, the engineering strike of August and September 1889 united skilled, semi-skilled and unskilled engineering workers together in the demand for a wage increase. This dispute exposed the genuine grievances of the working classes in Keighley who had been unfairly treated under the old system.[2] A speaker at a strike meeting reflected the new, less compliant, spirit of the workforce:

> Keighley was known throughout the country for two things. In the first place it was famous for science and art and technical education, and in the second place ... it was notorious, not famous, for low wages. He wanted to put the two together and he wanted to ask them seriously what was the benefit of science and art and technical education unless they put more money in their pockets.[3]

The men were also warned to 'see that no mischief was done, that they do not run themselves into the police court or into the hands of the magistrates, for they would find as a rule that those men were not on the side of Labour'.[4] In the wake of this dispute a Trades Council was formed, which was closely associated with the Keighley ILP in the early 1890s.

Of more lasting and pervasive influence was the Manningham Mills strike of 1890 and 1891. It was the product of the attempt by Samuel Cunliffe Lister and the shareholders of Manningham Mills to reduce the wages of their silk and plush weavers by amounts varying from 15 per cent to 33 per cent of their wages. During the course of the dispute the entire workforce, of several thousands, struck or were forced out of work, the Weavers' Association became embroiled in the dispute, the issue of free speech was raised, violence occurred and the riot act was read.[5] This dispute has been scrutinised by many historians, most notably E.P. Thompson.[6] They have demonstrated how vital it was to the political education of the working classes of West Yorkshire. Much contemporary evidence, and most recent interpretations, have stressed the way in which the political consensus between the Liberals and the working classes was destroyed and replaced by a sense of deep injustice amongst a significant proportion of the working classes in Bradford and West Yorkshire. The <u>Bradford Observer</u> reported that 'The struggle took on the character of a general dispute between capital and labour since it is well known that a large number of prominent Bradford employers agreed with the action Mr. Lister had taken'.[7] The strike evoked a remarkable display of local working-class solidarity, so much so that the <u>Yorkshire Factory Times</u>, the weekly newspaper which served the textile workers, announced the end of the strike with the prophetic statement that 'Labour has so associated itself that even defeat must be victory'.[8]

Indeed the Manningham Mills strike acted as a catalyst for many of those trade unionists and individuals who had begun to doubt both the impartiality of the Liberal Party and its willingness to represent their interests. The <u>Yorkshire Factory Times</u> was correct in its estimation of the impact of the strike for the process of disengagement from Liberalism had already begun before the end of the dispute. In April 1891, at a strike meeting at Peckover Walks a famous open-air meeting place in Bradford, speaker after speaker pinpointed the lessons of the strike. Charlie Glyde summed up the frustrations of many when he reflected that 'We have had two parties in the past, the can'ts and the won'ts and it is time that we had a party that will'.[9]

The 'party that will' was officially formed about six weeks later at Firth's Temperance Hotel, formerly Laycock's, in East Parade, Bradford. A meeting was called for Thursday 30 April. Very few attended; those present, however, included W.H. Drew, James Bartley, E.W. Roche, Edwin Tolson and George Minty, men who were to become prominent in the Bradford Labour movement. A small committee was set up and a further meeting was arranged at Firth's Temperance Hall for 25 May 1891. At this meeting the Bradford and District Labour Union was formed to 'further the cause of direct Labour representation on Local Bodies and in Parliament'.[10]

The formation of the Bradford Labour Union presaged the rapid formation of others. The Colne Valley Labour Union was formed on 21 July 1891, and others were formed soon afterwards. By early January 1893 there were at least eight Labour unions, or similar organisations, in the West

Trade Unions and the ILP

Riding textile belt. Indeed Yorkshire was the best represented county at the Independent Labour Party's Inaugural Conference in January 1893. Of the 120 delegates present, 48 came from Yorkshire and of these, West Yorkshire sent the largest number. The Bradford Labour Union was represented by 20 delegates, Leeds ILP sent three, Halifax three, Batley one and Huddersfield six. In addition, although the Colne Valley Labour Union did not send a delegate it was effectively represented by two men, Edward Hoskins, of Slaithwaite Labour Club, and France Littlewood.[11] In total, then, 35 of the 120 delegates in Bradford were drawn from the woollen district of Yorkshire.

Table 3.1 Labour Unions/ILP branches in West Yorkshire, 1891-5

Organisation	Formed
Bradford Labour Union	28 May 1891
Colne Valley Labour Union	21 July 1891
Huddersfield Labour Union	14 September 1891
Halifax Labour Union	July 1892
Keighley Labour Union	October 1892
Leeds ILP	November 1892
Batley ILP	1893
Dewsbury ILP	1893
Shipley ILP	1895

Sources: *Yorkshire Factory Times*, 29 May 1891, 25 September 1891; Colne Valley Labour Union, Minutes, 21 July 1891; *Keighley News*, 8 October 1892 and the accounts of the National ILP Conference of 1893 which appear in several newspapers.

The prominence of West Yorkshire is further demonstrated by the national figures of branch affiliation. In 1895, for instance, 102 of the 305 ILP branches were to be found in Yorkshire, compared with 73 in Lancashire and Cheshire, 41 in Scotland, 29 in London, 23 in the Midlands, 18 in the North-East, 8 in Kent, four in the Eastern Counties, three in Ireland, three in Southern England and one in Wales.[12] Although many branches collapsed over the next five years it is clear that the North, as E.P. Thompson suggested many years ago, was the real home of the ILP and that the West Yorkshire textile district was its heartland.[13] It is hardly surprising then that Bradford ILP members, in particular, should constantly echo their justifiable pride in the fact that the National ILP was formed in Bradford, and that W.H. Drew, a member of the Bradford ILP and the Bradford Trades Council, should remind J. Ramsay MacDonald, shortly before the Labour Representation Conference held in Bradford in 1904, that Bradford was the 'Birthplace of the political Labour movement'.[14]

The early Labour breakthrough in Bradford and the woollen district was largely based upon the fact that the Labour Union/ILP organisations were quick to capture the support of some local trade unions and trade councils, many of which had only emerged in the late 1880s and early 1890s. Indeed the late emergence of a well-organised trade union movement in West Yorkshire might well account for the slowness of Socialist and ILP politics to develop before 1890 and its rapid growth therafter.

Until 1885 there were only two trades councils in West Yorkshire, at Leeds and Bradford. By the end of 1890 there were seven, and by 1895 the number had increased to 14. Apart from Leeds and Bradford, the majority of the trades councils were relatively small, although there was significant expansion at Halifax and Huddersfield in the early 1890s. The membership of the Leeds and Bradford councils fluctuated around 10,000 members each in the mid 1890s; Huddersfield had 2,000 members in 1893 and about 3,300 by 1899; Halifax fluctuated between about 3,000 and 4,000 members in the 1890s; Keighley claimed to represent 1,302 members in 1895; Batley had 3,000 members by the late 1890s; and other trades councils appear to have had fewer than 1,000 members in their early years.[15]

The relative weakness of most of these trades councils was a reflection of the weakness of trade unionism in West Yorkshire as a whole. We have already noted that textile trade unionism was weak in this region and the Webbs emphasised this in their estimate of the strength of trade unionism in 1892. According to them there were only 141,140 trade unionists in the county out of a total population of 2,464,415. Since about 55,000 of these were members of the Yorkshire Miners' Association, and several thousand were metal workers in Sheffield, it is evident that only about three per cent of the West Yorkshire population was unionised in the early 1890s.[16]

Indeed, there was little semblance of trade-

Table 3.2 Trades Councils in the West Yorkshire Textile District up to 1895

Organisation	Formed
Leeds Trades Council	1860, reformed in 1865
Bradford Trades Council	1868, reformed in 1872
Huddersfield Trades Council	1885
Shipley Friendly and Trades Societies	1887
Halifax Trades Council	1889
Keighley Trades Council	1890
Morley Trades Council	1890
Dewsbury and Batley Trades Council	1891
Brighouse and District Trades and Labour Council	1891
Wakefield Federated Trades Council	1891
Spen Valley Trades Council	1892
Todmorden Trades Council	1892
Batley Trades Council	formed about 1895

Source: K. Laybourn, 'The Attitudes of Yorkshire Trade Unions to the Economic and Social Problems of the Great Depression, 1873-1896', unpublished PhD thesis, University of Lancaster, 1973, particularly chapters three and ten.

union unity or effective organisation in the woollen and worsted industry before the First World War. Many unions were formed during the nineteenth century but they were, invariably, small combinations of skilled men with a propensity to collapse when employers applied the least pressure.[17]

The great difficulty faced by the wool textile unionists was that the woollen and worsted industry was so diverse that it made it almost impossible for large unions to emerge and represent a wide variety of interests. Some areas produced woollen dress fabrics whilst others produced worsted coatings. Huddersfield produced heavy woollens on a one-loom system, whilst Bradford weavers, largely female in contrast to the more male-dominated weaving sections in Huddersfield, worked two or more looms.[18] Other areas, such as Dewsbury, produced 'shoddy cloth' from the wool recovered from used garments. The industrial diversity of local industry, local customs, and the power and independent action of many employers who wished to determine wage rates directly with their workers made it difficult for wool textile unions to attract wide support.

The fact that the Bradford, Leeds and Halifax trade union movements, and their trades councils, were reasonably powerful in the 1890s is due largely to the fact that the craft unions, and particularly the engineering unions, in these districts were well established and powerful in their own trade. The fact is that woollen and worsted textile trade unionism was never able to carry influence in the West Yorkshire trade union movement which was at all commensurate with the importance of the industry within the area.

Faced with this weakness of trade unionism the local Liberal parties practically ignored the demands of trade unions and trades councils during the 1880s. It was only the rapid emergence of trade unionism and trades council organisations during the late 1880s and early 1890s which led local Liberal parties to make political approaches to the trades councils, by which time the vast majority of these bodies had allied themselves with the emerging ILP organisations.

E.P. Thompson has rightly pointed out that trades councils formed around 1890 were quickly committed to the Socialist cause. He argued that 'In almost every case, they were formed by socialists and new unionists with the direct aim of promoting independent political action; in some cases, the Trades Council formed the local I.L.P. as its political arm'. He also noted that 'The Trades Councils, even more than the Labour Unions, were the organisational units upon which the West Yorkshire ILP was based'.[19] Certainly those trades councils formed in West Yorkshire after 1889 fitted this bill, though many of their early progenitors would hardly have described themselves as Socialists.

Between 1890 and 1892 the leaders of the Bradford ILP, acting through their supportive unions took control of the Bradford Trades Council, ousting from its executive almost all the representatives of the hitherto dominant Lib-Lab group. The subsequent resentments, which almost led Liberal trade unionists to leave the Trades Council and form their own body, subsided and were eventually, and apparently successfully, contained with the creation of the Workers' Municipal Election Committee in 1901, soon to become the Workers' Municipal Federation.[20] The value of the organisational strength thus obtained is incalculable.

In an earlier publication we outlined the major reasons for the growth of the Bradford ILP. The gist of our argument was that 'strong trade-union support proved to be an essential corollary of effective independent working-class action'.[21] Because of the Bradford Liberal Association's contemptuous rejection of the Bradford Trades Council's attempt to secure working-class School Board candidates in the 1880s Liberal support in the Council began to be eroded.[22] The dissatisfaction thus engendered was translated into political action by the formation of the Bradford branch of the Labour Electoral Association in 1887. This body was formed in February 1887, following a conference at Bradford in which the Parliamentary Committee of the TUC convinced men like John Hollings (tailor), president of the Trades Council, Samuel Shaftoe (skip maker), secretary, and John Sewell (tailor), treasurer, of the need for positive action on the question of labour representation. They were not, however, so convinced of the need for independent political action - preferring, as we have argued, to act as a Labour group within the Liberal Party. Shaftoe, particularly, had made his career within the Liberal Party. He was a member of the Bradford Liberal Six Hundred, on the Executive Committee of the Eastern Division of the Bradford Liberal Association, and he stood for East Bowling as a Liberal in the municipal elections of 1884. Like many of his type, he saw nothing incompatible between his membership of the Bradford Labour Electoral Association and his connection with the Liberal Party.

Other working-class political activists were of a different opinion. Fred Jowett, C.L. Robinson and James Bartley objected to the alliance with Liberalism. Bartley could write in 1887: 'I believe it to be extremely undesirable to mix trade unionism with politics'.23 Two years later, he led an attack on the dominant Lib-Lab faction in the Bradford Trades Council. In 1891, Robinson, elected unopposed at a by-election for Manningham Ward, became Bradford's first ILP councillor. The alliance between Socialism and trade unionism in Bradford had laid its roots. As a first step towards independence, the Socialists and their allies joined the

Bradford branch of the Labour Electoral Association. Like its parent body, the National Labour Electoral Association, the Bradford branch was divided into two camps from the start – the Liberals led by Shaftoe and the Socialists led by Jowett and Bartley.

It was the latter camp which began to win support on the Trades Council between 1888 and 1892. A number of issues, but most importantly the actions of Shaftoe, lost the Liberal Party much of its support on the Trades Council. Shaftoe became embroiled in conflict by his criticism of the typographers over the delay in printing the congress reports in connection with the TUC Conference which was being held at Bradford in 1888.[24] Shaftoe's action in supporting an 'unfair printer' in the School Board elections of November 1888, and the bitter debate which surrounded this affair drove the Bradford Typographical Society and other trade societies towards Bartley and the Socialist camp.[25] From 1888 to 1893, Trades Council meetings were dominated by conflict between Bartley and Shaftoe, and the Socialist contingent gained increasing support from both the old craft societies and the new societies of unskilled and semi-skilled which flooded into the Trades Council.[26]

The Manningham Mills strike of 1890 and 1891 helped push the Trades Council more firmly in the direction of Socialism and political independence, but the switch of political power on the Trades Council did not come until the summer months of 1892. The formation in the Bradford Labour Union, in May 1891, and its decision to support Ben Tillett's candidacy of the West Bradford parliamentary constituency in the 1892 general election were vital events in the conversion of the Trades Council. The formation of a Labour Union, whose club membership rose swiftly in 1891 and 1892, provided a focus for agitation against trade-union support for the Liberal Party; the majority of its support being drawn from the ranks of trade unionism.[27] The Tillett election campaign of 1892, a product of the formation of the Bradford Labour Union, forced the Trades Council to decide whether to support Tillett or Illingworth, the Liberal candidate and sitting MP.[28]

Matters came to a head at the Trades Council meeting in June, a month before the General Election. There had been a majority in favour of the policy of the Labour Union for some time – as the election of George Cowgill, of the Amalgamated

Society of Engineers, as president had indicated. Nevertheless, the Tillett issue was bound to be divisive. The Bradford Observer, 18 June 1892 reported that

> The proceedings of Tuesday's meeting of the Trades Council were very lively. The Labour union members were determined to get a general vote in favour of Tillett ... They have had a majority on the Trades Council for some time ... they managed to get their vote but only after heated discussion.

In the vote which followed, 47 delegates supported Tillett and 33 opposed him. The Labour Union won, but, as Walter Sugden, a staunch Lib-Lab pointed out, the victory was not an overwhelming one. Voting revealed 'that very strong differences of opinion existed within the ranks of the Trades Council itself. Some bodies have even gone to the length of publicly expressing their disapprobation - such as the overlookers, the stuffpressers and the amalgamated boot and shoe makers'. Sugden continued: 'May I assure Mr. Tillett that his candidature in West Bradford has driven a knife into every labour organisation in town, the realities of which will be felt dramatically in the year to come'.[29] It proved an accurate prediction. The political balance of the Trades Council was clearly altered - but the Labour Electoral Association and Liberal supporters had not been thoroughly routed and continued to fight a rearguard action for more than a year.

Yet the Labour Union went from strength to strength. Tillett's impressive performance in the 1892 general election, despite coming third, did much to enhance the support for the Labour Union. Trade unionists joined the Labour Union in increasing numbers, and a large number of clubs, connected with the Labour Union, had been formed by the end of 1892.[30] Meanwhile the LEA was becoming isolated from the mainstream of trade-union activity. Shaftoe was its only representative in the higher echelons of Bradford trade unionism and its only municipal representative, having been elected for West Bowling in 1891. C.L. Robinson referred to the LEA 'as fast becoming an extinct volcano'.[31] George Cowgill was later to call it 'a Liberal association for the defence of blacklegs',[32] and its leaders were left in no doubt that they were seen to have betrayed their class during the Tillett election. Shaftoe, as secretary of the Trades Council, was the obvious target for hostility. In the election of officials held in January 1893 he was opposed by George Cowgill, a leading figure in the Labour Union and the former president of the Trades Council, and defeated. Shaftoe was defeated by 48 votes to 38, and the <u>Bradford Observer</u> referred indignantly to the 'cliquism' which now dominated the affairs of the Trades Council, reporting that 'no fewer than 17 delegates of the Dyers' Society attended and voted as a man for Cowgill'.33

There was no doubt at all that in future the weight of the Bradford Trades Council would be thrown behind the ILP. Shaftoe had been ousted on the 4 January 1893, and within two weeks the Bradford ILP had strengthened its position. On 8 January the Labour Church and Institute was opened in Peckover Street, and the first National Independent Labour Party Conference was held in Bradford on 13 and 14 January. The success of the Bradford Labour Union/ILP was complete. The new balance of power was clearly established. By 1896, J. Sewell was the only member of the nine-member executive of the Trades Council who was not a member of the ILP.34

It is fair to assume that by the mid 1890s the Bradford Labour Union/ILP had established its firm control over the Trades Council and that it derived much benefit from this relationship. W.H. Drew, a prominent member of the ILP a trade unionist, and the leading organiser in the Manningham Mills strike, was emphatic:

> I do say without the slightest hesitation that, at the inception of the Bradford Labour Union (from which body, of course, sprang the present Bradford ILP), it was the avowed intention of members of the union that it should be an essentially trade-union organisation.35

Although there was some dissent from this opinion in 1895, some middle-class members of the ILP objecting to the predominance of trade-union opinion within the ILP, it is clear that an elemental connection had been forged between the ILP and the Trades Council.36

The Bradford Trades Council formally dropped its apolitical stance in 1895 by adopting the Dyers' resolution, introduced by Joseph Hayhurst: 'That no person be accepted by the Council as a candidate for an elective body who is not pledged to support the collective ownership of the instruments of production, distribution and exchange'.37 By this resolution the Trades Council formalised a relationship which had existed since 1892, although the Trades Council, with the support of many of its ILP members, was later to change the basis of that arrangement in order that Liberal and Tory trade unionists might be drawn into Labour politics.38

In some cases, particularly amongst the newer trades councils the situation was not one in which the local Socialist and ILP organisations had to win the support of the local trades council but rather one in which the trades councils formed the first Labour union or ILP organisations. Two particular examples stand out - those of the Keighley and Halifax trades councils.

It was the engineers' strike in Keighley during 1889 which caused the formation of the Keighley Trades Council in 1890. Because of the comparative weakness of trade unionism in Keighley the Trades Council founded the Labour Union in 1892 in order to widen its base.39 In the mid 1890s the two organisations pulled apart. A similar type of situation occurred in Halifax where the Trades Council was formed in 1889. Though the Council drew widely from the whole political spectrum of trade union opinion it very quickly gravitated towards Labour policies. It did so for two main reasons. In the first place it was a recently formed organisation, with no established ties with the Liberal or Conservative parties. Secondly, the dismissals of James Beever and James Tattersall, both prominent members of the Trades Council, by a firm whose directors were well-known Liberals made it difficult for trade unionists to side openly with the Liberal party.

Beever was dismissed from his employment in April 1892, after serving his employer as a silk spinner for seventeen years. An indignation meeting was held soon afterwards, and the local press acknowledged that

> The Labour Party has been very much in evidence during the past week, much more so in fact than it has been before. On Saturday evening the working class crowded the Mechanics' Hall to contemplate the position which Mr. Beever, President of the Trades and Labour Council, now occupies, forced from the services of Messrs. Clayton, Murgatroyd and Co. He is to be the first Labour Agent for the Labour Party in Halifax.

James Tattersall was also dismissed about two months later. Testimonials were arranged for the two Labour martyrs and, in August 1892, they were presented with funds which permitted them both to enter business on their own account.[41]

Beever and Tattersall were victimised because of their prominence in Socialist circles. Beever was President of the Trades Council, was a member of the Halifax Fabian Society from 1891 and the President of the Yorkshire Federation of Fabian Societies when it was formed in January 1892. At approximately the same time he left the Liberal Party, and soon afterwards the Trades Council 'asserted in the most unqualified manner that they would have no political connection with the Liberal party'.[42] It would appear that the spite of the Halifax Liberal Four Hundred, the policy making body within Halifax Liberalism, led to the dismissal of Beever. In Tattersall's case there may have been personal motives involved in his dismissal for during the 1880s he became the Secretary of the Boothtown Liberal Club in Halifax.[43] He ditched Liberalism and proclaimed himself in favour of Labour independence in 1890, representing the latter view on the Halifax School Board from November 1891.

In July 1892, in the wake of the Beever and Tattersall dismissals, the Halifax Labour Union was formed. The political reaction of Halifax Trades Council to the victimisation of some of its members was the decision to separate its trade functions from its political functions. As Councillor J.W. Crossland, a member of the Trades Council, later acknowledged:

> Some time ago the political element was separated from this organisation and the money which had been collected or contributed for political and electioneering purposes was taken over, and the Labour Union was formed for the purpose, so as to leave the Council untrammelled to deal purely and simply with trade and labour topics. I voted strongly against it at the time but it was passed.[44]

However, the Halifax Trades Council found it difficult to separate industrial and political activities and formally re-established the connection with the Halifax Labour Union, by now the ILP, in September 1894.

As Thompson suggests then, trades councils and ILP branches worked in close harmony, even to the

Trade Unions and the ILP

point of trades councils forming Labour Unions. Yet it is also true that the older trades councils could sometimes take some persuading to join the ILP cause, as was the case of Leeds Trades Council.

The Leeds Trades Council was slow to respond to the socialist pressures. It was not until the early twentieth century that the Leeds ILP and the Leeds Labour Representation Committee became influential within the Trades Council, and even then relations were often sticky.[45] Part of the problem may well have been that some of the leading Socialists came from outside Leeds and clashed with local trade union leaders in their presentation of their demands for Labour representation. Yet as Thompson has suggested, Leeds-based Socialists acted as the missionaries for the rest of the woollen textile area, attending meetings, organising labourers into the Gasworkers and General Labourers' Union, and encouraging Socialist groups in the district.[46] From the late 1880s Tom Paylor, William Cockayne, Peter Curran and J.L. Mahon took an active part in promoting the joint causes of Socialism and trade unionism. Whilst they succeeded well in the textile district they were much less successful in Leeds. The problem they faced was that Leeds was a multi-industry town, unlike many West Riding textile towns which were dominated by one industry. Therefore, Leeds was never likely to suffer the same level of economic dislocation experienced in some towns, for whilst some industries experienced economic depression others remained prosperous. This industrial diversity reduced the likelihood that economic factors alone would stimulate support for the ILP.

The Socialist challenge in Leeds began in the mid 1880s, with the formation of the Leeds branch of the Socialist League, but effectively dates from the formation of the Leeds branch of the Gasworkers' Union in October 1889.[47] Within months the gas workers had won a bloodless victory against the Leeds Gas Committee, obtaining reduced working hours and improved working arrangements.[48] This victory underlined the value of having full-time officials organising the district. William Cockayne acted as district secretary and Tom Paylor was district organiser. Both men had been involved in London Socialism and brought their experience to bear in organising the Union's Leeds District. Membership increased rapidly and was further stimulated by the victory of the Leeds gasworkers in the four-day lock-out imposed by the Gas Committee in June 1890.⁴⁹ This famous, and bloody, victory increased membership and led to the opening of new branches. By the end of 1891 the Leeds District had organised more than 8,000 workers into 29 branches, representing 15 different trades. Twelve of these branches, and more than half of the members, were located in Leeds.⁵⁰

This increase of membership altered the balance of Leeds trade unionism in three ways. In the first place, it brought a new section of workers into Leeds trade unionism which, although less stable, rivalled the membership of the Leeds craft unions. Secondly, it introduced militancy into Leeds trade unionism. Thirdly, it helped to neutralise the Liberals on the Leeds Trades Council, thus allowing the 'anti-political' faction to control the Council during the early 1890s.

All three factors were interrelated, and represented a progressive deepening and widening of Socialist activities. By 1889 and 1890 almost every unorganised Leeds workforce was attempting to establish its own union. In November 1889 the Wholesale Clothiers Operatives' Union was formed to unite male workers in the wholesale tailoring trade.⁵¹ This was followed by an attempt to form a tailoresses' union following the strike of 900 tailoresses at Messrs. Arthur & Co.⁵² The Leeds tramway men held organisational meetings on a night.⁵³ The Jewish tailors, pressers, and machinists, formed three separate branches of the Gas Workers' Union. Public meetings were held regularly on Sunday afternoons and invited speakers included Tom Mann, Ben Tillett and Will Thorne.

The 'outside' Socialists who had fuelled the surge of Socialist and trade-union agitation in 1889 and 1890 gathered around them a mixed body of locally-established trade unionists, writers and middle-class philanthropists, including Tom Maguire, Alf Mattison, John Brotherton, Isabello O. Ford and J.H. Sweeney.⁵⁴ As a group they challenged the precepts of established trade unions.

The activities of these Socialists were, at first, strongly opposed by the craft unions of the Trades Council. It is important to remember that, in 1890, William Marston, John Bune and Sergeant Ellis, president, secretary and treasurer of the Trades Council, respectively, were all Liberals. John Bune in fact was a ward treasurer for the Liberal Party and became a Liberal councillor in 1893. Only John Judge, the vice-president of the

Trades Council, of the leading officials was not a Liberal - regarding himself as an independent. Thus it is hardly surprising that the attempts of the Socialists to organise the unskilled and semi-skilled workers into unions were not supported by the Trades Council. Indeed, the Trades Council appears to have made a deliberate decision to stay out of the activities surrounding the famous Leeds Gas Strike of 1890, when the Liberal-dominated Gas Committee of the City Council attempted to win back the wage concessions and improved working conditions it had been forced to concede to the gasworkers in the previous year.

Relations between the Socialists and the Trade Council were, understandably, poor. The Socialist activists of the Gasworkers and General Labourers' Union formed the Yorkshire Labour League in early 1890, intending it to highlight their opposition to the Trades Council.[55] In the wake of the successful Gas Strike of 1890, there was an ill-fated attempt to bring the two sides together when the Labour Electoral League was formed in July 1890, with Tom Maguire as chairman and John Judge as president. But it foundered with the unsuccessful attempt to find a suitable municipal candidate in the autumn of 1890. Also, in May 1891 the Leeds Trades Council refused to be represented at the massive May-Day demonstration which was held in Leeds.[56]

The antipathy between the two bodies was obviously fuelled by a variety of political and economic eddies, many of which actually fragmented the Trades Council response to the Socialists. The traditional links with Liberalism had obviously enhanced the political careers of some of the Trades Council officials who were reluctant to have their good fortune impaired. Many of the leaders of craft unions were also sensitive to the Gasworkers and General Labourers' Union organising the semi-skilled workers in their industries which they had hitherto ignored. Some delegates to the Trades Council were clearly of the view that it should not attach itself to any political group.

Yet between 1891 and 1895 the hostility of the Trades Council to the Socialists did begin to falter. This was partly due to the fact that the Gasworkers and General Labourers' Union joined the Trades Council in the autumn of 1890, and that Mahon became one of its representatives. The fight was taken into the Trades Council. In the conflict which ensued the Trades Council produced some odd and inconsistent decisions. Yet there were signs of change. The conflict between the Socialists and Liberals on the Trades Council did permit the neutral, anti-political, independent and Conservative-minded factions to emerge. These various factions were led by John Judge, John Demaine and J.H. Maundrill. It was Demaine, of the Leeds Typographical Society, who had originally maintained the need for the Council to be represented on the Leeds City Council independently of the other political parties in 1887, and had revived the idea in 1891. John Judge supported this suggestion soon after his trial for intimidation in October and November 1887, which appears to have hastened his departure from the Liberal Party.[58] Together, they directed the Council on a rather precarious course to political neutrality, the first signs of which appeared at the municipal elections of November 1891, when the Trades Council supported James Leach, an independent candidate who was incidentally the President of the Co-operative Society. Subsequently, when Mahon attempted to contest the School Board elections of 1891 it opposed Mahon's candidature and supported the Conservative sponsorship of John Demaine, who was duly elected. On a later occasion, Mahon's desire for School Board honours was rejected because the Trades Council 'did not wish to become involved in party politics'.[59] At the municipal elections of 1891, the Trades Council supported three of its own candidates - Cockayne (Socialist), Childerson (Liberal) and Maundrill (ex-Liberal independent). During the early 1890s the Leeds Trades Council struggled to give the impression that it was not attached to any particular political party but that it supported trade unionists in politics because they were trade unionists. Political neutrality was to be its watchword.

In May 1892 the Leeds Trades Council acted to establish a Labour Electoral Union, a body consisting of two-thirds Trades Council members and one-third Socialist members. But it withdrew from this political organisation in October 1892, maintaining that industrial and political matters should be kept separate, though it advised its affiliated unions to join separately.[60]

The Trades Council's reluctance to join with the Socialists direct was partly conditioned by the bitter conflict which occurred between J.L. Mahon and John Judge. Mahon decided to settle in Leeds in 1890 and take up the leadership of the local Socialist movement.[61] Judge had first come to Leeds in 1877, was an active figure in the Leeds branch of the Rivetters and Finishers (Boot and Shoe Makers), had twice been found guilty of offences under the Conspiracy and Protection of Property Act and had been found guilty of slander his £300 liability being partly met by the Leeds trade unionists.[62] His martyrdom in the cause of trade unionism made him an attractive and popular leader. Judge's support for an independent, rather than Socialist, line made him an obvious target for Socialist propaganda. His uncompromising trade-union stance led him to criticise Mahan, who he felt was not a genuine trade unionist and who he accused of having deserted the London Postman's Union after having led them into strike activity in 1890. Mahon threatened to sue Judge, but in the end the affair was settled by an arbitration committee composed of the societies involved in the dispute.[63]

The weakness of the Leeds Socialists was fully exposed by the Mahon-Judge affair. They had little support amongst the Trades Council delegates, which is why Mahon became a delegate to the Trades Council in January 1892.[64] Despite, or perhaps because of, Mahon's efforts Socialism remained weak in Leeds. The Trades Council continued its uncompromising policy of independence, and when the relationship between it and the Leeds ILP was discussed in May 1894 the minutes reveal that 13 delegates spoke against the suggestion that the Council should unite politically with the ILP.

Yet such a policy proved difficult to sustain in the face of mounting unemployment. Between the autumn of 1894 and the spring of 1895 the Trades Council and the ILP came closer together in their attempts to offer solutions to rising unemployment. At this time it was varyingly estimated that between 5,000 and 10,000 workmen were unemployed 'in the worst year that the West Riding had known'.[65] Inevitably, both organisations were drawn into the unemployment agitation that occurred in Leeds, and throughout the West Riding textile district, and both were united in committee work designed to find a solution to the problem, an action which culminated in the joint publication of a pamphlet entitled The Unemployed: A Discussion of Causes and Remedies for securing of Employment - Special Reference to Leeds (Leeds, 1895), which advocated the introduction of the eight-hour day to all industries - a policy which the Trades Council would not have entertained in 1891 or 1892.

Mere agreement on one issue was not, however,

sufficient to cement an alliance between the Trades Council and the ILP. Indeed that alliance seemed increasingly remote in the mid 1890s. The Mahon-Judge affair and Mahon's criticism of John Lister in the Halifax parliamentary by-election of 1893 had worsened relations. The Socialist delegates on the Trades Council were reduced by the Gasworkers' Union failing to pay its subscription and Paylor, Cockayne and Mahon all disappeared from the Council. And William Marston, the long-serving president of the Trades Council, led the Liberal group in a staunch resistance to the Socialist and ILP challenge. Yet the threat of unemployment did produce a Leeds trade union movement which became more pugnacious and inclined to the left, and some of the new Trades Council leaders were equivocal in their relationship to Liberalism and Socialism. For instance, Owen Connellan, secretary from 1892 until the early twentieth century, was returned to East Ward in the municipal elections of 1895, with Liberal support, but sought the Labour candidature of the East Leeds parliamentary constituency, following the Leeds Trades Council's affiliation to the LRC in 1900.66 By 1900 the Leeds Trades Council was prepared to give its political support to the Labour Representation Committee, the non-Socialist Labour Party, though not to the Socialist ILP.

The support of trade unions and trades councils was clearly vital in explaining the growth, or lack of growth, of the embryonic ILP in West Yorkshire. It is obvious that the newer trades councils became quickly committed to the Socialist cause. It is equally obvious that the longer-established trades councils, such as Leeds and Bradford, gravitated more slowly to the ILP and the Labour Party. Yet the winning of trade-council support was not of itself a guarantee of local political success for the local ILP branch. Only where trade unionism was well organised by the relatively lowly standards of West Yorkshire was the local ILP or Labour Union likely to make a political impact.

Of those ILP branches which had trades-council support in the 1890s the most important were clearly Bradford and Halifax. With about 10,000 trade unions members affiliated to the Bradford Trades Council in the mid 1890s it is hardly surprising that the Bradford ILP could muster something in the region of about 2,000 members. The Halifax Trades Council with more than 3,000 members supported an ILP organisation which fluctuated between 600 and

Trade Unions and the ILP

700 members.67 Together, Bradford and Halifax provided more than half the paid-up ILP membership in West Yorkshire in 1895. Indeed, Paul Bland, a leading member of the Bradford ILP, claimed that in 1895 the Bradford ILP was providing one-thirteenth of the National Administrative Council of the ILP's entire income and one-sixth of its affiliation fees.68

In Keighley, which had a fairly sizeable ILP branch of 120 members throughout the 1890s, the Trades Council was far too weak and vacillating to carry it to much local political success, and it was unable to mount an effective parliamentary challenge to the Liberal Party through the ILP branch it supported. In other areas, such as Dewsbury and Huddersfield, a modestly successful trades council supported a modestly effective ILP. In those areas where the membership and funds of the trades councils were low, as in Brighouse, Elland, Sowerby Bridge, Todmorden and Spen Valley, the local ILP branches offered very little challenge to Liberalism - though there was some fitful success in Brighouse.

It is our contention that the support of an exuberant trade union movement was essential to the successes which the ILP and Labour Party achieved in West Yorkshire during the 1890s and early twentieth century. Where trade unionism was relatively ineffective political success was limited. Yet, it is argued, that there is at least one major exception to these observations. In his book Colne Valley: Radicalism to Socialism, David Clark has argued that trade unionism was not 'an essential pre-requisite for Socialism', by which he means the success of an ILP candidate.69 He has argued that Tom Mann was unable to enhance the claims of the local ILP organisation, the Colne Valley Labour Union, to political control in the area because the message he put forward, in his An Appeal to the Yorkshire Textile Workers, was the collective one of advising them to join their unions.70 The fact is that trade unionism was weak in Colne Valley, there being only 1,545 trade union members in 1895 and only 867 by 1905.71 It is hardly surprising, Clark maintains, that Tom Mann was unsuccessful in contesting Colne Valley in the 1895 General Election. What transformed Mann's defeat in 1895 into Victor Grayson's parliamentary by-election victory in 1907 was the continuance of Labour clubs which underpinned the rising Labour optimism of the early twentieth century, the increasing support of

Anglican priests and Nonconformist ministers, and the sustained propaganda work which went on between 1905 and 1907. The whole was topped off with the selection of a charismatic ILP candidate, Victor Grayson, who touched the right ethical and individualistic nerve of the Colne Valley community. Moral suasion sustained by a thriving club life was therefore responsible for converting Liberals into Socialists and Liberal voters into ILP voters.

We will deal with the Grayson saga in a later chapter. At this point we merely seek to suggest that in emphasising the ethical appeal of Socialism, which clearly did attract many small businessmen into the Colne Valley Labour leadership, David Clark has neglected to emphasise the importance of the trade union contribution to Grayson's success.

There was nothing particularly unusual in a West Yorkshire ILP organisation being sustained by the moral indignation of those who objected to the economic and social inequalities of Capitalist society. John Lister, the Halifax landowner, and Arthur Priestman, the Bradford businessman, were sustained by such an outlook. There was nothing unusual in ILP and Socialist clubs sustaining the movement throughout its difficult periods. There were nine local Labour clubs in Colne Valley in 1893, reducing to a core of three between 1895 and 1905; there were 29 ILP clubs or groups in Bradford by 1895, reduced to about 10 by 1900; and the Halifax ILP had at least 8 clubs in 1895.[72] Labour clubs were not inimical to trade unionism, and the majority of members in Bradford and Halifax were clearly drawn from the trade unions. One suspects that the situation must have been similar in Colne Valley.

Trade unionists also played an important part in the Colne Valley Labour movement. The Colne Valley Labour Union, formed on 21 July 1891, was largely achieved at the instigation of trade unionists.[73] The inaugural meeting was the result of a prior meeting of the Amalgamated Society of Railway Servants and was strongly advocated by George Garside, of the Amalgamated Society of Engineers. It was dominated by the representatives of the Weavers' Association and the outside speakers included James Bartley, the Bradford typographer who had been instrumental in the formation of the Bradford Labour Union, Allan Gee and Ben Turner of the Weavers' Association. Of the ten members who were elected as the first officials only one, a local millowner named George William Haigh, appears not to have been a member of a trade union.74 Many of these officials remained within the CVLU throughout their lifetimes and, though there was no trades council in Colne Valley, they drew support from the nearby Huddersfield Trades Council.

We are not disputing the sterling work which David Clark has undertaken on Colne Valley, we are merely suggesting that the emphasis is misleading. Clearly there was something beyond mere trade unionism which contributed to Grayson's success in 1907, but just as clearly Mann's defeat in 1895 could have been the result of the national swing against the ILP or the failure of the CVLU, for a variety of reasons, to win wider support in Colne Valley; just as Grayson's defeat in the 1910 General Election may well have been due to the lack of a large and firm trade-union base in Colne Valley.

Despite the fact that Labour clubs emerged, that in towns like Bradford and Leeds there were thriving Labour Church organisations, it is clear that strong trade-union support proved to be an essential corollary of effective independent working-class political action in the West Yorkshire textile district. In the woollen textile district progress had already been made to capturing trade-union support to the ILP well before Alderman Ben Tillett made his prophetic ambitions clear to the National ILP Conference at Bradford in 1893:

> ... in spite of all that had been said about the Socialists, he thought English trade unionism was the best sort of Socialism and Labourism ... He wished to capture the trade unionists of this country, a body of men well organised, who paid their money, and were Socialists at their work every day, and not merely on this platform; who did not shout for blood-red revolution, and, when it comes to revolution, sneak under the nearest bed.75

Weak as trade unionism was in the West Riding textile district it had committed itself to the cause of independent Labour with verve and zeal in the early 1890s, and had been responsible for ILP branches winning significant political support in the textile district. It is true that the parliamentary impact of West Yorkshire ILP branches was not great - Ben Tillett failing in his two West Bradford contests, John Lister being defeated in his two parliamentary contests in Halifax, and Tom Mann being defeated in the Colne Valley parliamentary

Trade Unions and the ILP

Table 3.3: The Membership of West Yorkshire ILP organisations in the 1890s

Constituency	Branch	1893	1895	1899
Bradford (three seats)	Bradford	2,000	2,000	1,000
Colne Valley	Delph			6
	Golcar			18
	Honley			44
	Meltham			24
	Milnsbridge			50
	Mossley			45
	Netherton			12
	Slaithwaite			36
		300-400	300	235
Dewsbury	Batley		300	
	Dewsbury		500	
	Thornhill Lees			120
Elland	Brighouse		60	60
	Elland			9
Halifax (two seats)	Eight clubs	500	600	591
Huddersfield	Huddersfield	300-400	120	84
	Lindley	30-60	defunct	defunct
	Lockwood	60-90	17	defunct
	Longwood	50	45	27
	Milnsbridge	130	33	59
	Paddock	50-70	defunct	defunct
	Salford	80	defunct	defunct
		780-880	215	170
Keighley	Cowling			20
	Keighley	30+	100	120
Leeds (five seats)	Armley			29
	Birstall			18
	Central			100
	Hunslet – East			30
	– West			25
	Middleton			40
	North			25
				267

Table 3.3 (cont'd)

Constituency	Branch	1893	1895	1899
Pudsey	Farsley			42
	Pudsey			
	Tong			9
	Yeadon			27
Shipley	Shipley			60
Sowerby	Hebden Bridge			14
	Sowerby Bridge			18
	Todmorden			
Spen Valley	Cleckheaton			54
	Heckmondwike			60
	Spen Colliery			25

Details for Holmfirth, Morley, Otley and Wakefield are not available.

Sources: ILP News, May, Jun. 1898, Feb., Mar. 1899; Labour Union Journal, for 1891 and 1892; Bradford Daily Telegraph, 27 Nov. 1893; Bradford Labour Echo, 17 Nov. 1897; D. Clark, Colne Valley: Radicalism to Socialism. The Portrait of a Northern Constituency in the formative years of the Labour Party 1890-1910 (Longman, London, 1981), pp. 109-12; R.B. Perks, 'Trade Unionism and the Emergence of the Labour Party in Huddersfield', forthcoming article in J.L. Halstead and W. Lancaster, (eds) Socialist Studies (Harvester, Brighton, 1984).

contest in the 1895 General Election - but a start had been made, and the ILP was beginning to make inroads into Liberal domination at the local level.

The most immediate evidence of a burgeoning ILP was the proliferation of branches and the initially rapid growth of membership before the difficult years of the late 1890s. Whatever the outward reaction of the Liberal leaders they must have been shocked by Labour's swift political progress. By 1893 there were probably about 4,500 or so ILP members in West Yorkshire, a number which remained fairly stable until the loss of support following the disappointments of the 1895 General Election. Even then, and despite the difficulties of obtaining accurate membership figures, there were probably about 3,250 members in 1899. Thereafter, ILP membership increased until the First World War and was added to by an enormous rise in Labour Party membership.

The ILP's impact had, of course, been immensely variable. Bradford and Halifax were centres of ILP activity, whilst Leeds, Huddersfield, Dewsbury and Colne Valley showed some fitful potential of being ILP strongholds. Keighley, many of the smaller towns and some outlying districts were much less promising. In many of these areas membership figures were in the tens rather than in the hundreds and in some areas, such as Wakefield there was no ILP branch in the 1890s: 'It was barren territory which contained not one known I.L.P. supporter. The trade unions were weak and there was no local trades council'.[76]

This patchiness of ILP support is further reflected in the municipal and local political successes of the ILP. The municipal successes of the ILP were confined to six West Yorkshire towns up to the mid 1890s, and there were only twelve municipal representatives in West Yorkshire in 1895, and 19 in 1900. Yet there were successes in other local political elections. George Garside was returned for Slaithwaite in the West Riding County Council elections of 1892 and sat as a county councillor until his death in 1907.[77] In addition there were some successes in the urban district council elections in Colne Valley and elsewhere, to which might be added the successes in School Board and Guardian elections. The overwhelming evidence suggests that Labour was making steady, if unspectacular, progress in the municipal and local elections in West Yorkshire; not enough to worry the Liberal Party in the district as a whole but sufficient to embarrass them in Bradford and foreshadow the great growth in Labour's municipal support which occurred in the twentieth century.

The 1890s saw the National ILP rise to political importance in local elections. In 1896 a 'suggestive figure revealed that it had at least 181 representatives on local bodies, a figure which rose to over 400 by 1905.[78] A detailed breakdown of its 247 local representatives in 1900 indicated that there were at least 63 town, four county, 36 urban district, three rural-district and 16 parish councillors; plus eight citizen auditors, 51 members of board of guardians and 66 members of school boards

Trade Unions and the ILP

Table 3.4: The Municipal Successes of the ILP in four West Yorkshire textile towns, 1891-1900.

Year	Number of Municipal Representatives				
	Bradford	Halifax	Huddersfield	Keighley	Total
1891	2				2
1892	2	3	1		6
1893	4	3	1		8
1894	4	1	1	1	7
1895	6	0	1	1	8
1896	4	0	1	1	6
1897	5	1	1	2	9
1898	5	1	1	4	11
1899	5	2	1	5	13
1900	6	2	1	5	14

Note: a. The Bradford figures for 1891 are composed of C.L. Robinson who was returned unopposed in a municipal by-election and C. Woods who was returned as a Conservative working man at the November elections, though he subsequently associated himself with the ILP.
Sources: These figures have been largely compiled from the November issues of the Labour Leader, ILP News, Labour Union Journal, Bradford Observer, Huddersfield Examiner, Halifax Guardian, Halifax Courier and Keighley News.

Table 3.5: The Number of ILP Representatives in West Yorkshire, 1891-1900

Year	Municipal	CC,UDC,RDC PC,LB	Board of Guardians	School Board	Total
1891	4			2	6
1892	7	2		4	13
1893	10	2		4	16
1894	10	2		5	17
1895	12	2		7	21
1896	11	2		7	20
1897	14	10		11	35
1898	15	9	3	15	42
1899	19	10	3	18	50
1900	19	10	3	21	53

Note: a. This list includes the details of the County Council, urban-district councils, rural-district councils, parish councils and local boards. These details are not always fully presented in the Labour press and should therefore be taken as the minimum numbers. It may well be that the particular columns, and thus the total number of ILP representatives have been underestimated.

Sources: These figures have been taken from the March, April, May and November editions of the Labour Leader, ILP News, Bradford Observer, Labour Union Journal, Bradford Telegraph, Halifax Guardian, Halifax Courier and Keighley News.

representing the ILP throughout the country.[79] Of these totals it is clear that at least 20 representatives were to be found in West Yorkshire in 1896 and 53 in 1900. In other words, West Yorkshire ILP representation had increased from eleven per cent of the total national ILP local representatives in 1896 to about 13 per cent by 1900. West Yorkshire was clearly becoming a major political centre for the ILP.

Yet whilst such local successes broke the mould of the two-party system in some Yorkshire textile communities, one should not expect the ILP's political successes to exert much impact upon the pattern of local political events. ILP representatives were still isolated voices in the political wilderness in the 1890s, and the real breakthrough in a local political sense did not occur until after 1906. Although ILP councillors had a vision of a collectivist society in which the municipality would be responsible for ensuring that poverty was tackled and employment guaranteed through municipal action, it is clear that in these early days they were able to do little more than register their political presence. They remained overwhelmingly outnumbered on local political bodies and were unable to do much about the rising problems of unemployment which afflicted most Yorkshire textile towns in the early and mid 1890s. ILP councillors were unable to move the local authorities to action despite the fact that one survey, in 1894, indicated that 27.1 per cent of the population of Bradford, 57,558 people, were affected by unemployment and that other less detailed surveys suggested that a similar situation pertained in Leeds, Huddersfield and other towns in West Yorkshire.[80] Boards of Guardians protested that unemployment was no more than 'average'. Town Councils did little more than set up temporary unemployment registers to help the unemployed, and the numerous Labour protest meetings remained largely ignored. The Yorkshire Labour Movement Conference, held at the Labour Institute, Bradford, in November 1893 brought together 70 delegates representing 6,000 ILP members and trade unionists. This mass meeting of ILP opinion offered the eight-hour day, public works and land colonies as the trio of policies which the Yorkshire labour movement was to pursue.[81] But none of these policies had the slightest chance of being accepted in the 1890s, or of offering a solution to unemployment. A solution to unemployment was well beyond the scope of local effort; it was a national problem which required national solutions, although the Yorkshire ILP branches did not appear to realise this until after 1906.

Yet whilst the big problem eluded the influence of the ILP, the smaller issues fell within their compass. Many local authorities - town councils, school boards and boards of guardians - had come to accept the need for some type of 'fair wages' or 'fair contracts' resolution by the mid 1890s, although the implimentation of such resolutions, whereby contracts were only given to firms paying trade-union wage rates, often necessitated great vigilance on the behalf of ILP representatives and trade union officials. In both Bradford and Leeds, the Liberals appear to have taken fright at the ILP challenges and offered more 'progressive' policies at the municipal elections in 1894. In Leeds this included a range of measures to cleanse the River Aire, to cheapen the cost of travelling by tram, and to extend the provision of public baths. The Leeds Mercury reflected that 'From the appearance of the Liberal Programme last year we shall come to date a new era in the history of the civic life of Leeds'.[82] In Bradford, J.W. Jarratt, an advanced Liberal, helped to formulate a progressive municipal programme for the Bradford Liberal Association, which included a commitment to introduce an eight-hour day and a forty-eight hour week for Corporation workers, Corporation control of nightsoil clearance and tramways, and the introduction of fair contracts. Jarratt maintained that if the Liberal Party adopted a progressive policy 'they could cut the ground from under the feet of the Independent Labour Party'.[83] The very fact that Liberals were persuaded to discuss the possibility of introducing progressive measures at this early stage is clear evidence that the ILP was exerting an impact upon local politics.

With a rapidly growing membership, at least before 1895, a measurable impact upon local elections and a modest influence upon the operation of municipal corporations, it is clear that the ILP organisations in West Yorkshire were exerting some pressure on the local Liberal organisations. The ILP was taking its first steps to political viability. Yet, despite its rapid growth in a very short period of time, the ILP was still a comparatively rudimentary and untried organisation. In the enthusiasm of youth it pushed forward to contest parliamentary elections, often without the administrative infrastructure, including funds and full-time local agents, which the Liberals and Tories deemed to be essential in such contests. Without adequate funds and full-time agents, the ILP organisations lacked the essential pre-requisites for winning political support amongst enfranchised working men. Notwithstanding such disadvantages, and mindful of the fact that it was not until 1906 that the ILP won its first parliamentary seats in West Yorkshire, it is clear that parliamentary contests between 1892 and 1895 indicated that the ILP had much to look forward to, despite some local difficulties.

The Bradford Labour Union, as we have seen, had been founded on a refusal to work within the Liberal Party. It was this sentiment which promoted the candidature of Ben Tillett, first suggested for Bradford East. The shift to Bradford West was above all a blow struck deep into the heart of the Lib-Lab alliance, for here was the domain of Alfred Illingworth. Tillett's refusal to accept the Liberal offer of a straightforward run in Bradford East in order to leave Illingworth's alliance with the LEA intact was probably decisive in confirming the split between the LEA and the ILP, the former emphasising the need to concentrate upon local action whilst the latter was prepared to risk a parliamentary contest.

In the early months of 1892, Katherine St. John Conway, Enid Stacey, Bernard Shaw, Tom McCarthy, and many other national Labour figures, came to Bradford and helped to keep the parliamentary ambitions of the Labour Union at fever pitch. As already seen, Tillett's candidature was an essential ingredient in converting the Trades Council to the ILP cause. In this respect the impact of a parliamentary candidate had proved decidedly helpful to the Labour Union cause at the local level. When the 1892 General Election was called it was clear that the Irish vote would be against him, largely on the grounds that he put social reform on a par with Home Rule, and that Bradford Nonconformity was with Illingworth rather than, the also Nonconformist, Tillett.[84] Despite the redoutable opposition, Tillett pressed forward with his demands for an Eight-Hour Bill, old-age pensions, and a whole range of Socialist policies. In the event, he lost the election, coming third, but indicated that the fledgling Labour Union (later ILP) was a political force to be reckoned with. Tillett obtained more than 30 per cent of the vote. Although his second contest in the 1895 General Election was disappointing, he philosophically reflected that the ILP was down to its hard-core support.

Whilst Tillett might have held modest ambitions of winning Bradford West in the 1890s it is equally clear that the ILP's entry into other contests was less optimistic, largely borne of a desire to register an ILP presence, to challenge Liberalism in its parliamentary strongholds and to give working-class voters an alternative to the established political parties. As a result, John Lister contested the Halifax by-election, shortly after becoming the treasurer of the National ILP at the Bradford Conference in January 1893, exceeding wildest expectations by obtaining 25.4 per cent of the vote.

Yet, although the ILP could do well in the odd isolated contest, where many of the ILP branches in the region would help out, it was patently obvious that its fragile political structure was not capable of finding the funds, organising the voters, and mustering the level of propaganda activity which was necessary for a more sizeable onslaught upon West Yorkshire Liberalism. This became obvious in the 1895 General Election in which the ILP contested six West Yorkshire constituencies, being badly defeated in four and doing modestly in two.

Table 3.6: West Yorkshire Parliamentary Contests fought by the ILP, 1892-5

Constituency	Date	Candidate	Votes Cast	Labour % of the poll
Bradford West	1892	B.Tillett	2,749	30.2
Halifax	1893	J.Lister	3,028	25.4
Bradford West	1895	B.Tillett	2,264	23.4
Colne Valley	1895	T.Mann	1,245	13.4
Dewsbury	1895	E.R.Hartley	1,080	10.5

Table 3.6 (cont'd)

Constituency	Date	Candidate	Votes Cast	Labour % of the poll
Halifax	1895	J.Lister	3,818	20.5
Huddersfield	1895	H.R.Smart	1,594	11.2
Leeds South	1895	A.Shaw	622	6.4

Source: F.W.S. Craig, <u>British Parliamentary Election Results 1885-1918</u>, (Macmillan, London, 1974).

Although the 1895 General Election was the nadir of the ILP growth it is clear that the confidence of the movement engendered the need to make a dramatic breakthrough into parliamentary politics. That this did not occur, and that the ILP temporarily declined is obvious, but it must be equally obvious that Liberalism did not escape unscathed. At the national level, the Conservative Party returned to office in place of the Liberals, and in the Yorkshire textile district the Liberal dominance was significantly eroded. In 1892 20 Liberals and three Conservatives were returned to the district. In the 1895 General Election, and indeed the 1900 General Election, 14 Liberals and nine Conservatives were returned to Parliament. The Liberals lost all three seats in Bradford, one seat in Halifax, one seat in Otley, one seat in Shipley, and regained the Huddersfield seat lost at a by-election in 1893. Although there had been a national swing against the Liberals, it did not go unnoticed that some of the most significant local losses occurred in areas where the Labour challenge was strong and where Labour candidates were either contesting seats or where Labour voters were refusing to vote for the other two candidates, operating their personal claim to the 'Manchester Fourth Clause' which so dominated the discussion at early National ILP conferences.[85]

It is clear that ILP candidates were often being put forward simply in order to demonstrate their independence by an open challenge to Liberalism. Ben Tillett had had the opportunity of a straight run against the Conservatives in Bradford East during the 1892 General Election but had opted to fight the more difficult seat of Bradford West in which Alfred Illingworth, the doyen of Bradford Liberalism, was the sitting MP. Similarly, Tom Mann, in giving his reasons for contesting Colne Valley in 1895 suggested that one of his reasons was 'that the sitting member was a prominent Liberal capitalist, the head of a well-known engineering firm in Leeds, Mr. James Kitson, afterwards Sir James'.[86]

It is hardly surprising that, given such tactics, the Liberal parties in the textile district began to fear the loss of some of the traditional working-class Liberal vote, and began to view the Labour challenge as a plot to let the Tories in. The 1895 General Election appeared to confirm these fears.

What then had the ILP organisations of West Yorkshire achieved by the mid 1890s. Although local electoral successes were modest, and parliamentary success was non-existent, the embryonic ILP organisations had demonstrated that they were committed to political independence and posed a threat to the traditional working-class support for Liberalism. Above all, they wrested control of the local trades councils, and thus the trade union movement, from the Liberal Party. Propelled forward by the intransigence of local Liberalism and fuelled by the political support which emanated from industrial conflicts, such as the Manningham Mills strike, local ILP organisations became almost synonymous with trade unionism. Many ILP members would have subscribed to the vociferous comment of Councillor C. L. Robinson, the first ILP councillor in Bradford:

> an ILP man cannot be a true Labour man unless he favours the principle of trade unionism, and that the position of a trade unionist is a very anomolous one when he be not also an I.L.P. man, or at any rate perfectly independent - that is, prepared to steer clear of Liberal and Tory alike. Yes, I certainly think that the "trade unionist" and the "I.L.P.ers" ought to be absolutely synonymous terms.[87]

By the mid 1890s this was largely the situation in West Yorkshire. Most trades councils were attached to the ILP and most members of the ILP were also trade unionists, although many trade unionists still needed to be won from Liberalism. By 1895 the ILP was prepared to act as the representative of trade unionism and the vehicle for working-class aspirations. It was already posing a threat to Liberalism and the Liberal Party in West Yorkshire had to decide how to react.

NOTES

1. *Bradford Observer*, 9 Dec. 1891. The comment was made by Alfred Illingworth, Liberal MP for Bradford West.
2. D. James, 'The Emergence of the Keighley Independent Labour Party', unpublished MA dissertation, Huddersfield Polytechnic, 1980, chapter three.
3. *Keighley News*, 7 Sep. 1889.
4. Ibid., 31 Aug. 1889.
5. K. Laybourn, 'The Manningham Mills Strike: Its importance in Bradford History', pp. 7-35; Reynolds and Laybourn, 'The Emergence of the Independent Labour Party in Bradford', pp. 327-31.
6. Thompson, 'Homage to Tom Maguire', pp. 305-7.
7. *Bradford Observer*, 28 Apr. 1891.
8. *Yorkshire Factory Times*, 1 May 1891.
9. *Bradford Observer Budget*, 25 Apr. 1891.
10. *Yorkshire Factory Times*, 29 May 1891.
11. A.W. Roberts, 'The Liberal Party in West Yorkshire, 1885-1895', unpublished PhD thesis, University of Leeds, 1979, p. 255.
12. Ibid., p. 256.
13. Thompson, 'Homage to Tom Maguire', p. 277.
14. Labour Party Archive, Labour Representation Committee, 11/69.
15. Laybourn, 'Yorkshire Trade Unions', particularly chapters three and ten; Board of Trade Reports on Trade Unions, 1896 (c. 8644), 1900 (cd. 773); James, 'Emergence of Keighley Independent Labour Party', p. 64; Labour Representation Committee 14/5, Leicester Trades Council Balance Sheet for 1902 and Directory of Trades Councils.
16. Sydney and Beatrice Webb, *The History of Trade Unions* (Longman, Green, 1920 edition), pp. 427-33.
17. J.A. Jowitt and K. Laybourn, 'The Wool Textile Dispute of 1925', *The Journal of Local Studies*, Vol. 2, No. 1, Spring 1982, pp. 11-12.
18. K. Laybourn, 'Yorkshire Trade Unions', chapter one.
19. Thompson, 'Homage to Tom Maguire', p. 309.
20. Bradford Trades and Labour Council, *Yearbook 1912* (Bradford Trades Council, Bradford, 1912), pp. 21-2.

21. Reynolds and Laybourn, 'The Emergence of the Independent Labour Party in Bradford', p. 313.
22. Ibid., 324-5.
23. Bradford Observer, 16 Jul. 1887.
24. Reynolds and Laybourn, 'The Emergence of the Independent Labour Party in Bradford', p. 324.
25. Ibid., p. 325.
26. Ibid., pp. 336-7.
27. Ibid., pp. 337-40.
28. Ibid., pp. 331-4.
29. Bradford Observer, 24 Jun. 1892.
30. There were between 19 and 21 ILP clubs by the end of 1892, and 29 by 1895, before a decline to about ten by the late 1890s.
31. Bradford Observer, 11 Jul. 1892.
32. Bradford Observer Budget, 2 Nov. 1893.
33. Bradford Observer, 6 Jan. 1893.
34. Bradford Trades Council, Minutes, Jan. and Feb. 1896.
35. Bradford Labour Echo, 1 Jun. 1895.
36. Reynolds and Laybourn, 'The Emergence of the Independent Labour Party in Bradford', pp. 337-40.
37. Bradford Labour Echo, 22 Jun. 1895.
38. Bradford Observer, 18 Jun. 1892.
39. James, 'Keighley Independent Labour Party' pp. 67-8.
40. John Lister, 'The Early History of the ILP Movement in Halifax', MSS. copy in the Archives Collection, Calderdale Library Services.
41. Beever was presented with £157 and became a coal merchant and Tattersall was presented with £130 and became a tobacconist and confectioner.
42. Lister, 'The Early History of the ILP Movement in Halifax'.
43. Yorkshire Factory Times, 27, 29 Apr., 11, 22 Jul. 1892.
44. Halifax Guardian, 29 Sep. 1892.
45. Thompson, 'Homage to Tom Maguire', p. 302.
46. Ibid., p. 294.
47. Yorkshire Factory Times, 13 Dec. 1889.
48. Thompson, 'Homage to Tom Maguire', p. 299.
49. Ibid., pp. 299-301; Yorkshire Factory Times, 4 Jul. 1890; Second Annual Report of the Gasworkers and General Labourers of Great Britain and Ireland (Gasworkers and General Labourers, London, 1891), p. 11.
50. Gasworkers, Second Annual Report, pp. 25-6.
51. Yorkshire Factory Times, 6 Dec. 1889.
52. Ibid.
53. Ibid., 1 Nov. 1889.

54. Mattison was a member of the Amalgamated Society of Engineers, and his personal letters and diaries are in the Brotherton Library, University of Leeds.
55. Thompson, 'Homage to Tom Maguire', p. 298 refers to the formation of a Yorkshire Socialist Federation in July 1889, though this appears to have given way to the Yorkshire Labour League in February 1890.
56. Yorkshire Factory Times, 8 May 1891.
57. The Leeds Typographical Circular produced by the Leeds Graphical Society in the late 1880s and 1890s provides extensive details on Demaine. It is still in the hands of the Leeds Graphical Society.
58. Yorkshire Factory Times, 1 Jul. 1892.
59. Leeds Trades Council, Minutes, 26 Apr. 1893.
60. Ibid., 14 Apr. 1892.
61. Thompson, William Morris: Romatic to Revolutionary, p. 563.
62. Leeds Trades Council, Minutes, 6 Apr. 1887, 10 Aug. 1887; Yorkshire Factory Times, 1 Jul. 1892.
63. Leeds Trades Council, Minutes, 22 Jan. 1892; Yorkshire Factory Times, 1 Jul. 1892.
64. Leeds Trades Council, Minutes, 22 Jan. 1892.
65. Ibid., 6, 12 Feb, 6 Apr. 1895; Yorkshire Factory Times, 1 Jul. 1892.
66. There is extensive correspondence between the Leeds Trades Council and the Labour Representation Committee in the Labour Party Archive, LRC Correspondence boxes. Although the Leeds Trades Council joined the national LRC in 1900 it was not immediately affiliated to the Leeds Labour Representation Committee, which caused some local political difficulties. See particularly Owen Connellan's letter to MacDonald, LRC/13/367. Connellan was the secretary of the Trades Council and had been nominated to stand for the East Leeds constituency by the Trades Council despite the Leeds LRC giving its support to O'Grady.
67. Annual Report of the Halifax ILP, 1897, for 1896; ILP News, May and Jun. 1898.
68. Reynolds and Laybourn, 'The Emergence of the Independent Labour Party in Bradford'. p. 315.
69. Clark, Colne Valley: Radicalism to Socialism, chapters four and nine.
70. Ibid., p. 195. There are copies of this particular document in the Webb Collection, the British Library of Political Sciences and in the G.H. Wood Collection, the Polytechnic Library, Huddersfield.
71. Clark, Colne Valley, Radicalism to

Socialism, chapter four.

72. I.L.P. Directory of 1895 (ILP, London, 1895) indicated that there were 29 branches or clubs in Bradford, eleven in Colne Valley, nine in Spen Valley, eight in Leeds, eight in Halifax, eight in Huddersfield and five in Dewsbury.

73. Clark, Colne Valley: Radicalism to Socialism, pp. 7-19; Colne Valley Labour Union, Minutes, 21 Jul. 1891.

74. Ibid.

75. Bradford Observer, 14 Jan. 1893.

76. Colin Cross, Philip Snowden (Barrie & Rockliffe, London, 1966), p. 55.

77. Clark, Colne Valley: Radicalism to Socialism.

78. Bradford Labour Echo, 11 Apr. 1896; Forward, 10 Jun. 1905.

79. R. Moore, The Emergence of the Labour Party 1880-1924 (Macmillan, London, 1978), p. 60.

80. K. Laybourn, '"The Defence of the Bottom Dog": The Independent Labour Party in Local Politics' in D.G. Wright and J.A. Jowitt (eds), Victorian Bradford (City of Bradford Metropolitan Council, Libraries Division, Bradford, 1982), pp. 229-33.

81. Yorkshire Factory Times, 1 Dec. 1893.

82. Leeds Mercury, 27 Oct. 1894.

83. Bradford Observer, 11 Oct. 1894.

84. Reynolds and Laybourn, 'The Emergence of the Independent Labour Party in Bradford', p. 332; Bradford Observer, 4 Aug. 1891, 21 Apr. 1892.

85. The 'Manchester Fourth Clause' was pushed forward by Robert Blatchford and the Manchester ILP members who felt that, if there was no Labour candidate standing at an election, the ILP voters ought to abstain.

86. Tom Mann, Memoirs (Labour Publishing Company, Lond, 1923), p. 95.

87. Bradford Labour Echo, 15 Jun. 1895.

Chapter Four

LIBERAL RESPONSES AND LABOUR DIFFICULTIES IN THE 1890S

The Liberal Party organisations were supreme in the local and parliamentary politics of West Yorkshire during the late 1880s and early 1890s. The Home Rule crisis had tended to consolidate Liberalism behind a small number of Liberal-Nonconformist mill-owners rather than to divide and weaken it. Self-confident and well-organised, West Yorkshire Liberalism tended to regard Socialist and Independent groups, such as the Independent Labour Party, as a mere irritation rather than a serious threat to its political dominance of the region. Indeed, Alfred Illingworth probably summed up the preponderant mood of West Yorkshire Liberalism when he described the Bradford Labour Union as 'one of the little breezes which occasionally crosses Bradford'.[1] Disdainful of the ILP challenge, and almost contemptuous of the power of local trade unionism, the leading West Yorkshire Liberals made few concessions to the working classes, were unwilling to allow working-class Liberals to stand in local elections and offered little in the way of progressive social policies at the local level. The Newcastle Programme of 1891 might have meant a lot to the Liberal Party's national leaders but was largely ignored by the Liberal millocracy of West Yorkshire. It was not until the 1895 General Election that the Liberals became aware of the serious nature of the Labour challenge, which some felt had cost them seats to the Conservative Party. But even then the West Yorkshire Liberal organisations began to see their main opposition as a revived Conservative Party rather than an embarrassing, and probably spent, ILP. In short, the Liberal Party ignored the ILP before 1895, and was too preoccupied with the Conservative challenge to give much thought to the ILP therafter. The problems which ILP organisations faced in the late 1890s

Liberal Responses and Labour Difficulties

tended to strengthen the resolve of Liberals that they should challenge Conservatism rather than confront the ILP. This led the Liberal Party to shore up its middle-class support rather than to cater to the interests of the working classes and trade unions.

The confidence which the West Yorkshire Liberal organisation revealed in the face of mounting Labour opposition was hardly surprising given the parliamentary and local electoral successes of the Party. Liberalism dominated the parliamentary representation of West Yorkshire and was overwhelmingly in control of most of the school boards in West Yorkshire and the municipal authorities. It was not until about 1895 that its political position began to slip and given that the main challenge appeared to come from the Conservatives it is hardly surprising that Liberal anxiety focused upon the Conservative, rather than the Labour, challenge.

Table 4.1: The Parliamentary Representatives for West Yorkshire, 1886-1900[a]

General Election	Liberals	Conservatives	Total
1886	19	4	23
1892	20	3	23
1895	14	9	23
1900	14	9	23

Note: a. A list of the constituencies is provided in note 7 of chapter one.
Source: W.F.S. Craig, British Parliamentary Election Results 1885-1918 (Macmillan, London, 1977).

Table 4.2: The Municipal Balance of Power in Bradford, Leeds and Huddersfield, 1890-1900

Year	Bradford				Huddersfield				Leeds	
	L	C	ILP	O	L	C	ILP	O	L	C
1890	42	17		1	37	19		3	46	18
1891	36	23		1	38	19		3	40	24
1892	32	27	2		39	18	1	2	43	21
1893	30	26	4		38	18	1	3	40	24

Table 4.2 (cont'd)

Year	Bradford				Huddersfield				Leeds	
	L	C	ILP	O	L	C	ILP	O	L	Ca
1894	29	27	4		38	18	1	3	36	28
1895	28	26	5	1	38	17	1	3	26	38
1896	28	27	4	1	37	17	1	5	30	34
1897	28	26	5	1	38	16	1	5	30	34
1898	26	29	5		39	15	1	5	26	38
1899	27	44	5	8	28	16	1	5	26	38
1900	28	42	6	8	37	19	1	3	27	37

Note: a. The abbreviations are L for Liberal, C for Conservative, ILP for the Independent Labour Party and O for Others.
Sources: Bradford Observer, Huddersfield Examiner Nov. issues; T. Woodhouse, 'The working class', in Derek Fraser (ed.), A History of Modern Leeds (Manchester University Press, Manchester, 1980), p. 363.

The Liberal Party clearly had control of the progressive vote in West Yorkshire and it is perhaps not surprising that local Liberalism was aggressive, abrasive and unwilling to compromise with Labour. The Huddersfield Examiner, the organ of the Huddersfield Liberal Association, attacked the programme of the Socialist Party as 'so impractical that Liberals and Radicals easily recognise how foolish it would be to take up the bulk of it ...'[2] Liberals in Bradford tended to dismiss the formation of the Labour Union as being an irrelevance and W.B. Priestley, who was to become the Liberal MP for Bradford East in 1906, summed up this attitude when he said that 'Liberals believed that the I.L.P. were thoroughly honest in their intentions but they were a little too previous'.[3]

Not surprisingly, the West Yorkshire Liberals tended to dismiss the growth of an independent Labour movement as either unnecessary, since the Liberals were effectively representing the interests of the working classes, or as a Tory plot to undermine the progressive vote and return Tories to public office. The Huddersfield Examiner declaimed that 'Every working man in the Liberal ranks knows that a vote given to the Socialists is in effect a vote given to the Tories, and that every alienation is a means of weakening the cause of progress'.[4]

Yet the West Yorkshire Liberals did little to endear themselves to the working-class electorate. After the parliamentary victories of 1892, and despite the good showing of Ben Tillett in Bradford West, the Liberal Party did not attempt to heal the rifts that were opening up between Liberalism and the working classes. The Tillett contest, indeed, had revealed how reactionary was the Liberal candidate, Alfred Illingworth, who favoured the continuance of the half-time system and opposed the eight-hour day for miners. Two parliamentary by-elections in early 1893 revealed further evidence of the continued intransigence of Liberalism. The Halifax parliamentary by-election of February 1893 saw a bitter contest in which John Lister, a local landowner, member of the Halifax Labour Union and treasurer of the newly formed National ILP, obtained a promising vote of more than 3,000 for Labour. Although the Huddersfield parliamentary by-election of February 1893 contained no ILP candidate, it too added to the increasing tensions between the Liberal Party and the working classes. The narrowly defeated Liberal candidate, J. Woodhead, the owner and editor of the Huddersfield Examiner, was firmly opposed to trade unionism and had run a non-union shop for more than 30 years. The Huddersfield Chronicle, maintained

> In Huddersfield not only have the Liberals ignored the Labour Party but they have literally courted destruction by flying in the face of the Labour Party by selecting a candidate who is chiefly known throughout Yorkshire by his hostility to the Labour movement; a man who has said ... that he would rather lose the election than vote for the Eight Hours Bill for miners ....[5]

The local Liberal parties also compounded their sins by victimising leading Labour Union and trade-union officials. It was such action which had given rise to the Halifax Labour Union in 1892.[6] The Keighley Labour Journal, the organ of the Keighley ILP, also reflected that

> It is not so long since a prominent Liberal candidate told a defeated Labour candidate "it was a good job for him that he had not won the election as if he had his whole future career would have been blasted". Nor is it

> very long since a son of one of our so-called Liberal employers told another with respect to a Labour candidate, that "they would not have such a man about the place" and this ... simply because of his political opinion.7

G.F. Wardle, who edited the Keighley Labour Journal, was also placed under considerable pressure to give up his political activities. He explained how

> Some of the employers in Keighley ... had persecuted him because he dared to have an opinion of his own ... he was brought to the headquarters (of the Midland Railway Company) and made to sign an agreement not to take part in any public meeting belonging to the Independent Labour Party. ... He signed for the sake of his wife and children.8

Similar pressure was applied to many ILP members and some of their religious supporters. The Rev. J. Goldsack, a Keighley Nonconformist minister and confessed Socialist, was forced to resign his pastorate. 'What is the reason for this', asked the Keighley Labour Journal, 'Can it be that there are some members of his flock who prefer the old darkness to the new light'.9 The Rev. R. Roberts, a leading ILP figure from the mid 1890s until 1903 and on the eve of the First World War, was forced to leave Frizinghall Congregational Chapel for Brownroyd Congregational Chapel, largely because of his political beliefs.10 Similarly, the Rev. W.B. Graham, a Church of England Minister who had been active in the Bradford and Colne Valley labour movements during the early twentieth century, found himself victimised in Colne Valley.11

Liberal organisations still tended to be dominated by a few, intermarried, Nonconformist woollen and worsted manufacturing families, as they had been in the mid 1880s, and, despite the rise of the ILP challenge, the working classes had little active involvement in the organisation of the Liberal associations. Samuel Shaftoe, secretary of the Bradford Trades Council throughout the 1880s and up to 1893, was one of a small handful of working men in the Bradford Six Hundred, the policy-making body for Bradford Liberalism as a whole.12 Given the difficulty of winning support for the return of working-class delegates to Liberal organisations it is hardly surprising that many working-class activists drifted into the ILP.

There appears to have been relatively little support either for Lib-Labism or the new Liberalism in West Yorkshire. Samuel Shaftoe and Walter Sugden, both Bradford Lib-Labbers, were active in the national Labour Electoral Association but, as previously suggested, they found it difficult to sustain the movement in the face of obvious Liberal opposition to their aim of supporting the candidature of working men in local and parliamentary elections.[13] New Liberalism, in the sense that it offered a positive set of social policies to benefit the working classes, was also thinly represented in West Yorkshire. It was only in Leeds that Lib-Labism made any positive showing and only in Shipley that there was anything like a success for the Lib-Labs and new Liberals. In both areas, it was the work of William Pollard Byles, sometime editor of the Bradford Observer, which encouraged a new more progressive Liberalism to emerge - although only briefly.

The established political consensus between old Liberalism and the working classes in the Shipley constituency had been largely based upon Sir Titus Salt, Saltaire and the continuing influence of the 'Salt Ideal', which had as its basis notions of responsibility to employer, deference, and a working class prepared to follow the political lead of the Liberal middle class.[14] The death of Salt in the mid 1870s had done much to undermine the perpetuation of working-class deference in Shipley. Neither his sons nor his fellow directors carried the same influence amongst the workforce, or the same interest in the firm. In 1892 a new company took over the firm, and the loyalty of the workforce to the firm declined with the removal of family control and the increasing remoteness of decision-making.[15] Even though the new company left W.C. Stead, a former fellow director of Sir Titus, in charge the administration remained aloof and remote. Stead had become one of Titus Salt's partners in 1852 and, in various capacities, maintained his position in the firm until his death in 1897. It was Stead who was the President of the Shipley Liberal Association in the late 1880s and early 1890s, and it was Stead who emerged as the chief opponent to the idea that working men might be allowed to choose the Liberal candidate, and thus the MP, for Shipley.

In 1891 J. Craven, the Liberal MP for Shipley, declared his intention of retiring at the next election. The Shipley Liberal Association therefore made its intention clear that it wished Alfred E. Hutton, a young man connected with a highly-esteemed business family, and a Congregationalist, to be the new Liberal candidate. Stead, managing director of Salts mills, pressed forward Hutton's name to the Liberal Two Hundred in Shipley. From the start, however, the intentions of Stead, and his supporters, were challenged by one member of the Shipley Liberal Two Hundred, W.P. Byles, one of the proprietors of the Bradford Observer.

Byles was the son of William Byles, who had founded the Bradford Observer in the 1830s, and was involved with the paper as owner and editor. Byles also had financial interests in other firms and was a shareholder at Lister's Manningham Mills. This situation permitted him to make representations on the behalf of the workforce during the Manningham Mills strike.[16] He and his wife suggested that a lower dividend would enable the firm to forego the imposition of wage reductions. From this time onwards, Byles became identified with the cause of improving the lot of working men.

Byles was a formidable adversary to Stead and the leading Shipley Liberals, for he could use the power of the press to illuminate the trenchant opposition of old, established, Liberalism to the desires of working men. In an extremely bitter conflict he used his political prestige and the power of the press to put forward his own claim for the Liberal candidature of Shipley in opposition to Hutton. Although the details of the conflict of opinion are very complex, it is clear that Byles put his name forward on the basis that the existing Shipley Liberal Two Hundred was coming to the end of its existence and that the issue of the new Liberal candidate should be left to the newly-elected body.[17] As a result, the selection of new delegates for the Shipley Liberal Two Hundred became fiercely contested as Liberal clubs in Shipley, Bradford, and other areas where Shipley voters were organised, selected their candidates.[18] Throughout January 1892 Liberal club after Liberal club selected its delegates, in the heady atmosphere of internecine conflict between the Byles and Hutton factions.[19] In February 1892 the new Shipley Divisional Liberal Association, the Shipley Two Hundred, was formed. It consisted of 142 delegates, 59 who supported Hutton, 72 who supported Byles or were opposed to Hutton, and 11 who were members by virtue of their £5 annual subscription to the

Liberal Responses and Labour Difficulties

Shipley Liberal Association. Of these, 133 attended the annual meeting and it is clear, from the voting that Byles had a majority of about six delegates, although voting on some official positions was sometimes narrower. The delegates decided, by 68 votes to 62, to reject Hutton's candidature, which had been approved by the previous body in August 1891.[20] Seth Bentley, manager of the Saltaire washhouse, replaced Charles Stead, the managing director at Salts, as president, and most of the other positions, of nine vice-presidents, treasurer, secretary and 20 Executive Committee members, were filled by Byles's supporters. By the end of March 1892, Byles was formally adopted as the Liberal candidate for Shipley and a month later Hutton decided to withdraw his name and to stand for the Morley Division.[21]

What is particularly interesting about this conflict is that organised labour supported Byles to defeat the representative of Liberal millocracy. In effect, what had happened was that the Lib-Labs had captured a Liberal Association. The Shipley Trades Council supported Byles and helped form the Shipley Labour Electoral Association towards the end of February 1892. James Tiplady, a prominent member of the Bradford LEA and a Shipley man, reflected upon what had been achieved at Shipley, and the chairman of the meeting stated that

> He was glad to say, however, that in Shipley the Labour Party was thoroughly united, and that the great bulk of the workers were working for the Liberal party. The workers in that district were not going in for an independent position, but they had taken a very unusual course. A good deal of hard work had been given by workers with the object of getting hold of the machinery of the Liberal party in the division, and the attempt had been successful. They had selected the Liberal Executive altogether, and most of the delegates to the Two Hundred were with them. This was, he thought, the right way in which the labour question should be advanced.[22]

Such sentiments had already been expressed more than a month earlier, whilst the Hutton and Byles contest was still in progress. A public meeting, organised by Byles's supporters, including James Tiplady, Isaac and J. Sanctuary, members of a prominent working-class Saltaire family, found the chairman reflecting that

> It had also been said that Mr. Byles and his friends were setting class against class. The Executive did not give them the opportunity of doing this. They set themselves against Mr. Byles and his friends from the very first, and the charge of setting class against class could only be brought against those who made it.23

Working-class Liberals certainly felt that their interests had been neglected by the previous Shipley Liberal Two Hundred and that they were justified in fighting for their interests within the Liberal Party. This is what they had done, and they had won.

By the early 1890s, then, W.P. Byles had already set course on his career of supporting Lib-Labism, with its political connotations of an alliance between Liberalism and working men, and the new Liberalism, with its desire to promote legislation to improve the conditions of the working classes. He was adamant that Liberal and Labour interests were identical and stated that

> I myself and my supporters, who form a very large party in the division, as you will all admit, say that a Labour candidate and a Liberal candidate ought to be one and the same thing (hear, hear). I say that it ought to be an absurd question to ask whether a man is a Liberal candidate or a Labour candidate. There are Liberals, it is true, who are trying to drive the Labour section of the Liberal party out of the Liberal party. There are Labour men, it is also true, for instance, the Labour Union in Bradford, who are trying to drive Liberals out of the party. But I and Mr. Bentley and Mr. Watson and my supporters are trying to keep the two together.24

Yet it is obvious that Byles blatantly failed to keep Labour and Liberalism together. The Bradford ILP was ambivalant towards him, at once criticising his ultimate ambition whilst offering him political support. George Cowgill, President, and later Secretary, of the Bradford Trades Council, and a prominent member of the ILP, supported Byles's candidature in the 1892 General Election, informing an audience that 'They had come to look upon

Liberal Responses and Labour Difficulties

Mr. Byles as one of the best friends of the working man (cheers)'.[25] The supporters of the previous Shipley Liberal executive were less undecided; they appear to have gone over to support Theo Peel, Byles's Unionist opponent. The <u>Bradford Observer</u> noted:

> All along Mr. Byles's supporters had felt that they were fighting three parties, and as one of those parties, whatever its size, was a section of the Liberal party, it lent to the contest all the keenness of internecine warfare. As one went about the division on Saturday the magnitude of the forces opposed to Mr. Byles was most apparent. The bill-posting places were deluged with hostile blue, white and yellow literature, and yellow cards bearing on them the words "Vote for Peel and the backbone of the Liberal party".[26]

Despite such opposition, Byles won the seat by 282 votes, with 5,746 votes to Theo Peel's 5,464, much less than the 2,197 majority which had been recorded by Craven at the last contested parliamentary election in 1885.

Byles represented the Shipley constituency in the House of Commons between 1892 and 1895 but was narrowly defeated in the 1895 General Election when J. Fortescue Flannery (Liberal Unionist) obtained 5,999 votes to Byles's 5,921. Although Joseph Craven, the first Liberal MP for Shipley, and Charles Stead gave Byles their official support it is clear that many old Liberals remained hostile to Byles, and some, such as A.E. Hutton, were to be found supporting the Liberal Unionist opponent.[27]

Therafter, some of the Labour supporters of Byles began to drift towards the ILP, and a Shipley branch of the ILP was formed in 1895 with Jacob Sanctuary to the fore. In 1898 there were 61 members of the Shipley branch of the ILP.[28] But the ILP and the Labour Party were never to be significant forces in Shipley until after the First World War.

Byles, on the other hand, continued to develop his Lib-Lab and new-Liberal ideas. His election address, published for the 1892 General Election, indicated how progressive a Liberal he was. Whilst he recognised that the main issue of the 1892 General Election was '<u>the treatment of Ireland</u>' he regarded the second great issue to be '<u>the condition of the people</u>'.[29] Under this second heading he indicated that he was more than a Lib-Lab, wishing to extend

the franchise, the abolition of plural voting and
the payment of MPs, but that he wanted to see a coherent social policy presented by the Liberal Party.
Having referred to the issue of land nationisation
and other issues which many Liberals would have
agreed upon he concluded that

> Beyond these things I hope it may be found that
> social reforms will take legislative shape.
> Owing to the complexity of modern society, and
> to the development of the industrial system,
> there are many thousands of men and women who
> can only earn their livelihood at the will of
> another. This state of things appears to me to
> impose on society increased duties towards
> those members of it who are unemployed, overworked, or underpaid, as well as towards the
> young, sick, and the aged poor. I am ready to
> support just and reasonable proposals which
> are designed to overtake such responsibilities,
> and to increase the comfort, the health, the
> leisure, and the education of the people.[30]

Byles's position on these issues had, if anything,
hardened by 1895 and once he was out of Parliament
he began to explore the possibilities of working
more closely with the ILP.

Byles's first direct approach to the ILP was,
however, a tempetuous one. Having been defeated in
the Shipley parliamentary election of 1895 he began
to search out future possible seats. That was not
easy. Byles, although he was reasonably wealthy
was not rich enough to be able to pay the expenses
of elections, of election agents, and the contributions to numerous societies, which most Liberal
Associations favoured. However, an opportunity
presented itself in 1896 when Byron Reed, the Conservative MP for Bradford East, died. For a while,
the Liberals were unable to find a candidate and it
appeared that Keir Hardie, the ILP candidate, would
have a straight fight with the Conservative candidate. But it was obvious that Alfred Illingworth
was looking for a suitable Liberal candidate and
Byles hoped to presume himself on to the Liberal
Party and the ILP alike as a compromise figure.
Byles's suit was unsuccessful, but his exchange of
letters with Hardie reflects the extent of his
personal commitment to the new Liberalism. Byles
wrote:

> When you say I vacillate between two opinions

Liberal Responses and Labour Difficulties

> and do not choose between Liberalism and Labour, you absolutely misunderstand my position. I will explain: you and I hold practically the same opinions. These opinions have led you to disbelieve in the Lib. party as an engine for the reforms you seek, and therefore to leave it and form a separate party. The same opinions have not led me to the same conclusions. Bad and reactionary as many Liberals are, I believe that salvation must come thro the Liberal party wh. still contains more friends of Labour than can be found outside it, and the destruction of which (if it were possible wh. it isn't) would set back the Labour clock a generation.31

By the end of the 1890s, having sold his shares in the <u>Bradford Observer</u> and having asked Charles W. Dilke to intervene on his behalf with Hardie, Byles stood as a Labour candidate for Leeds East, obtaining 1,266 votes or 20.1 per cent of the vote.

The circumstances of Byles's labour candidature in Leeds East were unusual and confused. There was extensive correspondence on Byles between the Leeds Trades Council and the Labour Representation Committee, or, more precisely, between Owen Connellan, Secretary of the Trades Council, and MacDonald.32 The gist of the correspondence was that Byles's candidature had been sought by the East Leeds branch of the United Irish League which had approached the Trades Council with a view to getting Byles accepted as a Labour and Home Rule candidate. The Trades Council endorsed Byles's candidature in September 1900 and it was clearly hoped that the Liberal Party would be persuaded to accept Byles as the Liberal candidate as well. These events were clearly deplored by a number of local Labour activists who considered the 'Byles business' to be 'disgraceful'.33 Owen Connellan, who hoped to be selected as Labour candidate for Leeds East, was Byles's bitterest opponent. Reflecting that the Labour Representation Committee ought to have been rather broader in its political approach, and selected its own Liberal-Labour man, Connellan trenchantly, but accurately, summed up the situation by suggesting that it would have been better than 'to see the Trades Council, ILP and Socialist influence used for the purpose of forcing an unpopular man upon his own party. And I believe it would have been easier to induce the Liberal party to accept a Labour man than to swallow Mr. Byles'.34 Byles soon returned to the

Liberal fold, left Bradford, and successfully sought his political fortune in Lancashire where his new-Liberal ideas appear to have gone down well. But he does not appear to have created much of a following in West Yorkshire. The old Liberal millocracy suspected him, and were positively opposed to him in Shipley, Bradford and Leeds. On the other hand, the ILP and Labour Representation Committee leaders were equally dubious of Byles and, urging him to join the ILP, one political commentator reflected that 'As a Liberal fighting on a Liberal platform, he is very little more to us than the rest of the plutocrats who are beguiling and misleading the workers'.[35]

There were very few victories for Lib-Labism and the new Liberalism in West Yorkshire throughout the 1890s. There is evidence of initiatives by the new Liberals. J.W. Jarratt, an advanced Liberal, helped to formulate a progressive municipal programme for the Bradford Liberal Association in 1894, which contained commitments to introducing an eight-hour day and forty-eight hour week for Corporation workers, Corporation control of nightsoil clearance and tramways, and the introduction of fair contracts, but it does not appear to have stemmed the flow to the ILP.[36] When this policy failed to achieve the desired result the Liberals began to make overtures to the ILP, and there were meetings between leading Liberals and ILP members in April 1897, orchestrated by W.P. Byles.[37] The opprobrious reaction within ILP circles quickly ended the initiative, though the <u>Bradford Observer</u> was proud to report that the Joint Committee of the Trades Council and the ILP after having put three test questions to all municipal candidates in 1898 had recommended 'working men to support Liberal candidates in all wards in which no Labour candidate had appeared'.[38] In 1899 the <u>Bradford Labour Echo</u> speculated that the feud between the 'Radical Socialists' in the Liberal Party and 'old-time Liberalism' could only end 'in the disappearance of old Liberalism'.[39] There was much optimism within some sections of Liberalism when W.E.B. Priestley's secret mission to H. Gladstone led to Jarratt's standing down from Bradford West, thus permitting Fred Jowett a straight fight with the conservative candidate in the 1900 General Election. But, in the end, the old Liberalism prevailed, a fact testified to by Byles's eventual departure from Bradford politics in 1903, for the more politically agreeable air of Manchester and Salford.[40]

Apart from Byles, there is little evidence of prominent Liberal politicians from West Yorkshire

Liberal Responses and Labour Difficulties

exhibiting much interest in the Liberal ideas of the 1890s. C.P. Trevelyan was only returned for the Elland constituency in the parliamentary by-election of March 1899 and there is little evidence that he was inclined to new Liberalism before 1906.[41] Old Liberalism, dominated by a Nonconformist textile millocracy remained dominant in West Yorkshire throughout the 1890s and remained almost impervious to the demands being put forward by advanced and new Liberals such as Byles. In the early 1890s old Liberalism refused to acknowledge the seriousness of the Labour challenge, and from 1895 onwards became increasingly preoccupied with the rise of Conservative fortunes which had reduced the parliamentary strength of Liberalism in West Yorkshire and removed it completely in Bradford.[42] In many respects this concern to meet the challenge of Conservatism was most sensible, given the problems which the ILP faced in West Yorkshire during the late 1890s.

The previous chapter suggested that ILP membership in West Yorkshire declined substantially after the 1895 General Election which pricked the bubble of support which had welled up for the ILP between 1893 and 1895.[43] Membership fell from about 2,000 to 1,000 in Bradford between 1895 and 1896, and many small ILP branches began to collapse throughout West Yorkshire. This situation was worsened by the internecine conflict which emerged within the Halifax ILP, one of the most powerful ILP branches in the country.

In its early years, the three leading political figures in the Halifax Labour Union had been John Lister, James Beever and James Tattersall. John Lister was the owner of the Shibden Hall estate, on the outskirts of Halifax, had been educated at Oxford, where he was greatly influenced by the writings of John Ruskin and William Morris, and was drawn into Fabianism in 1891. By 1892 he had joined the Labour Union and in January 1893 he had become the Treasurer of the National ILP, a post which he retained until he left the ILP in 1895.[44] Beever and Tattersall, on the other hand, had been drawn into the ILP by their trade union activities. As previously suggested, both had been victimised by their employer in 1892, and it was out of the indignation which followed that the Halifax Labour Union was formed.[45] Beever was an active Fabian, became President of the Halifax Trades Council, and effectively became the 'first Labour agent' for Halifax. Tattersall became the first president of the

Halifax Labour Union in 1892.

In a traumatic train of events all three were gradually forced out of the ILP between 1894 and 1895. The internal squabbles of the Halifax Labour Union were widely reported in the local and national press, doing much damage to the cause of independent Labour. They began in May 1894 when Lister, Beever and Tattersall, the ILP's three town council representatives, divided over the issue of the reorganization of the Town Clerk's Office. Lister voted in favour, and Beever and Tattersall against the motion for reorganization. Although this division appeared to be an isolated incident, the June meeting of the Halifax Labour Union, chaired by Montague Blatchford, decided that in 'future councillors were to confer with the Union' before voting on any item of the Council agenda.[46] Although the possibility of conflict appeared to subside, it is clear, from a letter which Henry Backhouse sent to Keir Hardie, that there was much indignation that the three representatives were divided. Discussing the rising political level of activities in anticipation of Town Council, School Board and Guardian elections, Backhouse reflected that 'Everything hinges on, whether these men (three) can be persuaded to fall into line to practice the teachings of socialism - to submit to the great heart of the people and to esteem it and honour it ...'[47]

Local tensions subsided until the 23 October 1894, the day before the municipal nomination deadline, when Lister sent a letter to Tattersall, and the Labour Union, asking for his nomination for Central Ward to be withdrawn. In a fit of pique, Lister informed Tattersall that

> I can't attend to the duties properly and I don't like the job. Moreover, I feel that I have not given satisfaction to the Labour Union during my term of stewardship, and I am not prepared to accept the new conditions that the Union has imposed upon its representatives. I cannot submit to having my opinion, even in matters of detail, cut and dried for me.[48]

During the next twenty-four hours the Halifax Labour Union attempted to find a suitable substitute candidate for Lister. None was forthcoming, although Beever intimated his willingness to contest Central Ward if some type of political arrangement could be made with the Tories. The Labour Union declined to accept the suggestion but, to its

consternation, found out on 24th October that
Lister's name had been put down for the North Ward
and that Beever's name had been put forward for
Central Ward. Beever was immediately asked to withdraw his nomination from Central Ward, but refused
to do so and Lister re-entered the affair with three
telegrams on 25th October, at first declaring his
intention to stand for Council but then indicating
his decision to retire from municipal work.[49] There
was a strong feeling amongst the Labour Union members that the Liberal Party was connected with the
fact that Beever had been nominated for Central as
well as Southowram Ward, and a meeting was held
that night, chaired by Alderman Tattersall, which
repudiated Beever's candidature by 88 votes to 68.
Beever still contested Southowram however, with the
support of the Southowram Labour Club.

When the November municipal elections occurred
Central Ward was uncontested, the three Labour
candidates, including Beever were defeated, and
only Alderman Tattersall was left on the Council.
Retribution was swift. Beever was expelled from the
Halifax Labour Union for 'insubordination' and
Lister was forced to make his apologies to the Coun-
cil of the Halifax Labour Union.[50]

The matter might have rested there had it not
been for the Clarion taking the issue as an opportunity to strike at the ILP executive in general,
and Keir Hardie in particular. Lister was the treasurer of the ILP and a friend of Hardie. Neither
Robert Blatchford nor Montague Blatchford cared for
either, there being differences of opinion over ILP
tactics, municipal policy and Socialist unity.
Robert Blatchford condemned Lister and Beever through the Clarion, pronouncing that

> In a Democratic body the rule of the majority
> must be obeyed. If the ruling of the majority
> is disobeyed, the fact that the rebel holds a
> high position in the party is the strongest
> argument in favour of his condign punishment.
> Socialism without Democracy would be an abom-
> inable tyranny.[51]

Whilst Blatchford emphasised the need for a
democratic body to have control over its members,
and argued that the Halifax affair had proved the
quality of democracy within the ILP, others begged
to differ. Edward Carpenter, the Sheffield-based
Socialist, was critical of what he called the
'dancing-doll delegate ... You know what I mean.

Liberal Responses and Labour Difficulties

The constituents (or is it not more often a caucus of the constituents?) pull the string; the delegate holds up his hand. They slacken and he drops it'.[52] John Burns felt that 'It is necessary to compromise in non-essential methods in order to achieve the essential things they were after'. Hardie felt that 'There is a spirit of distrust and suspicion abroad in our movement ... distrust and suspicion which is the reverse of our real purpose'.[53]

The petulant nature of this affair continued when, in mid-November 1894, James Beever was returned as a School Board candidate, whilst the Labour Union candidates, Montague Blatchford, Tattersall and Marsden, were all defeated.[54] The N.A.C. of the ILP requested that the Halifax Labour Union should consider reinstating Mr. Beever, but it declined to do so.[55] In addition, several of the local ILP clubs such as Southowram, Siddal and Caddy Field opposed the Labour Union, and the Caddy Field club informed the N.A.C. of the ILP that 'payment of affiliation fees would be paid direct to the treasurer' as it was 'now not part of the Halifax Labour Union'.[56]

Relations deteriorated in December 1894 when Montague Blatchford, and some of his supporters, demanded that Lister should be censured and stripped of his ILP parliamentary candidature for Halifax; he had stood in the parliamentary by-election of January 1893. Lister was in no hurry to attend a censure meeting and the threat to humble him before the Labour Union provoked fierce responses on both sides.

Lister wrote to Hardie explaining his actions and threatening to resign from the party rather than face a second meeting.[57] As the National ILP was in debt to Lister to the tune of about £135, and as Hardie expressed his personal obligation to pay off some of this debt, it is hardly surprising that Hardie was unwilling to lose the Treasurer of the ILP and its financial benefactor in one fell swoop. On Christmas Day 1894 he wrote to Lister giving him his support, suggesting that the Blatchford request was insulting, advising him to join another branch of the ILP, and noting that

> It might be as well to write to Tom Mann as secretary protesting against the Resolution already passed, and appealing to the N.A.C. against being condemned unheard. The upshot will probably be the severance of the Halifax Labour Union from the I.L.P. and for the present I see nothing better that could happen. If the

spirit of the Halifax Labour Union became general in the movement, I for one would clear out.[58]

The animus created by the Halifax events flowed over into the national movement. Hardie was criticised by Robert Blatchford and many local Halifax men for his public support of Lister in the Labour Leader. Robert Blatchford's relatively restrained letters to Hardie were laced with references to Lister being 'a weak man' and a 'wrong un'.[59] Others were less diplomatic. Robert Morley, a local engineering trade unionist who was subsequently to become closely involved in the formation of Tom Mann's Workers' Union,[60] criticised Hardie's 'one-eyed approach', and concluded one lengthy letter, in which he outlined the whole affair as he saw it, in the following manner: '"A score of sound honest men are better than 20,000 unreliable" so said Hardie in Halifax last June. We believe it still & are therefore safe. Hoping a similar judgement may possess you, & a less prejudiced position be assumed towards us'.[61]

In the event, Lister faced the second censure meeting on 3 January 1895. Despite strong criticism, and a 'lively discussion', Lister remained a member of the Halifax Labour Union, was not censured and remained the Labour Union's parliamentary candidate for Halifax.[62] Within a few weeks he was campaigning for the Halifax seat and in July 1895 he made a spirited attempt to win the seat for the ILP.[63] He subsequently contested the municipal elections in November 1895, but then quickly drifted out of the local and the National ILP.[64] Beever briefly returned to the Labour fold, to speak in favour of Lister at the 1895 General Election, but then re-established his Liberal credentials.

Alderman Tattersall also left the ILP, in November 1895. In 1892 Tattersall had been supported by the Conservatives who pushed for him to be raised to the aldermanic bench in preference to Beever who was favoured by the Liberals.[65] On the town council, Tattersall found that he gained most support from Alderman Whittaker, the Conservative party boss in Halifax, and maintained that 'so far as industrial legislation is concerned I am quite convinced that the Labour Party has more to hope for from the Conservative Government than they can possible get from a Liberal Administration'.[66] During the 1895 General Election, when he was the ILP candidate for Preston, he despatched An Appeal to the working men of Halifax in which he advised Labour voters to cast their second vote, Halifax being a two-seat constituency, 'against the most illiberal set of men in Halifax and the nominees of the so-called Liberal Association'.[67] The implication was that Labour voters should use their second vote to support the Conservative candidate. He also stressed that the split votes indicated that 1,351 Conservatives voted for Lister in the 1895 General Election whilst only 700 Liberals had done the same.[68] Eventually, in November 1895, Tattersall was drummed out of the Halifax Labour Union by the overwhelming majority of 75 votes to 15.[69] Soon afterwards he became a full-time agent for the Halifax Conservative Party.[70]

The Liberal Party and the nation's press made much sport out of the open conflict which had emerged between the factions of the Halifax Labour Union and the National ILP. Such internecine conflict was not the best way to approach a general election, and was obviously a contributory factor in the disappointing results achieved by the ILP in 1895.

The 1895 General Election was, indeed, a great setback for the national movement. The loss of Hardie's West Ham seat, the defeat of 35 ILP candidates, who could only muster 50,000 votes between them - about 15 per cent of the vote in what were considered to be improving seats for the ILP - told disastrously on the national movement. Membership slipped away following this political defeat for the party was not as yet established to fight on a comparatively large scale. Despite the relative strength of the ILP in West Yorkshire, Labour leaders were desperately sifting through the possibilities of reviving the movement. Stephen Yeo has suggested that it was at about this stage that the 'Cause' began to lose its sense of Socialist purpose and to concentrate its efforts upon improving its electoral performance. Yeo feels that at this stage the pursuit of electoral success began to undermine the Socialist purpose of the 'Cause'. The Socialist movement neglected its original aim of winning ground for Socialism and offering a Socialist way of life.[71] However, what is clear in West Yorkshire is that the spiritual and religious side of the movement continued to flourish at the same time as the movement became increasingly dominated by trade unions. Indeed, the Socialist Sunday school movement was only just beginning to get under way, the real growth occurring from 1899 onwards with the formation of the Central Socialist Sunday school in Bradford and the formation of the Yorkshire Socialist Sunday School Union.[72] Therafter the movement continued to grow until the First World War winning an increasing number of children, and their parents, to the pursuance of a Socialist way of life. And although the Leeds Labour Church was experiencing some difficulties, the Bradford Labour Church continued to act as an inspirational force in the Bradford Labour movement by providing lectures: 'Sunday after Sunday it brings to the town speakers of the first rank, and in many ways help to keep the good work going'.[73] It is clear that the various objectives of the independent movement were not so much countervailing as complementary in West Yorkshire. Out of the hardships of the late 1890s was forged a much more unified, realistic and tolerand independent Labour movement.

    The ILP contested six of the 23 seats in West Yorkshire during the 1895 General Election, and came bottom of the poll in all these contests.[74] The Bradford East by-election of November 1896, in which Keir Hardie stood for the ILP, and the Halifax by-election of 1897, in which Tom Mann stood for the ILP, did little to improve the prospects of the ILP, both candidates also coming firmly at the bottom of the polls.[75] Despite the growing unity of the working classes there was still enough fragmentations to make victory in a constituency like Bradford East difficult. There was undoubtedly a working-class enclave at the centre of the constituency - but this was surrounded by an equally numerous area of middle class and lower middle-class housing and flanked on the south by the Irish community whose voters still voted Liberal. Local election results were little better, though there were a few local and municipal successes. But these disappointments did not so much discourage the ILP as spur it on to examine ways of extending its support.

    In essence, the West Yorkshire Labour movement was faced with three possibilities. It could rejoin the Liberal fold, seek to establish a Socialist party uniting all Socialist and Labour groups throughout West Yorkshire or, as it finally did, strengthen its connections with trade unionism. The semi-autonomous nature of ILP branches could have militated against an effective attempt to tackle the problems of the ILP. The events in Halifax had demonstrated the dangers of the NAC of the ILP interfering in local matters. In the case of West Yorkshire, however, it is clear that the national and local leadership were moving in the same direction

Liberal Responses and Labour Difficulties

Neither were seriously prepared to examine the possibilities of an alliance with Liberalism or the establishment of Socialist unity. In the case of a projected Liberal-Labour alliance, it is clear that the Liberal leadership had, in general, set its face against such a possibility. In the case of the issue of Socialist unity it is clear that the West Yorkshire ILP organisations were largely opposed to it, as was Keir Hardie, on the grounds that they could not see the advantage of such an alliance and felt that it would lose them support. They appear to have been in tune with Hardie's sentiments, expressed in the pages of the Labour Leader and the I.L.P. News, which saw an alliance with the SDF, in particular, as an anathama to ILP success. Hardie expressed the view that 'Rigidity is fatal to growth as I think our S.D.F. friends are finding out', and reflected upon the possible loss of trade-union support for the two organisations if they merged.[76] His attitude was neatly presented in the I.L.P. News:

> It may be that there is something in the methods of propaganda, if not in the principles of the S.D.F. that not only renders it somewhat antipathetic to our members, but out of touch and harmony with the feelings and ideals of the mass of the people. If, too, it be the case that the S.D.F., even if not decaying, is not growing in membership, the indication would seem to be that it has not proceeded on the lines of British industrial evolution. It might be, therefore, that the introduction of its spirit and methods of attack would check rather than help forward our movement.

This view was strongly upheld by most of the ILP branches in West Yorkshire during the national debate which occurred between the ILP and SDF over the issue of Socialist unity in 1896, 1897 and 1898. Keir Hardie and the national leadership of the ILP opposed fusion with the SDF and it is clear that they obtained much support.

In Bradford the rejection of Socialist unity was very evident. In September and October 1897 there was almost total indifference to the issue when the national debate was at its height. Attempts to re-organise the Bradford ILP clubs in 1898, which followed the appointment of Sam Hemsley as the local agent in 1897, also clearly veered away from any implication that a Socialist unity group would be established. It is obvious that during the

Liberal Responses and Labour Difficulties

discussions various local Socialist societies had misinterpreted the intentions of the Bradford ILP. The General Council of the Bradford ILP had decided to meet with a committee of 15 'outsiders', in the hope of widening support for the ILP. Their action was misunderstood. As the <u>Bradford Labour Echo</u> reflected:

> They the outsiders endeavoured to ignore the fact that the meeting was an ILP branch meeting, and proceeded to treat the gathering as one specially called to bring into being an entirely new Socialist party. Some of the outsiders who proposed to serve on the committee withdrew their names, when the meeting passed the following resolution: "That the fifteen members elected from the meeting should declare themselves Socialists who are willing to become members of the I.L.P. under the reconstituted constitution". Carried by an overwhelming majority.[78]

The <u>Bradford Observer</u> report, contained in the same issue of the <u>Bradford Labour Echo</u>, was even more direct: 'One fact made quite clear was that no fusion of Socialist sections is intended. The representatives of various smaller Socialist bodies attended, and did their best to turn the discussion into this groove, but entirely without avail'.

The Halifax ILP assumed a similar stance to the Bradford ILP. The July 1898 issue of the <u>Record</u>, organ of the Halifax Independent Labour Party, did refer to the 'One Socialist Party' campaign being conducted in Bradford but played down its importance, doubting its 'practical superiority' to the existing situation. It was suggested that the term 'fusion' indicated a tightening and hardening of Socialist policies which did not fit the more general approach favoured by the membership of the Halifax ILP. Also most ILP members spent a working week protected by trade union surveillance, and weekends attending Labour Church activities, glee club meetings and rambles. Satisfied with their achievements they were not inclined to join forces with the SDF, which had little influence in Halifax and which played down the value of trade unionism. On the whole one is left with the impression that Socialist unity barely merited serious consideration in the new ILP strongholds of Bradford and Halifax. There only appears to have been marginal support for the notion in Keighley and perhaps some fitful support for it in the Huddersfield area.79

This situation is not wholly unexpected given the numerical support of the ILP over other Socialist parties in the West Riding. The ILP was broadly and firmly based, whilst the SDF carried little weight. Indeed, there was no active branch of the SDF in Halifax during the mid 1890s and only one small branch in Bradford. The Bradford branch had been formed in 1894 with six members. In 1896 it had reached a peak of 28 members, before collapsing in 1898.80 It was not revived until 1902. The only figures of real stature in the SDF, though neither appears to have been actively involved in local branch activities, were Charles A. Glyde and Edward Robertshaw Hartley. Glyde had been a member of the SDF since 1887 but was also active in the ILP and a trade-union organiser for the Gasworkers and General Labourers' Union.81 Hartley was an ILP member who joined the SDF about 1902. He was also the secretary of the Clarion Van movement in the early twentieth century.82 Neither of these local political figures was able to bridge the gap between the Bradford ILP and the Bradford branch of the SDF. The simple fact is that the ILP in Bradford, and throughout West Yorkshire, outnumbered the SDF members by more than 30 to 1 and, understandably, saw no advantage in uniting with an almost non-existent party.

The hopes and aspirations of achieving Socialist unity therefore remained unfulfilled. Some measure of unity was established with the formation of the Labour Representation Committee in 1900, to which the ILP and the SDF, temporarily, affiliated. But this was a federation of Socialist and trade-union bodies, not a Socialist party, and the SDF soon withdrew.

As indicated in chapter three, the ILP branches of West Yorkshire were closely interlinked with the local trade union movements. The formation of the Labour Representation Committee in 1900 was thus welcomed by West Yorkshire ILP branches, who had already gone some way in identifying with trade unions and their demands. With the local Liberal organisations showing remarkable indifference to the rising political challenge of Labour in the 1890s, it is hardly surprising that Yorkshire ILP branches continued to tap the sustaining power of trade unionism. It was this support which permitted the ILP to weather the parliamentary disasters of the 1895 General Election and the bout of internecine

Liberal Responses and Labour Difficulties

conflict within the Halifax ILP and between it and the leadership of the National ILP. It was also this support which proved inimical to the campaign for Socialist unity and paved the way for a revival of ILP fortunes at the turn of the century.

NOTES

1. Bradford Observer, 9 Dec. 1891.
2. Huddersfield Examiner, 13 Jul. 1895.
3. Bradford Observer, 4 Dec. 1896.
4. Huddersfield Examiner, 13 Jul. 1895.
5. Huddersfield Chronicle, 21 Jan. 1893.
6. Lister, 'The Early History of the ILP Movement in Halifax'.
7. Keighley Labour Journal, 8 Mar. 1896.
8. Ibid., 26 Mar. 1898.
9. Ibid., 20 Mar. 1897.
10. ILP News, Dec. 1902.
11. Clark, Colne Valley: Radicalism to Socialism, p. 149.
12. The Bradford Liberal organisation was divided into three Liberal Two Hundreds, which consisted of about 200 elected delegates and life members, one for each of the three Bradford constituencies. The three together formed the supreme policy-making body, the Liberal Six Hundred, which elected the Executive of the Bradford Liberal Association.
13. Reynolds and Laybourn, 'The Emergence of the Independent Labour Party in Bradford', pp. 314-5; Bradford Observer, 25 Sep. 1895.
14. Jack Reynolds, Saltaire: An Introduction to the Village of Sir Titus Salt (Bradford Art Galleries and Museums, City Trail No 2, Bradford, 1976), pp. 10, 28.
15. K. Laybourn, 'The Emergence of Working-Class Independence and the rejection of the Salt Ideal', a lecture delivered at the Victoria Institute, Saltaire, 7 Mar. 1979, copies of which are to be found in Bradford Central Library and various branch libraries in the Shipley and Saltaire districts.
16. Laybourn, 'The Manningham Mills Strike: its importance in Bradford history', p. 16.
17. Bradford Observer, 16 Oct. 1891.
18. Ibid., 6, 8, 9, 14, 15, 18, 19, 23 Jan. 1892.
19. Ibid., 2, 18 Feb. 1892.
20. Ibid., 22 Feb. 1892.
21. Ibid., 28 Mar, 21 Apr. 1892.
22. Ibid., 29 Feb. 1892.

23. Ibid., 15 Jan. 1892.
24. Ibid., 9 Jan. 1892.
25. Ibid., 9 Jul. 1892.
26. Ibid., 18 Jul. 1892.
27. Ibid., 28 Mar., 18 Jul. 1892.
28. ILP News, May and June 1898.
29. Mr. Byles's Address to the Electors: General Election, 1892, Shipley Parliamentary Division, Bradford Archives Collection, 40D78/150.
30. Ibid., p. 3.
31. ILP Archive, Francis Johnson Collection, 1896/84, letter from James Keir Hardie, dated 21 Nov. 1896.
32. Labour Party Archive, Labour Representation Committee, 1/224, 2/192.
33. Ibid., 2/17.
34. Ibid., 2/192.
35. Bradford Labour Echo, 25 Sep. 1897.
36. Bradford Observer, 11 Oct. 1894.
37. Bradford Labour Echo, 17 Apr., 1 May 1897. Meetings took place at the Gladstone Liberal Club and the house of Rev. R. Roberts.
38. Bradford Observer., 2 Nov. 1894.
39. Bradford Labour Echo, 4 Feb. 1899.
40. Bradford Daily Telegraph, 31 Mar. 1903.
41. A.J.A. Morris, C.P. Trevelyan, 1870-1958: Portrait of a Radical (Blackstaff Press, Belfast, 1977).
42. See Table 4.1.
43. ILP Archive, Francis Johnson Collection, 1895/105, F.W. Jowett to J.K. Hardie, 6 Jul. 1896 suggests that the Bradford ILP's financial membership had declined to 1,600.
44. H.J.O. Drake, 'John Lister of Shibden Hall, 1847-1933'.
45. Lister, 'The Early History of the ILP Movement in Halifax'.
46. Drake, 'John Lister of Shibden Hall', pp. 448-9.
47. ILP Archive, Francis Johnson Collection, 1894/116.
48. Halifax Guardian, 27 Oct. 1894.
49. Drake, 'John Lister of Shibden Hall', pp. 449-51; Bradford Observer, 27, 30 Oct. 1894.
50. Drake, 'John Lister of Shibden Hall', pp. 453-4; Bradford Observer, 17 Nov. 1894.
51. Clarion, 2 Nov. 1894.
52. Drake, 'John Lister of Shibden Hall', p. 456; Clarion, 24 Nov. 1894.
53. Labour Leader, 3 Nov. 1894.
54. Bradford Observer, 13 Nov. 1894.

55. National Administrative Council of the ILP, Minutes, 4 Dec. 1894.
56. Ibid.
57. ILP Archive, Francis Johnson Collection, 1894/212.
58. Ibid., 1894/213.
59. Ibid., 1894/214.
60. R. Hyman, The Workers Union (Clarendon Press, Oxford, 1972).
61. ILP Archive, Francis Johnson Collection, 1895/2.
62. Drake, 'John Lister of Shibden Hall', p. 464.
63. Lister won 20.5 per cent of the vote, in this two-seated constituency, compared with the 29.3 per cent and 27.2 per cent of the Conservative and Liberal victors, respectively. He obtained 3,818 votes, 790 more than at the by-election in 1893.
64. Drake, 'John Lister of Shibden Hall', pp. 470-4.
65. Lister, 'The Early History of the ILP Movement in Halifax'.
66. Halifax Guardian, 19 Oct. 1895.
67. Drake, 'John Lister of Shibden Hall', p. 466.
68. Halifax Guardian, 20 Jan. 1895.
69. Ibid., 23 Nov. 1895.
70. Drake, 'John Lister of Shibden Hall', p. 470.
71. Stephen Yeo, 'A New Life: The Religion of Socialism in Britain 1883-1896', History Workshop, issue 4, autumn 1977.
72. Bradford Labour Echo, 24 Jun. 1899, Forward, 14, 21 Jul., 22 Sep. 1906.
73. Bradford Labour Echo, 1 Feb. 1896.
74. Labour candidates were defeated in Bradford West, Colne Valley, Dewsbury, Halifax, Huddersfield and Leeds South.
75. Hardie obtained 1,953 votes, or 17.1 per cent of the poll and Tom Mann obtained 2,000 votes, or 15.5 per cent of the poll.
76. Labour Leader, 4, 18, 25 Sep., 2 Oct. 1897.
77. ILP News, Aug. 1897.
78. Bradford Labour Echo, 20 Aug. 1898.
79. I am indebted to David James, the Bradford Archivist, for this information on Keighley, and to Robert Perks, until recently a Research Assistant in the Humanities Department of Huddersfield Polytechnic.
80. Justice, 8 Feb. 1896.

81. M. Cahill, 'C.A. Glyde' in J. Bellamy and J. Saville (eds.), Dictionary of Labour Biography, vol. 6 (Macmillan, London, 1982).
82. K. Laybourn and J. Saville, 'Edward Hartley 1855-1918', in J. Bellamy and J. Saville (eds.), Dictionary of Labour Biography, vol. 3 (Macmillan, London, 1976).

Chapter Five

LABOUR RESURGENCE 1900-6

The formation of the Labour Representation Committee in 1900 was to quickly transform the sagging fortunes of the West Yorkshire Labour movement. Whilst it brought the ILP and other political labour organisations more closely into line with each other its greatest benefit was that it encouraged the involvement of non-Socialist trade unionists in the demand for an independent political voice for the working classes. Labour representation committees were quickly formed in Leeds, Wakefield, and in other West Yorkshire towns.[1] Most of the leading West Yorkshire trades councils joined the LRC and there was a proliferation of intermediary bodies, such as the Workers' Municipal Federation in Bradford and the Halifax Workers' Election Committee, which facilitated the alliance between trade unions and Labour's independent political organisations.[2] What was impressive about the West Yorkshire Labour movement in the early years of the twentieth century was the immense energy it exerted in its urgent task of widening the appeal of Labour. Encouraged by the missionary work being conducted by members of the ILP and the LRC, trade unions were constantly joining the LRC, or declaring their intention to join once their financial conditions permitted. Even the relatively supine Keighley and District Trades and Labour Council reflected the new strident tone in Labour circles when, in April 1901, it announced 'That in the opinion of our Council the time has arrived when our new democratic party should be formed in the House of Commons to give national expression to the democratic ideals among the labouring masses'.[3] The fact that the West Yorkshire Labour movement moved quickly, and that Liberalism failed to rise to the challenge this posed to its working-class electorate, has led one writer to conclude that

Labour Resurgence 1900-6

'The evidence suggests that, notwithstanding its success in the General Election of 1906, the Liberal Party in West Yorkshire was in a state of irreversable decline by the outbreak of the First World War'.[4] This is a view with which we concur. But it is clear that the seeds of Liberal decline and Labour resurgence in West Yorkshire were sown between 1900 and 1907.

For more than 50 years historians have attempted to explain how the Labour Party was able to break the two-party system in the early years of the twentieth century whilst its forbears made only fitful headway in that direction during the 1880s and 1890s. A variety of explanations have been offered. Some historians have suggested that the growth of social control in the second half of the nineteenth century, whether in the form of better wages for some skilled workers or in the growth of leisure and sporting activities, had an enervating effect upon Socialist and Independent Labour movements.[5] Patrick Joyce provided a regional variant of this social control argument in his work on factory politics in Lancashire.[6] What he suggests is that between the 1850s and the 1890s a few large mill-owning families were able - owing to their economic power, their exploitation of a deferential relationship between master and operative, and their involvement in the politics of their local community - to impose the culture of the factory upon their workers and submerge demands for political independence. As a supplementary to this argument, and by way of contrast, Joyce has suggested that the later arrival of mechanisation to the woollen and worsted, as opposed to the cotton, industry permitted the independent-craftsman tradition to persist in Yorkshire until the late 1880s when the radicalism it portended flowed into the ILP and Socialist movements at the end of the century. Only in a few areas, such as Keighley did the influence of factory politics appear to exert the same degree of influence which existed in some Lancashire textile towns.

The most common explanation of the ILP's halting growth in the 1890s is that it lacked trade-union support.[7] The failure of ILP candidates in the 1895 General Election, the Bradford East by-election defeat of 1896, the disastrous Barnsley by-election of 1897, and many other political disappointments convinced Keir Hardie, and other ILP leaders, that it was the lack of trade-union support which was responsible for the failure of the ILP to

Labour Resurgence 1900-6

become a mass political party.

But these checks on Labour's political growth appear to have dissipated within less than a decade. During the period between about 1895 and 1905, factory politics began to be extinguished, for a variety of reasons, and trade unions were won over to the idea of independent working-class politics by a flurry of industrial disputes and court decisions which undermined the old attachments to the two-party system in general, and Liberalism in particular. Serious attention has been paid to the Taff Vale Decision of June 1901 as a catalyst in this change of political emphasis within trade unionism.[8]

These general and particular observations on the rise of Labour are partly reflected in the events that occurred in West Yorkshire. Whilst the pervasiveness of social control and factory politics is difficult to measure, just as much as is the independent and radical spirit which survived between the Chartist period and the Socialist revival, it is equally evident that the Taff Vale decision did convert many trade unionists to the ILP and LRC. But it is clear that in West Yorkshire, at least, the process of accretion to the Labour movement had begun before the Taff Vale decision was announced.

The formation of the Labour Representation Committee at Memorial Hall, London, on 27 February 1900 may not have attracted the interest and attention it deserved but it was certainly of vital importance to the continued development of the Labour movement in West Yorkshire. A large number of West Yorkshire delegates attended on the behalf of trade union and ILP branches. Allan Gee, Secretary of the General Union of Textile Workers and an active figure in Huddersfield Labour politics, became a trade-union member of the National Executive of the LRC and James Parker, an engineering warehouseman, trade unionist and a leading figure in the Halifax ILP, became, with Keir Hardie, one of the two ILP representatives on the National Executive.

This early interest is, perhaps, best reflected in the fact that the Bradford and Leeds trades councils had affiliated to the LRC within a few months of its formation. In April 1900, W.H. Drew, Secretary of the Bradford Trades and Labour Council, wrote to Ramsay MacDonald, stating that 'an an individual member of it (Bradford Trades Council),I shall have pleasure in doing all that lays in my power to induce the Council to affiliate'.[9] His efforts were clearly successful for in May 1900 he wrote again to MacDonald informing of his Trades Council's decision to affiliate.[10] In April 1900 Owen Connellan, secretary of the Leeds Trades and Labour Council, wrote to MacDonald on the advisability of contesting the Leeds East constituency in the forthcoming general election, although the Trades Council does not appear to have officially joined the LRC until July 1900.[11] In May 1900 the Huddersfield Trades Council contacted MacDonald, seeking clarification about whether or not it was eligible to join the LRC, though it did not affiliate for some time afterwards.[12] In the first two or three years of the LRC's existence then it was through the trades councils rather than through the creation of separate local LRCs that it extended its influence in West Yorkshire. The basis of that approach had been firmly laid down before the end of 1900.

Table 5.1: West Yorkshire Trades Councils affiliated to the Labour Representation Committee

Trades Council	Affiliation date
Bradford Trades Council[a]	May 1900
Leeds Trades Council	July 1900
Todmorden Trades Council	4 May 1901
Halifax Trades Council	23 June 1902
Wakefield Trades Council	August 1902
Keighley Trades Council	19 February 1903
Dewsbury, Batley Trades Council	March 1903
Huddersfield Trades Council	March 1904
Shipley Trades Council	between 1902 and 1904

Note: a. Only the brief title of the various trade councils is given. In most cases the full title includes 'and Labour' or 'and District'.
Source: Details have been extracted from the Labour Party Archive, Labour Representation Committee Correspondence, boxes 1-31.

Notwithstanding this early domination by the West Yorkshire trades councils, many unions began to affiliate to the LRC in their own right, and most of the leading Yorkshire textile unions were affiliated to the LRC by early 1903.[13] Imposed upon this structure of affiliation was a further layer of organisation - the local LRCs. According to the national constitution of the LRC, local LRCs could only

Labour Resurgence 1900-6

be formed by trade unions and Socialist societies in districts where there was no trades council affiliated to the LRC or where an affiliated trades council had been consulted and was agreeable to a local LRC being formed. Not surprisingly the local LRCs were formed in the wake of the earlier activity of the trades councils and trade unions. The first in West Yorkshire appears to have been formed at Leeds in October 1902, quickly to be followed by the Batley LRC in December 1902. Within three years most of the West Yorkshire towns had their own LRC branch, although no unifying body appears to have been established for Bradford. Some organisations, such as the Leeds LRC, appear to have spawned many district organisations within their town or city borders.

Table 5.2: Local Labour Representation Committees in West Yorkshire

Organisation	Formed	
Huddersfield LRC	November	1900
Leeds LRC (also Central)	September	1902
District LRCs		
East Hunslet LRC	March	1905
Armley & Wortley LRC	May	1905
New Wortley LRC	November	1905
Heavy Woollen LRC (Batley and Dewsbury)	March	1903
Wakefield LRC	June to September	1903
Huddersfield LRC	January	1904
Keighley LRC		1904

Source: Labour Party Archive, Labour Representation Committee Correspondence, boxes 1-31.

Moreover this support for the West Yorkshire Labour movement was quickly transmitted into both parliamentary and local election results. For the first time, as Table 5.3 indicates, the Labour movement made tremendous gains in the parliamentary general elections. This was complimented by the steady progress which was made in local elections throughout this period, as indicated in tables 5.4 and 5.5. Although Labour's big breakthrough in local politics did not occur until after 1906, the period 1900 to

Table 5.3: The Number of Votes and the Proportion of Votes received by the leading political parties of West Yorkshire at general elections, 1885 - 1910

Year		Liberals Votes	%	Conservative and Liberal Unionist Votes	%	Labour Votes	%
1885		113,712	59.1	78,640	40.9		
1886		66,903	56.4	51,759	43.6		
1892		107,777	54.0	88,844	44.6	2,749	1.4
1895		106,861	49.0	100,899	46.1	10,623	4.9
1900		105,960	48.3	104,034	47.4	9,491	4.3
1906		113,194	50.3	72,913	32.4	38,925	17.3
1910	(J)	140,586	49.2	100,257	35.7	42,871	15.1
1910	(D)	94,681	47.5	76,601	38.5	27,962	14.0

Source: F.W.S. Craig, British Parliamentary Election Results 1885 - 1918 (Macmillan, London, 1974).

1906 did see tangible gains.

The first success by a legitimate Labour candidate at Leeds did not occur until 1903, but by November 1906 there were nine Labour representatives on the City Council. The euphoria which resulted from such growth led the Leeds LRC to push for the contesting of three Leeds parliamentary seats in the 1906 general election. J. O'Grady was the LRC candidate for Leeds East, after a bitter and protracted contest with Owen Connellan, Secretary of the Trades Council, for the nomination.[14] But there were feelings expressed that O'Grady should contest Leeds South instead, and John Macrae wrote to Ramsay MacDonald expressing his view that 'Our most tried and fullest strength is in South & West divisions and it is galling to them to be without a candidate'.[15] In the final analysis, only Leeds East and Leeds South were contested, though, as we shall see, a determined effort was made to put a candidate forward for Leeds West. The determined resistance of MacDonald, and his control over central funds, made a contest in Leeds West impossible.[16]

Municipal successes in Bradford were more gradual and, on the whole, led to less ambitious parliamentary aspirations in 1906[17] Elsewhere in West Yorkshire there was a steady accretion of municipal, urban district and local successes for Labour.

Labour Resurgence 1900-6

Table 5.4: The Number of Municipal Representatives returned for Labour in Four West Yorkshire Towns and Cities, 1900-6

Year	Bradford	Halifax	Huddersfield	Leeds	Total
1900	6	2	1	0	9
1901	8	5	1	0	14
1902	8	6	1	0	15
1903	7	6	1	1	15
1904	10	6	4	4	24
1905	10	5	6	8	29
1906	11	4	8	9	32

Sources: November issues of Bradford Observer, Halifax Guardian, Huddersfield Examiner; T. Woodhouse, 'The working class', in Derek Fraser (ed.), A History of Modern Leeds (Manchester University Press, Manchester, 1980), p. 363.

Table 5.5: The Number of Labour Representatives on Local Political Bodies in West Yorkshire, 1900-6

Year	Municipal	CC,UDC RDC^a,PC	Board of Guardians	School^b Board	Total
1900	19	10	3	21	53
1901	26	20	8	24	68
1902	26	13	8	22	69
1903	27	15	8	22	72
1904	37	21	6	22	86
1905	41	34	6		81
1906	47	36	6		89

Note: a. County Council, urban-district councils, rural-district councils and parish councils.
   b. School boards were abolished in April 1904 and their functions assumed by the West Riding County Council and the municipal authorities.
Sources: Labour Leader, ILP News, Bradford Observer, Halifax Guardian, Huddersfield Examiner and the records of a number of trades councils and Labour Party branches.

What is evident, from both local contests and

parliamentary activity, is that the West Yorkshire Labour movement was gathering pace from 1900 onwards. It is clear that it was not particularly hampered by the Boer War nor was it overly encouraged by the Taff Vale decision of June 1901. The organisational changes which went on in the Labour movement paved the way for steady and real improvements in Labour's position before 1906.

In recent years the political impact of the Boer War has been subjected to close scrutiny. In the early 1970s, Richard Price took to task those historians who have suggested that the Conservative government's conduct of the war attracted significant support from the working classes who were largely in support of aggressive imperial policies. Price suggests that most working-class organisations were divided over the war, that despite the relief of Mafeking, and 'Mafeking Night', the war did not spark widespread interest and that this is reflected in the fact that the 'Khaki' election of October 1900 provoked much less interest, and a smaller turnout, than did the 1895 General Election.[18]

It is clear that the implications of the Boer War for the ILP and LRC, who opposed the war, would either be politically disastrous as the tide of working-class support for imperialism swept Labour's parliamentary, and local, challenge aside, or irrelevant owing to the relatively unimportant nature of the issue amongst working-class supporters. The evidence of West Yorkshire tends to support the latter assumption. On the whole the Boer War made little difference to the prospects of the independent Labour movement in West Yorkshire, and there is no evidence to suggest that the movement found its political hopes blighted by the war.

Part of the reason for the drop in Labour's proportion of the parliamentary vote in the 1900 General Election, as indicated in Table 5.3, is that the West Yorkshire Labour movement fielded fewer candidates than in 1895. In the 1895 General Election there were five Labour candidates whilst in the 1900 General Election there were only three, and only two of those, Jowett, in West Bradford, and Parker, in Halifax, could be accurately described as Labour candidates.[19] Byles, who stood for East Leeds, was, as previously suggested, imposed upon Labour with the support of the 'Irish party'.

All three ILP/Labour candidates were opposed to the Boer War, supporting the official ILP line, presented forthrightly at the Seventh Annual

Conference of the ILP, at Leeds in 1899, that it was 'a capitalist clique, who are seeking, through Mr. Chamberlain, his colleagues or the Government, and an unscrupulous Press, to further their own ends against what we believe to be the true interests of England' and calling the Government to cease the war and 'submit all subjects of difference to arbitration'.[20] Jowett promoted the joint ILP and Trades Council anti-war public meeting which was held in the Bradford Mechanics' Institute in September 1899 and was prominent in organising and speaking at a peace demonstration at Peckover Walks, Bradford, in March 1900.[21] Byles was the leading force in the Bradford South African Conciliation Committee, and James Parker actively opposed the war.[22]

Fenner Brockway, in his biography of Jowett, suggested that despite the unpopularity of the pro-Boer stance adopted by Jowett he continued to press the 'peace' campaign during the election.[23] More recently this view has been challenged by two historians, one of whom has argued that Jowett and the ILP 'deliberately avoided the issue during the election'.[24] Indeed, Jowett does appear to have played down the significance of the Boer War and concentrated upon the issue of social reform. Yet his pro-Boer position was well known and his Tory opponent did concentrate upon the war. Moreover, Jowett, admittedly in a two-cornered election, did come within 41 votes of victory. The war was clearly the key issue being fought out in the 1900 General Election, and the key issue in the Bradford campaign, and yet the ILP candidate was almost successful. Similarly, the Boer War was important in the contests fought by two other Labour candidates, and whilst both lost the contests they polled quite well; Byles obtaining 20.1 per cent of the vote in Leeds East and James Parker obtaining 16.3 per cent of the vote in the four-way Halifax contest. As with the national trend, the turnout in all three contests was lower than in the 1895 General Election contest.[25] Political apathy rather than political bellicosity appears to have been the major feature of the 1900 General Election. The independent labour position does not appear to have been worsened by the Boer War, and Jowett's impressive performance in West Bradford gave the ILP/LRC hope for the future.

Part of the explanation for Labour's relative success in riding the patriotic tide which could have overwhelmed it may be that there was still a strong sense of Liberal Nonconformist opposition to the war which still espoused the old Liberal shibboliths of 'peace, retrenchment, and reform'. H.J. Wilson, the Liberal MP for Holmfirth, was vehemently opposed to the war, as were most of the leading Bradford Liberals, such as Alfred Illingworth.[26] Indeed, there was no Liberal Imperialist group active within Bradford Liberalism, though one suspects that there were many individuals within the Liberal Party who kept silent and either did not vote in the 1900 General Election or voted Conservative.[27] J.H. Whitley, one of the two Halifax MPs, was also staunchly opposed to war, as was Sir J.T. Woodhouse in Huddersfield.[28] There were, of course, exceptions, Sir James Kitson, the Leeds engineering employer and one-time organiser of Leeds Liberalism, was a fervent imperialist and projected his views on the Colne Valley electorate in 1900.[29] On balance then, there was a substantial proportion of West Riding Liberalism which was just as much opposed to the war as was the ILP and LRC. Although 'peace' or 'pro-Boer' meetings were broken up by a few activists, there is sufficient evidence to suggest that a large proportion of the voting public, were equivocal about the war, admiring the British victories but leaning back to their Liberal upbringing on the matter of seeking peace. The political climate was by no means hostile to the pro-Boer opinions held by ILPers and Liberal alike and the Conservative Party, which pressed the war issue, did not improve its parliamentary position in West Yorkshire, still holding nine of the 23 seats as it had done in the 1895 General Election.[30]

The identification of Liberal and Labour candidates on the war issue could, of course, have blurred the distinctions between the organisations and tended towards the submergence of Labour within Liberalism. This was a possibility which could have been further galvanised by the common stance which the Labour and Liberal parties assumed in opposing the 1902 Education Act, which transferred elementary education from school board to local authority. But in reality this did not occur for at least two reasons. The first is that most sections of West Yorkshire Liberalism were opposed to compromising with Labour. In Halifax and Leeds East both the ILP and Labour candidates were opposed by Liberals, whilst in West Bradford, a good portion of the Liberal Party, led by Alfred Illingworth objected to Fred Jowett being given a straight run with the Conservatives after the Liberal progressives had secured the withdrawal of Jarratt, the Liberal candidate.[31]

Labour Resurgence 1900-6

Liberals, such as Illingworth, were prepared to share the 'peace' platform with Labour but were unprepared to endorse a Labour candidate in the place of a Liberal. As previously suggested, this arrangement in West Bradford led to Illingworth's temporary departure from the Bradford Liberal Association. The second reason why Labour's submergence within Liberalism did not occur is that neither the ILP nor the LRC in West Yorkshire were prepared to entertain such an alliance, as is witnessed by both the volumnious correspondence which flowed by Keir Hardie and Ramsay MacDonald in the eventful years of the early twentieth century.[32] On the whole, West Yorkshire Labour leaders favoured more parliamentary contests whilst the ILP and the LRC national leaderships were intent upon keeping the number of contests to a minimum.[33]

Thus the Labour movement was growing rapidly and independently of the Liberal Party from 1900, barely touched by any unpopularity which might have resulted from the Boer War because of the strong Nonconformist tradition of West Yorkshire which tempered the patriotic fervour of war. The Bradford Trades Council and the Leeds Trades Council, the General Union of Textile Workers, and many other trade union organisations had been won to the LRC by the end of 1900. The Taff Vale decision of 1901 merely galvanised an existing trend in West Yorkshire. The events are well known enough not to need recounting in detail. The Taff Vale Railway Company successfully sued the Amalgamated Society of Railway Servants for damages incurred by picketing and won its case in the High Court. The Court of Appeal reversed the decision; but the company won damages against the ASRS in the House of Lords in 1901.[34] The immediate significance from the Bradford point of view is that the chairman of the ASRS at this time was J.H. Palin, a prominent member of the Laisterdyke branch of the ASRS and a leading figure on the Trades Council and in the ILP. He broadcast his views to the Trades Council and the Bradford ILP and gained further support for the LRC.

In Huddersfield the situation was similar to that of Bradford. The ILP-dominated executive of the Trades Council had established an LRC as early as November 1900,[35] and the Taff Vale decision, and other similar legal positions at this time, merely served to strengthen the trade union link with Labour. Although the Huddersfield LRC floundered, William Pickles, President of the Huddersfield Trades Council, wrote a letter to MacDonald in

Labour Resurgence 1900-6

January 1902 asserting that

> with the organisation of capital for defensive and aggressive purposes ... we see that in industry as well as politics, the next step must be in the direction of socialisation of the means of production ... This step the Liberals are not prepared to take.[36]

Many trade union organisations within the Huddersfield Trades Council still showed reluctance to drop Liberalism, but the Taff Vale decision did help the ILP and LRC to win over the waverers.

Faced with a growing Labour movement the Liberals in West Yorkshire attempted to use political tactics to thwart Labour rather than to offer the new Liberal ideology as an alternative to the collectivist tendencies of the ILP and the LRC. In Leeds, the Liberals had attempted to control the Trades Council by offering some of the officials opportunities to stand as Liberal municipal candidates.[37] In Bradford, Liberals had resorted to a similar tactic in 1891, after the Bradford Labour Union had begun to challenge Liberal hegemony on the Trades Council.[38] In Huddersfield, the Liberals constantly claimed Allan Gee to be a Liberal councillor, despite the fact that he was a member of the ILP, the only Labour councillor for Huddersfield in the 1890s, and a leading national figure in the LRC from 1900 onwards.[39] Where Labour was making some inroads, and where there was still Liberal support amongst trade unions and within the trades councils, the West Yorkshire Liberal parties appear to have made some minor concessions to working-class representation.

But these palliatives did not halt the growth of the ILP and local Liberal parties were forced to campaign more solidly for working-class support in 1902 and 1903. Attempts at a Liberal <u>rapprochement</u> with Labour were inaugurated, and in May 1903, one prominent Bradford ILPer noted that 'every effort is being made by the Liberals to draw the Trade Unionists into an alliance'.[40] But such efforts evaporated quickly in the face of ILP and LRC campaigning amongst trade unionists and as the euphoria of rising municipal success drove the Labour movement forward in Halifax, Huddersfield, Bradford, Leeds and other Labour centres.

The definite turning-point for Labour appears to have been 1903. In that year the Leeds ILP/LRC won its first seat on the municipal council.[41]

Labour Resurgence 1900-6

This was also the time when, according to David Clark, there was the beginnings of a massive swelling of support and activity within the Labour movement of Colne Valley.42 In many respects the final dashing of Liberal hopes of compromise was symbolised by Keir Hardie's clear hostility to the established parties at a May Day Demonstration in Bradford when he stated that 'Liberalism and Toryism had divided the workers, Independents had come to unite them'.43 This statement was taken to be an irrevocable declaration of war against both Bradford and West Yorkshire Liberalism. It was an attack born of confidence rather than hope for Labour. Indeed, the local election result began to reveal that Labour was undermining Liberal domination in several municipalities between 1900 and 1906, and in areas such as Bradford the Liberal Party was beginning to face financial strains as well as a loss of support.

Table 5.6 The Municipal Balance of Power in Bradford, Leeds and Huddersfield, 1900-6

Year	Bradford				Huddersfield				Leeds		
	L.	C.	Lab	O.[a]	L.	C.	Lab	O.	L.	C.	Lab
1900	28	42	6	8	37	19	1	3	27	37	0
1901	42	31	8	3	33	24	1	2	28	36	0
1902	45	29	8	2	33	24	1	2	30	34	0
1903	49	26	7	2	30	27	1	2	29	34	1
1904	45	28	10	1	32	22	4	2	40	20	4
1905	42	31	10	1	32	19	6	3	37	19	8
1906	38	34	11	1	32	17	8	3	34	21	9

Note: a. The abbreviations are L for Liberal, C for Conservative, Lab for Labour and O. for Others.
Sources: Bradford Observer, Huddersfield Examiner, Nov. issues; T. Woodhouse, 'The working class' in Derek Fraser (ed.), A History of Modern Leeds (Manchester University Press, Manchester, 1980), p. 363.

Clearly then, the formation of the LRC had achieved the object of strengthening the independent Labour movement. Yet there were other factors at play which also furnished support for that movement. One was the emergence of workers' election committees outside the LRC. A second was the extension of the cultural activities of the ILP and wider Labour movement.

From the outset many trades councils joined the LRC and, in some areas, additional LRC branches were formed. In Bradford and Halifax, however, no LRC branch organisation was formed. Instead workers' electoral or municipal committees were formed to act as go-betweens for trades unionists and ILPers, very much the same role as LRC branches without actually joining the National LRC.

In Bradford the Workers' Municipal Federation was formed - as a more formal organisation than the Municipal Election Committee which had been formed in 1900 - in order to 'secure the return of Labour representatives on the City Council, Board of Guardians and the now defunct School Board'.[44] Thus it sought to avoid the truculent political conflict within the Bradford Labour movement which had emerged in the late 1890s when the Trades Council had insisted that its candidates for local office should be Socialists.[45]

Notwithstanding an early setback, when the ILP eventually decided not to join the WMF, the formation of the new organisation anticipated a movement towards political unity within the ranks of the Bradford Labour movement. Even without formal membership the ILP found its views well represented on the WMF through the many trade union and Trades Council representatives, such as W.H. Drew, George Licence, A.T. Sutton, Tom Brown and James Bartley, all of whom were leading figures in the ILP.[46] Of the first 16 members of the Executive at least five were pominent ILP members.[47] It was this informal presence which helped to pave the way for more formal consultations between the two bodies. In 1904, the WMF resolved to endorse the ILP nominees contesting municipal elections and, in 1905, the Executive Committee of the WMF decided to 'receive a deputation from the I.L.P. with a view to avoid clashing in contest of seats'.[48] In 1907 relations were so good that it helped form a committee to run ILP and WMF candidates jointly in municipal elections. Although formed to get the best arrangements from any political party, the WMF in reality worked with the ILP and in opposition to Liberals and Tories. In effect, they fought as a united group on the City Council. The WMF was partly encouraged in this policy by the continued intolerance of the Bradford Liberal Association, which had been unwilling to withdraw its candidate and allow A.N. Harris, president of the WMF, a straight run with the

Conservatives in the 1902 municipal election in Listerhills ward.[49] This experience imbued the WMF with a sense of its own independence which meant that subsequent Liberal overtures were rejected.[50] After the events of 1902 Liberal vicissitudes had no place in the discussions and debates of the WMF and the organisation looked to its own strength and the ILP for political gains. By 1905 it could claim five representatives on the City Council, half the Labour group at that time.

The Halifax Workers' Election Committee fulfilled a similar role to the WMF. It was formed in 1900 and by 1905 had 22 trade societies plus the ILP affiliated to it, representing between 4,000 and 5,000 workers. The Committee was responsible for all the local election work of the local Labour movement, had six borough council representatives and four board of guardian representatives by 1905. It was reported that although the Halifax Trades Council was affiliated to the LRC 'they do no election work'.[51] Labour's unifying force in Halifax was the Workers' Committee.

Underpinning much of this political work, and that undertaken by the ILP and the LRC, was the growth of Labour's cultural and social institutions. We have already suggested that there was such growth in the 1890s and the early twentieth century, with the rapid emergence of clubs, Labour churches and Socialist sunday schools. It is true, as previously suggested, that the number of ILP clubs diminished in the late 1890s and that the Labour churches began to lose their appeal. By 1900 the Keighley and Leeds Labour churches were clearly experiencing difficulties, and the Leeds organisation was toying with the idea of joining with the Bradford Labour Church.[52] The Spen Valley Labour Church had apparently ceased to exist by the turn of the century and the three Labour churches in Huddersfield, at Lockwoold ILP club, Longwood and Milnsbridge, had practically expired by 1895, following the defeat of H.R. Smart, a leading Labour Church activist, in the 1895 General Election.[53] There is certainly evidence that the cultural side of the movement was declining, but Yeo has clearly written the obituary of the 'religion of socialism' for too early a date.[54] The Labour churches in Bradford and Halifax were still active, the Clarion movement and the Socialist sunday schools were just emerging, and the general cultural side of the movement was still prevalent until the First World War.[55]

There is strong evidence that the Clarion

movement, formed by Robert Blatchford in the early 1890s, had begun to expand its activities in the years between 1900 and the First World War. The Clarion movement had always been well-established in Keighley, Bradford and Halifax, where there were numerous cycling, field, scout, glee and vocal unions in existence. In Keighley, the movement had its own brass band.56 From 1900 the membership of some sections of the movement, particularly the Clarion cyclists, began to increase. From about 1903 the Clarion movement also became better organised in areas where its impact had, hitherto, been limited. The movement began to make an impact in Huddersfield after 1902 and by 1906 the Huddersfield movement had a glee club, a vocal union, a brass band, a swimming club and a cycling club.57

It was not until the formation of the Yorkshire Socialist Sunday School Union in 1900 that Socialist sunday schools began to emerge with vigour, though there had been some earlier attempts to form such schools, most notably at Bradford in 1895 and in Huddersfield in 1896.58 The Yorkshire Socialist Sunday School Union was committed to the Hardie, rather than Blatchford, strand of the movement, desiring to capture youngsters for Socialism whilst 'their minds and suspectibilities are plastic and impressionable'.59 Its emergence quickly strengthened and spawned other similar organisations throughout West Yorkshire.60 The Bradford Central Socialist Sunday School was formed in June 1899. This organisation, which was started by Sam Wood, initially attracted about 90 children and their parents to the one-hour long Sunday meetings which it held in the Labour Institute.61 It was the only organisation of its type in Bradford until 1905 when the Great Horton, Manningham and Little Horton Socialist sunday schools were formed.62 Similar schools were established in West Bowling and East Bowling in 1906, to be followed by another three schools in later years.63

Always limited to a minority of Socialists, the Socialist sunday schools nevertheless provided an important strut to the Labour movement, underpinning the wider movement with a solidity of support and commitment. In 1900 the Bradford school had 112 scholars, the Halifax school 159 and the Huddersfield school 40.64 By 1906 the movement had widened considerably and in Bradford alone there were between about 250 and 300 regular scholars attending these schools, plus their parents. In total there were probably 150 or more families involved in

Labour Resurgence 1900-6

Bradford Socialist Sunday schools, probably representing 700 or more people, and the movement was still growing. They included such prominent figures as Nora Fineburgh, the daughter of Joseph Burgess, the famous editor of Labour newspapers, and her son Willie Fineburgh who was later to become a Labour MP.65 The Fineburghs attended the Great Horton Socialist Sunday School. Victor Feather, as a young lad, attended East Bradford Socialist Sunday School.

Although these Sunday schools helped to swell the support for the Labour movement in West Yorkshire, their primary aim was to produce the next generation of Socialists. This objective was the crux of their activities. The normal Sunday meeting took place between 2 pm and 3 pm and consisted of children singing some Socialist hymn, group discussion, further singing and a rendering of the 'Socialist Ten Commandments', which would have been attached to the wall throughout the proceedings. The group discussion consisted mainly of moral instructions drawn from a variety of texts. At East Bowling, Bradford, in 1906, J.J. Gould's book <u>The Child's Book of Moral Lessons</u> was used.66 The adult classes, usually held at the same time, were based mainly on a variety of lectures, such as George H. Froggett's 'Labour Attitude towards Religion', which was delivered at East Bowling in 1906. On occasions specific lectures led to the formation of other classes which might meet in the houses of members during the week. One lecture on Esperanto led to the formation of an Esperanto class in connection with the East Bowling Socialist Sunday School.67 These activities, with the formation of drama societies and other organisations, formed the basis of what was a thriving Socialist culture in West Yorkshire until the end of the First World War. Like the chapels and churches of Victorian England, the ILP was providing what, in fact, was a total way of life in which whole families could participate. Indeed, one of the most notable features of such cultural activity was that it encouraged, and attracted, family participation.

It was the conflation of a variety of factors - the formation of an LRC, the rapid extension of trade-union support, for a variety of reasons, the emergence of workers' election committees, and the development of the cultural side of the movement - which explain the dramatic improvement in the political fortunes of independent Labour in the period between 1900 and 1906. Yet what made this growth insuperable was the emergence of class conflict and class division over many of the vital issues which separated the Labour and Liberal parties. The most dramatic divisions in policy occurred over the problems of unemployment and the attitudes of Liberals towards municipalisation.

Unemployment was the most important economic issue in West Yorkshire in the early years of the twentieth century. The woollen and worsted textile economy had suffered badly in the 1890s, due largely to foreign competition and foreign tariffs which reduced the demand for West Yorkshire woollen and worsted pieces. The manufacturers' response to these pressures had been to speed up machinery, rather than to introduce new machinery, and to reduce wages. In addition unemployment, or 'broken time', the gap between a weaver's completing one piece and taking an order to produce another piece of cloth, increased. Unemployment was usually high but, intensified by tariff restrictions, was appreciably higher during the period between the autumn of 1891 and the early months of 1895 and between the winter months of 1902/3 and 1905/6. We have already noted that the high unemployment of the early 1890s nurtured support for independent Labour from a number of quarters, and it is clear that similar support was forthcoming between 1902 and 1906.[68]

The return of high unemployment provoked the town and city councils of West Yorkshire to take action. Most set up a Lord Mayor's Fund in order to finance relief for the unemployed and their families, and some set up their own unemployment committees, which occasionally led to the formation of joint unemployment committees between the municipal authorities, boards of guardians and voluntary organisations.[69] Labour registers for the unemployed were also opened by town, or city, councils. Bradford City Council set up such a register in the winter of 1902/3, and repeated the operation in the winter months of 1903/4 and 1904/5.[70] Leeds City Council did much the same from the autumn of 1902 onwards, continuing the operation for a number of winters.[71] Leeds City Council also provided £10,000 from the City funds to relieve unemployment, and there was discussion about employing the unemployed on the town hall extension being built in Bradford.[72] Bradford Corporation sent a deputation to the Nidd Valley to see whether the land there was was suitable for farm colonies, and <u>Forward</u>, the journal of the Bradford ILP, eagerly supported the intention behind the visit, arguing that 'if you could experimentally place 100 unemployed Bradford men on the land and give them a chance of living upon it, you would not displace more than the farmer and his family.[73] There was a scheme to send some of those on the Bradford Labour Bureau register to Canada.[74] There was certainly no lack of schemes to deal with the unemployed in West Yorkshire.

Most of these schemes were cosmetic. There were many schemes blending both charity and public relief into the relief of the unemployed but they were trifling when compared with the scale of unemployment. In the autumn of 1903, before the onset of winter which would add many outdoor workers to those unemployed, it was 'computed by workmen that in the industrial centres of the West Riding there are 20,000 unemployed, and what is nearly as bad, an equal number of operatives only partially employed'.[75] In Bradford alone it was suggested that at least 6,000 men were unemployed, plus a large number of women who were employed in the woollen and worsted industries, by December 1903.[76] The distress was equally severe in Leeds and Owen Connellan, Secretary of the Leeds Trades and Labour Council, stated in December 1903 that 'As a matter of fact he believed that in Leeds several industries were suffering from very great depression indeed, notably in the engineering and clothing trades'.[77]

Trades councils were to the fore in pressing the municipal and local authorities to offer relief to the unemployed, and in passing motions that the Government ought to take action to deal with the problem.[78] Numerous unemployment demonstrations and conferences were organised by trade unions and trades councils. The <u>Yorkshire Factory Times</u>, the journal of textile trades unionists in the West Riding, ran regular columns on the problems of the unemployed, as did the local Labour press. What became obvious is that unemployed registers barely reflected the true extent of unemployment. The unemployed register set up in Bradford in the autumn of 1902 attracted only 335 men - most of them woolcombers - though there were 61,355 textile workers in the city. But as a correspondent to the <u>Yorkshire Factory Times</u> noted:

> It is convenient to forget that those employed were male workers and that the lower-paid labour of women had displaced men in the textile industry. Further, hundreds of dyers and other operatives refused to register their names

> because they were unable to bear the strain of
> outdoor labour, and a little army of out of
> work, who were in receipt of out of work
> pay from the trade union, because of their an-
> tipathy to a free labour agency avoided the
> Corporation Bureau as a pesthouse.79

Even when a large number of unemployed registered with a labour bureau it was highly likely that the bureau would, for a number of reasons, only deal with a small section of those registered. In the winter of 1904/5 there were almost 4,500 unemployed registered with the Bradford Labour Bureau. Of these, 1,303 found regular work before they were dealt with, 534 were put on relief work, and the other 2,660 were either out of work, had been lost sight of, transferred to a new register, or had been struck off the register because they were not sufficiently destitute.80 The Labour bureau registers thus proved to be an inefficient tool for dealing with the unemployed. The Labour bureaus failed to offer relief work to the vast majority of those unemployed workers who even bothered to register.

The inadequacy of public relief and charity did much to bring the Liberal and Labour parties into conflict in West Yorkshire. The local Liberal organisations, and their spokesmen, did much to extoll the virtues of charity and essential, if limited, public provision. Their view tended to be that if charity was failing then it had to be re-organised, not abandoned. The independent Labour organisations, on the other hand, stressed the need for an extension of municipal provision. The difference of approach adopted by the two political parties produced bitter conflict over the scale of relief for the unemployed, the issue of municipal contracts, school feeding and other related issues.

It is beautifully demonstrated in the struggle to provide free municipal school meals in Bradford.81 Despite the fact that the Bradford Cinderalla Club admitted that it was unable to provide a sufficient number of free meals for the children of the unemployed, though it had provided 110,000 free meals in the winter months of 1903/4, and that is was practically without funds, the Liberal Association in Bradford refused to consider the necessity of municipal provision. It was only political expediency, forced upon it by the impending municipal elections of November 1904, which eventually led the Liberal-dominated Bradford City Council to accept the possibility of municipal school feeding in October 1904, an action which it reversed immediately after the municipal elections. For almost three years, until the early months of 1907, the Bradford Liberals resisted the demand for municipal provision of free school meals, largely on the grounds that such an action would lead to the widespread municipalisation of poverty. Instead they supplemented the work of charity by setting up a Lord Mayor's Fund, which was to be administered by the representatives of the City Council and of the Cinderella Club. When the Fund was exhausted the task of feeding the children of the poor was passed on to the Board of Guardians, who quickly demonstrated their inability to deal with the full extent of the problem. It was only when the actions of Charity and the Poor Law had foundered, when the Bradford Liberals began to experience political reverses in local elections, when the Liberal government passed a permissive act providing for municipal school feeding in December 1906, and when Alfred Illingworth - a leading opponent of municipal school feeding - died in February 1907 that the Bradford Liberal Association capitulated and accepted the need for municipal school feeding.[82]

It is clear that faced with the obvious failings of charity Liberals were, on the whole, inclined to favour its re-organisation rather than to engineer moves towards municipal responsibility. Charity began to alter its form to deal with the new scale of economic problems in West Yorkshire. For many years the Charity Organisation Society had been offering relief to the poor by providing the worthy with money for self-help activities. In Bradford, when the Charity Organisation Society appeared to be faltering, many of its leading figures, such as H.B. Priestman, the leader of Bradford Liberalism, decided to set up an entirely new body, the Guild of Help, in 1904.[83] The main purpose of this body was to tackle poverty at its source, rather than to examine it before a committee, which had been the style of the Charity Organisation Society. The Guild of Help established a network of helpers throughout Bradford who would enter the houses of the poor and provide help and relief for these people. Social casework was to be the focus of its work, and poverty was to be grappled at first hand. Guilds of Help were formed in other parts of the country and in West Yorkshire, one of the most notable organisations being formed at Huddersfield in 1908.[84]

On the whole, however, Labour politicians were sceptical of these cosmetic exercises. To them, rising unemployment, and its consequential poverty, had exposed the failures of charity and the Poor Law. Harry Smith, Secretary of the Bradford Cinderella Club, and a leading member of the ILP, considered that 'at best in Yorkshire there exists a state of things that no system of private almsgiving can alleviate'.85 To him, and many other members of the ILP and trade union organisations, what was required was the two-fold intervention of local and central government to provide relief, investment and jobs. The focus of ILP and trade union activity was, therefore, to pressure for municipalisation at all levels - whether it be of hospitals, industry, coal supply or school feeding. On the issue of school feeding, the Bradford ILP vigorously demanded 'the provision of at least one free meal a day at each school' for each child.86 Whilst strongly advocating municipalisation, however, there were some ILPers who were willing to entertain Liberal attempts to re-organise charity. Harry Smith, for instance, was quite prepared to join in the activities of the Bradford Guild of Help, though many ILP members, such as James Bartley, were bullish in their opposition to the Guild.87

In the end, however, charity and the Poor Law were left to provide relief. Charity was incapable of dealing with the problem and the Guardians, who assumed more responsibility for school feeding in 1905, following an instruction from the Local Government Board, were clearly seen to be incapable of dealing effectively with the issue.88 The established means of dealing with unemployment and poverty were effete.

There is no doubt that the failure of the local Liberal-dominated town and city councils to consider and tackle the problems of unemployment, and the recourse which was made to charity and the Poor Law, forced many trade unionists and workers over to the ILP and LRC. The surge in Labour's local representation partly reflects the concern for unemployment and also partly reflects the rising concern for a municipal solution. In addition, however, there was the issue of fair contracts, the payment of trade union wage rates, which it became clear could only be firmly established on public bodies if there was adequate Labour representation.89 ILP and LRC members, most of whom were also trade unionists, were quick to seize the problem of enforcing fair contracts resolutions to strengthen their support.90 They were also adept at using the attempts of employers to increase work burdens to enlist support. This was particularly obvious in the Huddersfield

Labour Resurgence 1900-6

Labour movement, where there was strong Labour and trade union opposition to the moves by employers in the woollen industry to introduce the two-loom system, whereby weavers minded two looms instead of one.[91]

Yet the course of Labour growth did not run smoothly in the early years of the twentieth century. In West Yorkshire there appear to have been two main problems which created difficulties. The first is that, despite its weakness in West Yorkshire, the Social Democratic Federation created tensions within the Labour movement in both Dewsbury and Bradford. The second is that the exuberance of many local Labour leaders led them to demand that Labour candidates should be put forward in their constituency at the next general election, despite the entreaties of Ramsay MacDonald that only a few prime constituencies ought to be fought.

The SDF had never been well-established in the West Yorkshire textile district in the 1890s, nor had it ever made the efforts to win support as it had done in London and Lancashire.[92] Although there were a number of prominent individuals who were members of the SDF there were few SDF branches in West Yorkshire. There had been an SDF branch in Leeds during the 1880s and a small Bradford branch was in existence between 1895 and 1898, but by the end of 1901 there was probably only one branch in West Yorkshire, at Dewsbury, though a Bradford branch was re-established soon afterwards.[93] It was the Dewsbury branch which caused most difficulty for the ILP and LRC, and which created related problems in Bradford.

The conflict between the ILP and the Trades Council, on the one hand, and the SDF, on the other, was most protracted between October 1901 and January 1902. As we have already suggested, Dewsbury was a promising centre for ILP activity in the mid 1890s. The constituency contained ILP branches in Dewsbury itself, Batley and Thornhill Lees and a membership of 800 to 900 by the mid 1890s. During the late 1890s, however, this support had been partly dissipated by the fact that the local ILP had appointed an SDF man from Lancashire as its local agent, and he had converted the Dewsbury ILP into a Socialist Society and, finally, into an SDF branch.[94] Much of the old ILP support had drifted away quickly, and by 1901 the SDF branch in Dewsbury had only about 40 or 50 members.[95] The ILP, weakened as it was, still retained a substantial membership in

125

Batley, where Ben Turner the ILP was active, and in Thornhill Lees, where Tom Myers was prominent.96 Turner and Myers, were both active members of the Dewsbury Trades Council and kept support for the ILP strong in that organisation.

Relations between the local ILP and the SDF organisations were never very easy, but they deteriorated markedly when the SDF pushed for a local conference with other Labour organisations in November 1901, and then pre-empted the issue by announcing their intention to contest Dewsbury with Harry Quelch, a leading figure in the SDF and the editor of *Justice*, before the local conference was held. Although the SDF argued that it took such action because it felt that the Trades Council and the ILP would accept Sam Woods, the Liberal nominee, as the effective Labour candidate it was well known that the Trades Council and the ILP would support E.R. Hartley who had unsuccessfully contested Dewsbury in 1895. The spurious claims of the SDF did much to fuel the fusillade of abuse hurled at it by the leading figures in the ILP. The *Labour Leader* registered the official ILP view, as presented by its sub-committee set up to examine the affair, that Quelch and the SDF were the first in the field 'only by breaking away from the starting line'.97

Although the focus of much of the ILP criticism was that the SDF had cheated whilst the ILP and the Trades Council had played by the rules of selection, many ILP leaders felt that the affair had demonstrated what was to be expected of the much lauded Socialist unity campaign which was being waged by the SDF. One writer reflected that 'The S.D.F. has taken up the attitude of having its own isolated impossibilist way, and setting at defiance the I.L.P. and the Trades Council. It is unity, no doubt - the unity of itself'.98 The same writer later added that

> We are disputing the pretence under which he has been placed in the field as "the Socialist and Trades Union candidate", and we are disputing the suggestion that his candidature can result in anything but an unnecessary and humiliating reproach upon the reputation of Socialism.

The *ILP News* felt that the imposition of Quelch would be disastrous for Socialism:

> An isolated S.D.F. candidate would prove a very lamentable and futile political escapade, and

would provide a very bad advertisement for Socialism in the West Riding of Yorkshire. Without the cardinal co-operation of the Trade Unions, no third, not to speak of a fourth candidate, would receive an effective vote in the division.[99]

Despite the criticism of Keir Hardie, Bruce Glasier, Philip Snowden, and local figures, such as Ben Turner and Tom Myers, the tactical advantage was with the SDF who were supplied with the additional bonus of the decision of Hartley, mooted as the ILP and Trades Council candidate, to stand down in favour of Quelch. The defeat of Quelch in the January 1902 by-election - where he obtained 1,597 votes or 13.6 per cent of the vote - was not the end of the affair for its ramifications extended into Hartley's position with the ILP in Bradford. Hartley was a highly respected figure in the ILP and when the NAC of the ILP censured his action the Bradford movement came to his defence.[100] But he was soon to develop his relations with the SDF alongside his ILP and Clarion Van activities. He joined the SDF in 1902 and helped the re-formation of the Bradford SDF branch in the same year. He also pressed to be adopted by the ILP as the Socialist candidate for Bradford East, in tandem with Fred Jowett who had been endorsed by the ILP and the LRC for Bradford West. In this action, many Bradford ILPers saw him acting as the representative of the SDF and feared that the SDF was attempting to obtain ILP support to secure the return of a parliamentary candidate. Neither the Bradford ILP nor Fred Jowett were prepared to divide the resources of the Bradford ILP between Bradford West and Bradford East[101]and Keir Hardie reflected the official ILP line on Hartley's candidature when he wrote to Cunninghame Graham, who had been to Bradford East to help Hartley's campaign, in vitriolic style - arguing that Hartley's candidature was the outcome of 'vanity', that the SDF had refused to find 'money for the candidature' and that Jowett's prospects of winning Bradford West would be impaired.[102] Hardie also noted that MacDonald, and the LRC, agreed with this advice not to divide the ILP forces.

The Quelch affair and the Hartley action continued to fuel hostility between the ILP and the SDF in West Yorkshire up to the First World War. In a broader sense, however, the whole issue of the selection of candidates was encapsulated within the events which took place at Dewsbury. Both the ILP and the LRC were very much feeling their way in the selection of candidates. Whilst the National ILP appears to have been less pedantic; it is clear that both the ILP and LRC were concerned that proper and extensive consultations with all local labour organisations should take place and that only seats capable of returning a Labour candidate should be contested. This approach was evident in Hardie's attitude towards Hartley's contesting Bradford East and putting Bradford West at risk. But it was even more evident in the relations between the LRC and local LRC constituency organisations. MacDonald, Secretary of the LRC, was strongly opposed to the assumption by many constituency organisations that they should run a Labour candidate in the parliamentary elections just because a local LRC had been formed or because the local trades council had affiliated to the National LRC. The resulting correspondence was often heated.

In West Yorkshire the LRC gradually adopted seven candidates for the forthcoming election
- James O'Grady (Leeds East), Fred Jowett (Bradford West), James Parker (Halifax), Ben Turner (Dewsbury), T.R. Williams (Huddersfield), A. Fox (South Leeds) and Dr. Stanton Coit (Wakefield). Most of these candidates were selected without acrimonious debate. Some discussion was raised about Fox standing for Leeds when, at one time, it appeared to be the view that only Leeds East, of the five Leeds constituencies, would be contested by Labour.103 But MacDonald fought a determined rearguard action against the promotion of Labour candidates for other seats.

Joe Walker of the Pudsey ILP tried to pressure MacDonald to find a 'Trade Union candidate (a Socialist preferable) who is yet without a constituency' to fight Pudsey.104 The difficulty with the enormous Pudsey division, which surrounded Bradford, was that the ILP was weak; the trade union movement insignificant, that there was only one small trades council, at Stanningley, and, above all, that about 5,000 Leeds freeholders were to be found amongst its electorate of between 15,000 and 16,000.105 Despite some minor political successes which were achieved in the Pudsey constituency, MacDonald was forced to conclude that the area was not worth fighting.106 Similarly in Todmorden, though the Trades Council advocated the selection of a Labour candidate for the Sowerby Division, James Parker, the Halifax ILP man who, with Keir Hardie, was one of the two ILP representatives on the LRC Executive, advised that 'The Sowerby Division is a hopeless place for a Labour candidate, it is a county division, very little trade unionism in the division & Todmorden itself has very few voters in the division'.[107]

Whilst the situations in the Pudsey and Sowerby divisions were not promising, and MacDonald was probably wise not to get the LRC to give its support, this was not the situation in all constituencies. Bradford East was a promising area for a Labour parliamentary candidate, but animosity towards Hartley ruled out LRC support there. In Leeds West it was the secret pact of 1903, between Herbert Gladstone and Ramsay MacDonald which intruded into relations between the Leeds LRC and the National LRC. Relations between MacDonald and the Leeds LRC had never been particularly easy but they worsened considerably when J.D. Macrae, Secretary of the Leeds LRC, wrote to MacDonald indicating the intention of his organisation to contest Leeds West as well as Leeds East and Leeds South. The argument which Macrae put forward was that the November 1905 municipal elections suggested that there was more support for Labour in Leeds West than there was for the Liberal Party.[108] Indeed, Macrae had been returned for Armley/Wortley ward and A. Shaw had been returned for New Wortley. Two of the four wards in West Leeds had been won by Labour in the 1905 municipal elections. MacDonald's reaction to Macrae's letter was to suggest that the LRC would probably pass a strong resolution against the contest, that O'Grady' society, which permitted him to stand for Leeds East on the understanding that he would be the only Labour candidate in the Leeds constituencies, would probably have to be contacted, and that 'my Executive will even go to the length of publishing a condemnatory resolution in the newspaper if you insist upon a third candidate'.[109] The riposte to MacDonald and J.S. Middleton was impressive, and clearly touched a nerve. Macrae replied in mocking style:

> What is the matter with West Leeds? Dear me, national responsibility, only one candidate, condemnatory resolution in the newspaper, national movement has suffered, dissociating ourselves from such a policy. What a flutter in the dovecotes. What did you say? Chief Liberal Whip, how very rude, it really is too bad for you. Now do be good boys, remember the honour and dignity of the movement depend upon your conduct.[110]

MacDonald's furious reply complained of Macrae's 'reckless charges' regarding the 'Chief Liberal Whip'.[111] But Macrae had hit bullseye, for MacDonald did not wish to endanger the secret agreement he had made with Gladstone, to avoid needless Liberal and Labour clashes in certain constituencies, by allowing a Labour candidate to be put forward against Herbert Gladstone in Leeds West. In the end, MacDonald successfully blocked the efforts of the Leeds LRC.

The West Yorkshire Labour movement progressed enormously between 1900 and 1906. Traditional areas of Labour strength - such as Bradford and Halifax - continued their inexorable growth. More unstable areas of Labour support - such as Huddersfield, Leeds and Dewsbury - showed real signs of Labour's improving position. On the other hand, the once promising Keighley constituency saw a regression in Labour support after 1900. There had been a marked improvement in Labour's position in 13 of the 14 constituencies covered by these six towns in the period 1906 to 1914. The other ten constituencies in West Yorkshire experienced more mixed fortunes. Labour strength was only marginally improved in Otley, Sowerby, Elland, Holmfirth, Morley, Pudsey, Spen Valley and Shipley. Yet, as David Clark has ably revealed, there were major improvements in Labour's propaganda work, lecturing activities and club activities in Colne Valley, although the constituency was not contested by Labour in the 1906 General Election.[112] Yet the most dramatic improvement for Labour in West Yorkshire occurred at Wakefield.

Wakefield was a traditional stronghold of Conservatism. A Conservative or Unionist candidate had been returned for the constituency in all the general election contests since the mid 1880s, though the margin of victory was often comparatively small. This Conservative dominance had been confirmed in the 1900 General Election when the Unionist candidate, Viscount Milton, had been returned unopposed. Up to that time the Liberal Party was effete and the Labour movement had barely begun to stir. The Wakefield Federated Trades Council had been formed in 1891, but is remained a weak and ineffective organisation throughout the 1890s. There does not appear to have been an ILP organisation in the constituency, though there were clearly some ILP members in Wakefield. The meaningful starting date of the Wakefield Labour movement was March 1902 when, due to Viscount Milton's becoming Earl Fitzwilliam, there was a by-election at Wakefield. Since the Liberals did not intend to contest the by-election Philip Snowden stepped in and, with both Liberal and Labour support, recorded just under 2,000 votes, or just over 40 per cent of the vote, in a two-sided contest. It is true that Snowden acted as the radical candidate, and that there was some criticism from the SDF which claimed to have given him some support at Blackburn in the 1900 General Election, but it is also clear that his entry transformed Labour's position in Wakefield. In the wake of his campaign, the Wakefield Trades Council affiliated to the LRC about September 1902 and a Wakefield LRC was formed in the late spring or summer of 1903.[113] By June 1903, the Wakefield LRC was requesting a list of Trade Union/Labour candidates from the National LRC and showing distinct signs of wishing to make Wakefield one of the official LRC seats to be contested at the next general election.

Initially, it was Robert Morley, one of the stalwarts of the Halifax ILP, who acted as the organising secretary of the Wakefield LRC,[114] and it may have been his influence which provoked the formation of the Wakefield ILP. This became very active throughout 1903.[115] By the end of 1903, the ILP, the LRC and the Trades Council had gone through the business of selecting Dr. Stanton Coit, from London, as the Labour candidate for Wakefield.[116] Once selected, Stanton Coit set about strengthening Labour's position within Wakefield, and did so dramatically by purchasing the <u>Wakefield Echo</u> at the end of April 1905. Coit informed Arthur Henderson, of the LRC, that

> I have just taken over, in the interests of the Labour Party, the "Wakefield Echo", a halfpenny eight-page paper which has been in existence 27 years. The first issue under the new regime will appear on Friday morning of this week. As you are well known to all the people of Wakefield, I write to ask whether you will not send us a short letter ... expressing your good will and congratulating the Labour Party here upon having an organ which will set forth its principles.[117]

The Wakefield movement had indeed surged forward and, despite some concern at the appearance of a Liberal candidate, Dr. Coit came within an ace of winning Wakefield for Labour in the 1906 General

Election.[118]

The 1906 General Election marked the breakthrough of Labour into national politics, with the return of 29 Labour/ILP MPs. The events in West Yorkshire were a mirror image of the euphoria which overtook the national independent Labour movement at the beginning of 1906. Nine Labour or Socialist candidates contested seats in West Yorkshire, seven for the ILP/LRC, one for the ILP, and one for the SDF.[119] Of these, three were returned to Parliament - Fred Jowett (Bradford West), James Parker (Halifax) and James O'Grady (Leeds East) - all of them for the ILP/LRC. Admittedly, O'Grady won a straight fight with the Conservatives and Parker had only one Liberal opponent in the two-seat Halifax constituency, but elsewhere there were victories and narrow defeats for Labour in the face of stiff Liberal opposition. Jowett was an impressive victor in Bradford West, forcing the Liberal candidate into third place, T. Russell Williams was only narrowly defeated by Sir J.T. Woodhouse in Huddersfield, and Stanton Coit pushed the Conservative candidate close in Wakefield, and was well ahead of the Liberal candidate. As Table 5.3 indicates, the Labour Party did remarkably well in West Yorkshire in an election which saw the Liberals recover some of their vote and the Conservative vote collapse. Labour did remarkably well on the progressive tide.

There were, however, deep divisions between Labour and Liberalism which made the contests in Yorkshire more overtly based upon the conflict of class issues than any previous General Election. In Bradford, the Liberal and Conservative parties were united over the issues of

> Free Trade, Welsh Disestablishment and Tariff Reforms, with reference to Home Rule for Ireland, religious teaching in schools, licencing reforms and 'Chinese slavery" in South Africa. Jowett gave most attention to the poverty question, and particularly to unemployment and school feeding, and showed that on these issues there was little difference between the Conservatives and Liberals.[12]

Even though the O'Grady victory in Leeds East was due to the Gladstone-MacDonald pact arrangement, Tom Woodhouse concludes:

> If allowing James O'Grady a free run in

> East Leeds is seen as an example of progressive Liberalism it must be observed that the concession was opposed as damaging by local Liberal activities. The reason was that the Labour Party in Leeds simply did not respect the policy of <u>rapprochement</u>. Given its head in East Leeds it was all the more ready to attack the other Liberal seats. Joseph Henry watchdog of Liberal interests in their stronghold of West Leeds, pointed out the effects of the policy: 'I hope the party is not going to go as it did at the last election - leave the Labour man at liberty to fight a Tory and then allow him to fight a Liberal whenever he likes ...[121]

In Halifax, James Parker, despite effectively running in tandem with a Liberal in the two-seat constituency, pressed home the issues of unemployment and poverty at the general election. E.R. Hartley, though officially an SDF candidate, held joint meeting with Fred Jowett, at St. George's Hall, where poverty and school feeding were on the menu of topics for discussion.[122]

It was the exigencies of working-class life which both coloured the Labour campaigns throughout West Yorkshire in the 1906 General Election and distinguished them from the Liberal and Conservative campaigns. This distinction of approach persisted even where Liberal candidate had given way to Labour candidates, and it is wise to remember that, whatever MacDonald might have arranged with the Liberal leadership at the national level, the local Labour leaders in West Yorkshire were resolute in their opposition to the ideas of an alliance with Liberalism. Contrary to the views recently expressed by David Howell, a Progressive unity between the Liberal and Labour parties did not dominate the political events surrounding the growth of Labour in Bradford, and evidence of such a Progressive alliance is thin for the West Yorkshire area as a whole.[123] The political and social divisions between the Labour and Liberal parties were, by now, too deep to permit such an accommodation. The intransigence of Liberal industrialists and the aloofness of Liberal politicians to the need for municipal provision, and their penchant for charity provision, cast them adrift from an increasing proportion of the working class whose economic and social conditions required more than the limited financial resources of charitable institutions. The infrequent parliamentary contests cannot accurately and precisely chart this loss of Liberal support over a short period of time and their unrepresentative nature can often obscure the political metamorphosis which was occurring. In contrast, the more representative local elections and muncipal contests provide a more accurate year by year benchmark of Labour's growth.[124] Between 1900 and 1906, as Table 5.5 reveals, that growth was steady. As we shall argue in the next chapter, Labour's growth became more rapid therafter.

On the face of it, the Liberal Party had done well in West Yorkshire at the 1906 General Election. It had increased its parliamentary representation from 14 to 19, the Conservatives were reduced to one representative instead of nine, and Labour was still only a modest parliamentary opponent with three representatives, though they were the first parliamentary victories for Labour in West Yorkshire. But any complacency that such a Liberal victory engendered was short-lived in the face of the furious assault of Labour in local contests which was eating into the grass-roots support for Liberalism. All was not well with West Yorkshire Liberalism.

P.F. Clarke has argued that Progressive Liberalism changed in order to accommodate the newly-emerging working-class aspirations within the Liberal fold, that this was successfully accomplished in Lancashire and probably achieved in other areas. But there is little evidence that this occurred in West Yorkshire. There are, perhaps, two main reasons for this absence of Liberal approbation of working-class interests. In the first case, West Yorkshire Liberalism was still overwhelmingly dominated by the Nonconformist textile magnates such as Alfred Illingworth, James Hill and John Brigg. These men, and their like, continued to dominate West Yorkshire Liberalism, dominated local politics, and stifled opposition to the old Liberalism. Under their rule there was no synthesis between Liberalism and Socialism. Secondly, it is quite clear that the unrestricted Labour challenge in local politics, and the rising grass roots demand for political independence, prevented the Liberal Party from re-absorbing Labour supporters into the Progressive fold.

The years between 1900 and 1906 had seen the revival of the West Yorkshire Labour movement from its nadir of the late 1890s. Many factors account for this revival. The steady expansion of the cultural side of the movement and the continued and growing support of religious leaders helped broaden the appeal of the ILP and LRC. But, in the end, the revival of Labour fortunes was largely achieved by the mere formation of the national LRC, which broadened the possibility of obtaining trade-union support which was not Socialist. Typical of the new trade unionist who was active within the LRC was Ernest Wimpenny, a leading figure in the General Union of Textile Workers and prominent in the Huddersfield LRC. It was written of Wimpenny that he 'sailed his political craft under the LRC flag. He is not a Socialist, but a sound trade unionist'.[125] By winning this type of support the West Yorkshire Labour movement was able to quickly expand its activities. The events of Taff Vale were of marginal importance to this growth of Labour support for major inroads had been achieved before the decision of the House of Lords in the summer of 1901. The 1906 General Election was the icing on the cake for the West Yorkshire Labour movement. One local Labour leader, Robert Morley, of Halifax and Wakefield fame, noted that some Labour MPs were 'flushed with victory and talking foolishly' and that, in some areas, the ILP was buzzing with activity: 'Huddersfield & the District is simply alive with ILPism'.[126] However, from the 1906 General Election onwards, the West Yorkshire Labour movement had to settle down to the responsibility of consolidating its position. It became highly attuned to its new role, expanding its activities as the vehicle of working-class aspirations at a rate which the West Yorkshire Liberal parties were unable to withstand.

NOTES

    1. Labour Party Archive, LRC Correspondence 5/233,10/453.
    2. Ibid., 20/112; Workers' Municipal Federation Minutes, Bradford Trades and Labour Council Collection, Archives Department, Bradford Central Library.
    3. Labour Party Archive, LRC Correspondence 3/191.
    4. Roberts, 'The Liberal Party in West Yorkshire', epilogue.
    5. J. Foster, <u>Class Struggle and the Industrial Revolution</u> (Weidenfield and Nicolson, London, 1974).
    6. P. Joyce, <u>Work, Society and Politics: The Culture of the Factory in Later Victorian England</u>

Labour Resurgence 1900-6

(Harvester Press, Brighton, 1980).
7. H. Pelling, The Origins of the Labour Party (Macmillan, London, 1954), chapter x.
8. J. Saville, 'Trade Unions and Free Labour: The Background to the Taff Vale Decision' in A. Briggs and J. Saville, (eds.) Essays in Labour History (Macmillan, London, 1960, 1967), pp. 348-50.
9. Labour Party Archive, LRC 1/58.
10. Ibid., 1/53.
11. Ibid., 1/219-24, 2/192.
12. Huddersfield Trades Council, Minutes, 24 Feb. and 23 Mar. 1904; Yorkshire Factory Times, 1 Apr. 1904.
13. The General Union of Textile Workers appears to have joined the National Labour Representation Committee at its formation in Feb. 1900.
14. Labour Party Archive, LRC 13/267, 13/269, 14/212, 15/52, 15/54, 20/145.
15. Ibid., 20/149.
16. J. O'Grady fought Leeds East and A. Fox fought Leeds South in the 1906 General Election.
17. The Bradford ILP concentrated upon the return of Fred Jowett for Bradford West and though it gave its general support for E.R. Hartley, a member of both the ILP and the SDF, it put no resources into Hartley's Bradford East contest.
18. R. Price, An Imperial War and the British Working Class (Routledge and Kegan Paul, London, 1972), introduction and chapter three.
19. Jowett and Parker were both active in the ILP and the LRC; Byles does not appear to have been directly connected with either organisation.
20. Seventh Annual Report of the I.L.P. at Leeds, April 1899; Bradford Observer, 11 Jan. 1900.
21. Bradford Observer, 15 Sep. 1899, 26 Mar. 1900.
22. S.J. King, 'Bradford Politics and the Boer War', unpublished M.A. dissertation, Huddersfield Polytechnic, 1982.
23. Brockway, Socialism over Sixty Years, pp. 64-7.
24. King, 'Bradford Politics and the Boer War', p. 26.
25. Price, An Imperial War and the British Working Class, chapter three.
26. A. Illingworth, Fifty Years of Politics: Mr Alfred Illingworth: Retrospect (Bradford & District Newspaper Co. Ltd., Bradford, 1905).
27. The poll was low and the progressive vote ought to have been larger, which implies that there was a significant proportion of abstensions.

Labour Resurgence 1900-6

    28. One of the significant exceptions was C.P. Trevelyan, the Liberal, and later Labour, MP for Elland. Refer to Morris, <u>C.P. Trevelyan 1870-1958: Portrait of a Radical</u>, p. 35.
    29. E.D. Steele, 'Imperialism and Leeds Politics, c. 1850-1914' in D. Fraser (ed.) <u>A History of Modern Leeds</u> (Manchester University Press, Manchester, 1980), pp. 335-7, 343-6.
    30. Table 5.3 suggests that the 1900 General Election saw the Liberals reach a new low in parliamentary popularity in West Yorkshire, though there was comparatively little deterioration from the 1895 General Election position.
    31. W.E.B. Priestley had led a secret delegation to meet Herbert Gladstone in order to secure Jarratt's withdrawal.
    32. ILP Archive, Francis Johnson Collection and the Labour Party Archive, LRC Correspondence 1900-7 contains numerous examples of advice tendered against Labour being involved in alliances with the Liberals. Labour Party Archive, LRC 8/24 illustrates the hostility of the Bradford ILP to an alliance with the Liberals.
    33. ILP Archive, Francis Johnson Collection, 1907/70, 1908/156, 1908/159, 1908/199, 1908/202.
    34. Pelling, <u>Origins of the Labour Party</u>, pp. 225-7.
    35. <u>Yorkshire Factory Times</u>, 30 Nov. 1900; <u>Huddersfield Chronicle</u>, 24 Nov. 1900.
    36. Labour Party Archive, LRC 1/466.
    37. Woodhouse, 'The Working Class', p. 361.
    38. Samuel Shaftoe, Secretary of the Trades Council from the 1870s to 1893, was returned as a Liberal councillor for West Bowling in 1891.
    39. Gee was on the Executive Committee of the LRC in 1900.
    40. Labour Party Archive, LRC 8/34.
    41. Woodhouse, 'The Working Class', p. 363.
    42. Clark, <u>Colne Valley: Radicalism to Socialism</u>.
    43. <u>Bradford Daily Telegraph</u>, 4 May 1903.
    44. Workers' Municipal Federation, Minute Book, 1902-19, Archives Department, Bradford Central Library. The Constitution appears at the beginning of the book.
    45. Bradford Trades and Labour Council, Minutes, 1895, <u>passim</u>.
    46. Drew was the first Secretary of the WMF and Secretary of the Bradford Trades Council at the same time, as well as being a prominent member of the ILP. G. Licence was Secretary of the WMF between 1905 and 1909. A.T. Sutton became a member of the Executive

Committee of the WMF in 1905, at a time when he was also Secretary of the Bradford ILP, and became President of the WMF in 1913. Tom Brown was on the Executive Committee of the WMF in 1902 and, again, between 1902 and 1908. He acted as Fred Jowett's election agent during the 1906 General Election contest for Bradford West. James Bartley was on the first Executive Committee of the WMF in July 1902.

47. W.H. Drew, Tom Brown, James Bartley, J.H. Palin and G. East.
48. WMF, Minutes, 17 Jul. 1905.
49. Ibid., 3 Oct. 1902.
50. Ibid., for 1904.
51. Labour Party Archive, LRC 20/112.
52. James, 'The Emergence of the Keighley Independent Labour Party', charts the rise and fall of the Labour Church in Keighley.
53. K.S. Inglis, Churches and the Working Classes in Victorian England (Routledge and Kegan Paul, London, 1963), chapter six; Labour Prophet, May 1893, Jan., Mar., Apr., 1894; Yorkshire Factory Times, 3 Mar. 1893, 11 Jan., 1 Feb., 15 Feb. 1895.
54. S. Yeo, 'A New Life: The Religion of Socialism in Britain 1883-1896', History Workshop, issue 4, autumn 1977, pp. 5-56.
55. K. Laybourn, 'The Trade Unions and the ILP: The Manningham Experience' in J.A. Jowitt and R.K.S. Taylor, Bradford 1890-1914: The Cradle of the Independent Labour Party (Bradford City Occasional Papers No. 2, University of Leeds Centre of Adult Education, Bradford, 1980), pp. 34-40.
56. Keighley Labour Journal, 24 Mar., 30 Dec. 1894, 24 Apr., 2 Jun. 1897, 26 Jan. 1898.
57. Huddersfield Examiner, 14 Apr. 1906, 16 Feb. 1907.
58. Labour Leader, 15 Sep. 1900; Young Socialist, Mar. 1901.
59. Labour Leader, 25 Mar. 1895; F. Reid, 'Socialist Sunday Schools in Britain, 1892-1939', International Review of Social History, X1(1966), pp. 18-47.
60. ILP Archive, Francis Johnson Collection, 1917/61.
61. Bradford Labour Echo, 24 Jun. 1899.
62. Forward, 14, 21 Jul. 1906.
63. Taped interview with Ada Dalby, August 1979. In the possession of Dr. K. Laybourn.
64. Labour Leader, 15 Sep. 1900.
65. Burgess was the editor of the Yorkshire Factory Times and the Workman's Times in the early 1890s, fell on hard times in 1894, and went to live

in Scotland for a number of years before coming to live in Bradford. Mrs. A. Dalby remembered Burgess and his daughter attending the Great Horton Sunday School and provided Dr. Laybourn with photographs of the Fineburghs.

66. Forward, 27 Oct. 1906.
67. Ibid., 24 Nov. 1906.
68. Laybourn, '"The Defence of Bottom Dog": The Independent Labour Party in Local Politics', pp. 229-33.
69. Such a body was set up to deal with unemployment and the provision of school meals in Bradford at the beginning of 1905.
70. Yorkshire Factory Times, 4 Dec. 1903.
71. Ibid.
72. Ibid., 28 Oct. 1904.
73. Forward, 11 Feb. 1905.
74. Ibid., 9, 16, 23 Sep. 1905.
75. Yorkshire Factory Times, 30 Oct. 1903.
76. Ibid., 18 Dec. 1903.
77. Ibid., 4 Dec. 1903.
78. Ibid.
79. Ibid., 13 Nov. 1903.
80. Forward, 18 Mar. 1905.
81. Laybourn, '"The Defence of Bottom Dog": The Independent Labour Party in Local Politics', pp. 237-9; K. Laybourn, 'The Issue of School Feeding in Bradford, 1904-1907', Journal of Educational Administration and History, Vol. XIV, No. 2, Jul. 1982, pp. 30-8.
82. This change in direction occurred dramatically, and swiftly, between December 1906 and March 1907, and was partly implemented by the fact that the medical evidence supplied by Dr. Crowley, son-in-law of H.B. Priestman, the Bradford Liberal leader, revealed the acute problem of starvation and undernourishment which faced many children in the winter months.
83. M. Cahill and T. Jowitt, 'The New Philanthropy: The Emergence of the Bradford City Guild of Help', Journal of Social Policy, Vol. 9, Pt. 3. Jul. 1980, pp. 359-82.
84. C. Parton, 'Liberal Individualism and Infant Mortality: The Infant Welfare Movement in Huddersfield 1900-1918', unpublished dissertation, Huddersfield Polytechnic, 1982.
85. Yorkshire Factory Times, 30 Oct. 1903.
86. Forward, 29 Oct. 1904.
87. Cahill and Jowitt, 'The New Philanthropy', p. 377.
88. Forward, 10 Feb, 17 Feb., 30 Jun. 1906.

89. Bradford Trades and Labour Council Year Book, 1903 (Bradford Trades and Labour Council, Bradford, 1903), p. 11; Year Book, 1904 (Bradford, 1904), pp. 39-41; Year Book, 1905 (Bradford 1905), pp. 93-101.
90. ILP Manifestoes. Deed Box 13, Case 64, Archive Department, Bradford Central Library.
91. Yorkshire Factory Times, 27 Nov. 1903, 2 Feb. 1894, 27 Nov. 1895.
92. P.A. Watmough, 'The Membership of the Social Democratic Federation, 1885-1902', Bulletin of the Society for the Study of Labour History, no. 34, Spring 1977, pp. 35-40; ILP News, April 1902.
93. Hartley was responsible for re-starting the SDF branch in Bradford during 1902.
94. ILP News, Nov. 1901.
95. Ibid., Dec. 1901.
96. Yorkshire Factory Times, 19 Feb. 1904.
97. ILP Archive, Francis Johnson Collection, 1901/49, 1901/53-4, 1901/68; Justice, 2 Nov. 1901.
98. ILP News, Oct. 1901.
99. Ibid., Oct. 1901.
100. Ibid., May 1902.
101. Forward contains numerous references to this throughout 1905.
102. ILP Archive, Francis Johnson Collection, 1906/6.
103. Labour Party Archive, LRC Correspondence 24/263, 28/211.
104. Ibid., 17/534.
105. Ibid.
106. Ibid., 17/536.
107. Ibid., 8/298.
108. Ibid., 28/215.
109. Ibid., 28/216.
110. Ibid., 28/217.
111. Ibid., 28/218-19.
112. Clark, Colne Valley: Radicalism to Socialism, pp. 112-16.
113. Labour Party Archive, LRC 9/443.
114. Ibid., 10/454.
115. Ibid., 11/487.
116. Ibid.
117. Ibid., 23/54.
118. Coit obtained 2,068 votes, only 217 less than his Conservative opponent and more than 800 ahead of the Liberal candidate. The Snowden by-election candidature of 1902, when there was no Liberal candidate, appears to have established the credability of Labour.
119. The ILP/LRC candidates were O'Grady (Leeds

East), Fox (Leeds South), Coit (Wakefield), Turner (Dewsbury), Parker (Halifax), Jowett (Bradford West) and Williams (Huddersfield).Newlove was endorsed by the ILP for Keighley and Hartley had SDF support, and some ILP sympathy, in Bradford East.

    120.   Brockway, Socialism over Sixty Years, p. 68.
    121.   Woodhouse, 'The working class', p. 361.
    122.   Forward, 13 Jan. 1906.
    123.   Howell, British Workers and the Independent Labour Party 1888-1906, p. 197.
    124.   M.G. Sheppard, 'The Effects of the Franchise Provisions on the Social and Sex Composition of the Municipal Electorate 1882-1914', Bulletin of the Society for the Study of Labour History, no. 45 (Autumn, 1982), 19-25.
    125.   Yorkshire Factory Times, 4 Mar. 1904.
    126.   ILP Archive, Francis Johnson Collection, 1906/55.

Chapter Six

LIBERAL DECLINE AND LABOUR GROWTH 1906-14

The ever-increasing pace of working-class defections from Liberalism to Labour prior to the 1906 General Election turned into a torrent in the years immediately prior to the First World War. Although the Liberal Party did increase its parliamentary representation from 19 to 20 in 1910, and despite the fact that it recovered some municipal ground in 1908, it is evident that Labour was enhancing its political claims to West Yorkshire after 1906. Grayson's Colne Valley by-election success of 1907 temporarily increased Labour's parliamentary representation in West Yorkshire to four, reducing the number of Liberal MPs to 18, and it is evident that much of the Liberal parliamentary success of 1910 was based upon a dip in Conservative rather than Labour support. Liberalism was no longer garnering the working-class support which it once commanded and the real drift of that support to Labour appears in the enormous surge of Labour's municipal and local victories, especially after 1910. The inexorable political growth of Labour was borne upon the development of class politics, which had seen trade unionism, and through it the working class, attach itself to the Labour Party. Had the parliamentary franchise been more democratic, and had the financial position of the Labour Party been stronger, there is little doubt that Labour's parliamentary position in West Yorkshire would have risen as dramatically as did its local and municipal successes. Despite this, it is clear that by the First World War, the Labour Party was much stronger than the Conservative party in the whole spectrum of politics and if not as comprehensively powerful as the Liberal Party it was challenging it for political predominance in some areas of West Yorkshire. Indeed there is little to suggest that the Labour and

Liberal parties could be 'subsumed in Progressivism'[1] or that Labour 'fared abysmally' in all contests with the Liberals from December 1910 to the outbreak of war.[2] In West Yorkshire, Labour was pressing Liberalism on all political fronts between 1906 and 1914 and there are few signs of Liberalism arresting the development of the ILP/Labour Party.

West Yorkshire Liberal leaders were well pleased with the result of the 1906 General Election. The party had regained the five seats it had lost in the 1895 General Election. But they soon realised that there was no ground for complacency. The Liberal candidate had been pushed into third place in Bradford West and the Labour candidate had come within 400 votes of victory in Huddersfield. Whilst Liberals could quickly come to terms with the influence which Fred Jowett exerted over Bradford West they were less enamoured of the Labour challenge in the southern parts of the region, where Liberalism had shown few signs of weakness. Two parliamentary by-elections, at Huddersfield in 1906 and Colne Valley in 1907, did much to puncture Liberal confidence.

The resignation of Sir J.T. Woodhouse as Liberal MP for Huddersfield led to a parliamentary by-election in November 1906. The Liberal candidate, A.J. Sherwell, was returned despite the stiff opposition of Williams, the Labour candidate, and in the face of the revival of a serious Conservative challenge: Sherwell receiving 5,762 votes, Williams 5,422 and Fraser, the Conservative, 4,844. The closeness of the contest, which was said to have swung to Sherwell 'in the closing hours of the campaign' was reflected in the statement of Bruce Glasier, one of the leading ILP figures, when he wrote of the by-election that it was the 'most distinctively socialist contest fought in this country'.[3]

The Liberal Party had been shocked by the narrowness of their victory particularly since it had begun to re-organise itself in Huddersfield following the closeness of the Labour challenge in the 1906 General Election. Throughout 1906 the Liberals had been improving their organisation. The Huddersfield Liberal Association had increased its organising body from 300 to 500, divided the constituency into six districts, and re-organised the Liberal Club. It has been argued that the Huddersfield Liberal Association did respond to the Labour challenge and thus stifled its growth before the First World War.[4] Even so, and assuming that this view is correct, what is evident is that there was no attempt to offer a new progressive Liberalism to the constituency. What was offered was the old Liberalism based upon an improved organisation.

As for the Labour Party, it is clear that Williams was not an ideal candidate for Huddersfield. His ethical brand of Socialism, emphasising that 'all things socially needed should be socially owned', was not specific enough for many trade unionists looking for trade union policies in his manifesto and his speeches.[5] His employment as a mill manager in the Keighley area also presented him with difficulties from trade unionists in Huddersfield. It is clear that relations between Williams and the local Huddersfield Labour Party were by no means harmonious. The local trade-union dominated ILP and LRC organisations appear to have considered him to be a Socialist of the quasi-Marxist SDF type, whilst more extreme Socialists of the SDF type were inclined to dismiss his credentials as a serious Socialist candidate.[6] Ben Riley summed up the prevailing Labour opinion in Huddersfield, however, when he wrote to Keir Hardie after the by-election discouraging haste in the selection of a Labour candidate for Huddersfield and suggesting that 'we require a man for Huddersfield' of 'good Trade Union standing' and a 'thoroughly competent Labour politician'.[7]

Notwithstanding such criticism of Williams, it is evident that the internal conflict within Labour was confined to Williams and the trade unions. If it did anything to harm Labour support then the performance of Williams at the 1906 General Election and the by-election were even more impressive. The Liberals were badly shaken on both occasions by the narrowness of their victory.

If growing Labour support found expression in the Huddersfield parliamentary contests then there was even more evidence of Labour breakthrough in Victor Grayson's dramatic and 'splendid victory' in the Colne Valley by-election of July 1907. This victory provoked one national newspaper to write, exaggeratedly, that 'The Red Flag Waves over the Colne Valley ... the fever of Socialism has infected thousands of workers who ... seem to think that Mr. Grayson's return means the millennium for them'.[8]

Colne Valley had been an early centre of ILP activity in the 1890s. The Colne Valley Labour Union had supported Tom Mann's parliamentary contest there in the 1895 General Election and, despite a decline in the movement in the late 1890s there had been an enormous resurgence of Labour support in the

Liberal Decline and Labour Growth 1906-14

valley from about 1903 onwards. David Clark has suggested that much of this growth occurred outside the trade-union movement, which was weak in Colne Valley, and was to be found emerging from the ethical side of the movement, Labour club organisation, religious support for Labour, and in the frustrations of Liberals at the lack of democratic decision-making within their party.9 But Colne Valley was one of the seats which MacDonald had given to the Liberals in the secret Gladstone-MacDonald pact of 1903, and it was not contested by Labour at the 1906 General Election. Acutely annoyed at this failure to contest, the local ILP organisation, the Colne Valley Labour League as it was by 1907, decided to contest the seat at the earliest opportunity.

That moment arrived with the raising of Sir James Kitson to the House of Lords in the summer of 1907. For some time there had been rumours of this possibility. There was speculation about an impending by-election in April 1906 and in December 1906 Ben Riley wrote to Keir Hardie on the matter asking to be informed when Sir James Kitson was raised to the House of Lords and informing him that the Colne Valley branches were 'sure to insist upon a fight if possible'.10

Both Reg Groves and David Clark have examined the Grayson candidature and the campaign in detail.11 Their accounts of the events differ slightly but what is evident is that the local Labour movement was determined to contest the by-election. Indeed, the Colne Valley Labour League had already begun the process of selecting a candidate in April 1906, when the Executive Committee put forward four names, including Victor Grayson, as possible candidates.12 Behind the scenes, there had been a good deal of discussion and confusion as letters flew from Sam Eastwood, the Secretary of the CVLL, to the ILP and Labour Party, though it was not always clear which of the two, about the selection of a candidate and the possibility of the CVLL forming the basis of a Colne Valley LRC.13 As David Clark has explained, the confusion partly arose from the fact that whilst the CVLL should have only communicated with the National Administrative Council of the ILP, it was the practice of ILP branches to seek endorsement of all organisations within an area who were attached to the Labour Party. In addition, confusion often occurred over the fact that Ramsay MacDonald was Secretary of the LRC and Chairman of the ILP.14 Despite feverish activities and tactical moves by both national and local Labour figures it was decided not to select a Labour candidate until the end of January 1907.[15] After a protracted process of discussion, two ballots, and the withdrawal of W.C. Anderson as one of the two names put forward by the Executive of the CVLL to the whole membership, it was eventually agreed to nominate Grayson in February 1907.[16]

The eventual election of Grayson for Colne Valley created difficulties for both the Liberal and Labour parties. In the first instance, it is quite clear that local Labour groups, and especially the ILP organisations, considered themselves to be autonomous, or semi-autonomous, bodies, to which the national ILP and LRC organisations should pay due respects. If the national leadership intervened in local difficulties, as it did in Halifax in 1894 and 1895, then it was swiftly given its marching orders in no uncertain terms. But in the late 1890s and early twentieth century the balance of power had swung more to the national leadership which, through its increasing control of party organisation and funds was able to impose some semblance of discipline upon local Labour organisations, although its efforts to do so often provoked conflict and bitterness.[17] But even the national Labour leadership of the ILP/LRC had limits to its power. Since the normal practice was for the local bodies to pay for the election expenses of candidates and for the national organisations, and particularly the LRC, to help support Labour MPs who were returned and to pay about a quarter of the registration officer's fee, the real problem was that if local bodies could comply with the procedures imposed by national Labour organisations then they could do practically what they wanted and impose a financial burden upon the national organisations. The only way in which the national organisations could control local events was thus to find fault with the selection procedure and thus threaten to withhold funds. This is precisely what the ILP and the LRC tried to do with the Grayson candidature.

Both the ILP and the LRC examined the selection procedure in Colne Valley. The ILP, which agreed to pay for the services of a full-time organiser for three months, sent a deputation consisting of Philip Snowden and J. Howard to meet the Executive of the CVLL in April 1907.[18] They found the CVLL in healthy condition and resolute in its determination to contest the seat with Victor Grayson.[19] They recommended that 'in the circumstances the NAC try to meet the branches' desire'. In the event the

Liberal Decline and Labour Growth 1906-14

NAC procrastinated and the Annual Conference of the ILP at Derby in 1907 resolved to invoke a rule that all ILP candidates, except in exceptional circumstances, should be chosen in accordance with the Constitution of the Labour Party. This necessitated that all organisations affiliated to the Labour Party in any locality should be drawn together in a properly convened conference.20 MacDonald used this resolution to suggest that the CVLL should first of all approach the NAC before calling a conference, whilst the CVLL rightly pointed out that the resolution was passed after it had selected Grayson as its candidate.21 The animus created by these tactical ploys of the ILP and LRC national organisations lapped over into the acrimonious correspondence between Eastwood and Grayson, on the one hand, and MacDonald on the other. In the confusion of debate, and the occurrence of the by-election, Grayson and the CVLL fought without the endorsement of the Labour Party and with only partial support from the ILP.22 At one point, the Labour Party Executive advised that no Labour Party member should go to Colne Valley to aid Grayson but the ILP eventually approved of the contest and appealed for funds in the columns of the Labour Leader.23 For the independent political Labour movement the Colne Valley by-election proved to be an embarrassing episode revealing difficulties within the Labour movement which will be examined later. The core of this was MacDonald's attitude towards the relationship between the Labour and Liberal parties and the relationship between trade unionists and individual Socialists within the Labour movement. Although the Labour movement went through the whole gamut of public internecine conflict for which it has become famed, the fact is Grayson was victorious.

A second consequence of the Grayson by-election victory was clearly the traumatic impact which it exerted upon Colne Valley Liberalism. Sir James Kitson, the Liberal candidate, had been unopposed in the 1906 General Election and it was expected that his successor, P. Bright, would have little difficulty holding the seat, especially given that it was the Liberals who held the ultimate control over the timing of the by-election and held the advantage of prior knowledge: One local writer recalls how 'the result dumfounded everybody, more especially the Liberals, who imagined that their candidate, Philip Bright, would be safely returned.24 The editor of the Colne Valley Guardian, a staunch opponent of Socialism, reflected that

> Last week's election result suggests the historic question, 'Stands Colne Valley where it did?' The answer to which is emphatically 'no'. In the estimation of the country, Colne Valley has greviously fallen and it will take a decade, perhaps a generation, to restore it to its former position.[25]

In the event, the Liberal Party recovered the seat in the January 1910 General Election. Yet one must reflect that, given that Colne Valley was considered to be a staunch Liberal seat and that the trade union movement was weak in the area, the seat should never have been lost in the first place.

The Huddersfield parliamentary by-election of 1906 and the Colne Valley by-election of 1907 disabused West Yorkshire Liberals of the idea that their traditional centres of support were sacrosanct. The Labour Party and the ILP had delivered a political jolt to which they were forced to respond. That Huddersfield Liberalism did respond to make the parliamentary seat safer and that Grayson was beaten into third place in the 1910 General Election is not proof positive that the West Yorkshire Liberal parties were absorbing the Labour challenge on the eve of the First World War. The fact is that the Labour vote was increasing in local elections and that the Labour Party was doing well in parliamentary by-elections, despite the apparent tensions which were occurring within Labour ranks.

M.G. Sheppard and John L. Halstead have suggested that there was a strong upward trend in the Labour vote and the number of Labour candidates returned at municipal elections in provincial England and Wales from 1900 onwards, and that despite fluctuations from year to year the Labour Party's position was strengthened, not diminished, after 1910.[26] The municipal and local returns for West Yorkshire support this viewpoint. Table 6.1 indicates the extent to which progress was made in some of the more successful Labour areas. Table 6.2, on the other hand, indicates the full extent of Labour representation on local bodies in West Yorkshire. Taking them both, it is clear that despite some political setbacks in 1908 and 1909, Labour was rapidly cutting into the Liberal political stronghold of West Yorkshire on the eve of the First World War.

Faced with the municipal and local challenge of Labour the Liberal organisations in West

Liberal Decline and Labour Growth 1906-14

Table 6.1 Municipal Representation in Four West Yorkshire Municipalities, 1906-14

Year	Bradford	Halifax	Huddersfield	Leeds	Total
1906	11	4	8	9	32
1907	13	6	6	10	35
1908	10	7	5	4	26
1909	8	8	3	6	25
1910	8	7	2	6	23
1911	13	7	4	10	34
1912	17	8	5	11	41
1913	20	8	5	16	49
1914	20[a]	8	5	16	49

Note: a. A political truce operated in Bradford, Halifax and Leeds in November 1914.
Sources: November issues of Bradford Observer, Halifax Guardian, Halifax Courier, Labour Leader; T. Woodhouse 'The working class', A History of Modern Leeds (Manchester University Press, Manchester, 1980), p. 363.

Table 6.2 The Number of Labour Representatives on Local Political Bodies in West Yorkshire, 1906-14

Year	Municipal	CC, UDC, RDC, PC	Board of Guardians	Total
1906	47	36	6	89
1907	51	39	18	108
1908	44	45	18	107
1909	47	53	21	121
1910	44	60	24	128
1911	61	69	24	154
1912	70	68	24	162
1913	85	70	33	188
1914	85[a]	77[b]	40	202

Note: a. The municipal returns are the same as in 1913 as a result of the political truce which operated at the beginning of the First World War. Only Huddersfield appears not to have operated such a truce in November 1914.

b. The numbers of local labour representatives indicated are, if anything, likely to be underestimates. Whilst it is possible to obtain reasonably accurate information on municipal authorities and boards of guardians there is the possibility that the Labour press have not provided full details on the urban-district, rural district and parish council results where by-election and election successes may have gone unnoticed. Also since rural-district councils often acted as local board of guardians as well no attempt has been made to distinguish such bodies as guardians.
Sources: <u>Bradford Observer, Halifax Courier, Halifax Guardian, Huddersfield Examiner, ILP News, Labour Leader</u> and the records of a varied assortment of trades councils and Labour Party branches.

Yorkshire preferred, where necessary, to join with the Tories in a local alliance against Labour rather than to offer a more progressive form of Liberalism. Liberal-Tory alliances were not uncommon, especially where the Labour challenge was considered to be serious. Tom Woodhouse notes that 'A Tory-Liberal alliance had actually come to pass in Armley and Wortley in 1907', though there appears to have been some Liberal reluctance to enter such an agreement therafter.[27] A Liberal-Tory alliance sprang up at Halifax in 1906 when the ILP and the Trades Council put forward 13 candidates for the municipal elections. 'This challenge, says the Yorkshire Observer, was accepted, and as a result of an arrangement between the Liberal and Tories, three-cornered contests were avoided in wards where there was a Labour candidate'.[28] In the 1908 urban-district council elections for Farsley and Pudsey, where Labour was beginning to make a minor mark, a similar agreement was forged. 'A dead set was made by a Liberal and Tory combination at Farsley, resulting in the loss of Allerton and Walker. At Horsforth a ratepayers' association composed of the old parties combined, managed to throw Hazelip out'.[29]

What is clear, however, is that such alliances were of only marginal value in stemming the tide of Labour successes. The position of the ILP/Trades Council strength on Halifax Town Council was only marginally reduced, from five in 1905 to four in 1906. They appear to have worked best between about 1907 and 1910. Even then the advantage was often gained by the Tories rather than the Liberals. In Bradford, for instance, the Tories did much better out of the arrangement. Between 1906 and 1913,

Liberal Decline and Labour Growth 1906-14

16 of the 21 Bradford wards were involved in the local Tory-Liberal alliance and, as Table 6.3 indicates, the Tories had a higher ratio of success than the Liberals. In addition, it is clear that the Liberal control of the council was weakened not

Table 6.3: The Liberal-Conservative Municipal Pact in Bradford, 1906-13

	Liberal straight fights with Labour		Conservative straight fights with Labour		Total	
Year	Contested	Won	Contested	Won	Contested	Won
1906	3	2	4	4	7	6
1907	4	2	1	1	5	3
1908	4	4	4	3	8	7
1909	5	5	4	4	9	9
1910	3	1	2	2	5	3
1911	3	1	4	4	7	5
1912	1	0	1	1	2	1
1913	3	2	5	4	8	6
Totals	26	17	25	23	51	40

Source: *Bradford Observer*, Nov. issues between 1906 and 1913.

strengthened during the period in which the alliance operated. In November 1905 the Bradford Liberal Association had 42 representatives on the City Council, compared to the 31 of the Conservatives, the ten of Labour and the one Independent. By November 1913 the Liberals were down to 29 representatives, the Conservatives had 34, Labour had 20 and there was one Independent. Labour also gained 43.1 per cent of the municipal vote in the 1913 municipal elections, compared with the 27.2 per cent gained by the Liberals and the 29.7 per cent of the Conservatives.

The evidence suggests that West Yorkshire Liberalism preferred to enter an alliance with Conservatism where its municipal position was particularly vulnerable to the Labour challenge, rather

Table 6.4: The Municipal Balance of Power in
Bradford, Leeds and Huddersfield, 1906-13

Year	Bradford				Huddersfield				Leeds		
	L.	C.	Lab.	O	L.	C.	Lab.	O	L.	C.	Lab.
1906	38	34	11	1	32	17	8	3	34	21	9
1907	30	40	13	1	37	15	6	2	26	28	10
1908	32	42	10	2	37	16	5	2	23	36	4
1909	33	41	8	2	40	14	3	2	23	34	6
1910	35	39	8	2	42	15	2	1	26	31	6
1911	36	34	13	1	34	20	4	2	28	26	10
1912	35	31	17	1	27	25	5	1	33	34	11
1913	29	34	20	1	28	26	5	1	18	34	16

Note: a. The abbreviations are L. for Liberal, C. for Conservative, Lab. for Labour and O for Others. Sources: <u>Bradford Observer, Huddersfield Examiner</u>, Nov. issues; T. Woodhouse, 'The working class' in Derek Fraser (ed.), <u>A History of Modern Leeds</u> (Manchester University Press, Manchester, 1980), p. 363.

than offer a new more progressive type of Liberalsim which might attract the working-class vote. Its emphasis was to harness the anti-Labour or anti-Socialist vote rather than to unite progressives under the 'new' Liberal label.

It is true that the parliamentary position of Labour did not improve in West Yorkshire, and that this could be construed to suggest that Labour was being held in check by the Liberals. But even this evidence is not as clear as it seems. The Labour Party continued to poll well in general elections, and its by-election record was quite impressive in West Yorkshire. Table 5.3 has already suggested that the Labour proportion of the general election votes decreased from the 17.3 per cent peak in 1906 to 15.1 per cent in January 1910 and 14.0 per cent in December 1910. Yet at the same time, the Liberal proportions fell from 50.3 per cent in 1906 to 47.5 per cent in December 1910. It was not the Liberal Party which was reducing the parliamentary vote of Labour so much as the Conservative Party staging something of a political revival at the expense of both Labour and Liberalism, though it held no parliamentary seat in West Yorkshire from December 1910 to the war. Also, whilst the number of

Liberal Decline and Labour Growth 1906-14

Labour candidates, of all types, increased from the 1906 election to the January 1910 election, the 14 per cent of the vote obtained in the December 1910 General Election derived from only four contests; three in the Labour seats of Bradford West, Halifax and Leeds East, the fourth in Huddersfield where Harry Snell came bottom of the poll. What this indicated, as we shall stress, was the weak financial state of the West Yorkshire Labour movement rather than its lack of electoral support. Despite the class-representative nature of the unequal parliamentary franchise, it is evident that the Labour Party was doing particularly well in West Yorkshire constituencies. In the four seats it contested in the December 1910 General Election - admittedly including three Labour strongholds where there was no Liberal opposition - it obtained just over 41 per cent of the vote.[30]

Labour's performance in parliamentary elections was also very encouraging, particularly so after 1910. The Labour Party contested eight by-elections between 1906 and 1914, winning only the Colne Valley seat in 1907. All these contests were three-sided affairs and, as Table 6.5 suggests, the tendency was for Labour to improve its percentage of the poll.

Table 6.5: Parliamentary By-Elections in West Yorkshire at which Labour candidates were involved

Constituency	Date	Labour % of poll		Previous Labour % of poll	
Colne Valley	July 1907	35.2	(Victory)	1895	13.4
Dewsbury	April 1908	20.2		1906	21.3
Holmfirth	June 1912	28.2		(J)1910	14.9
Huddersfield	November 1906	33.8		1906	35.2
Keighley	October 1911	28.9		1906	26.6
Keighley	November 1913	29.8		1911	28.9
Leeds South	February 1908	19.4		1906	32.6
Pudsey	June 1908	10.7[a]			

Note: a. J. Benson stood as an Independent Labour candidate in the June 1908 parliamentary by-election for Pudsey, though he was not officially sanctioned by the ILP or the Labour Party.

Liberal Decline and Labour Growth 1906-14

Source: F.W.S. Craig, <u>British Parliamentary Election Results 1885-1918</u> (Macmillan, London, 1974).

As we have already suggested, Labour did well in Huddersfield and Colne Valley in 1906 and 1907. In 1908, a bad year for Labour in local contests, Labour lost three by-elections with substantial reductions in its support, but from 1910 onwards, the period in which P.F. Clarke suggests that the Liberals were winning by-elections and Labour was doing badly, it is evident that Labour was making progress. In Keighley there was a steady improvement of the Labour position. In Holmfirth, Labour almost doubled its percentage vote in two and a half years. The switch of allegiance amongst miners, from the Liberal Party to the Labour Party, might help explain the improvement in Holmfirth, but the fact is that Labour's position in by-elections does not suggest the enervating impact of Liberal progressivism existed in West Yorkshire. The dwindling trade-union support for Liberalism was, incidentally, further proof of the inroads which Labour had made into trade union, and working-class, support.

By any yardstick, Labour had made substantial political gains in West Yorkshire between 1906 and 1914. Whilst Liberalism remained the preponderant force at the parliamentary level, the roots of its parliamentary success were being rapidly eroded by Labour at the local level. When Labour chose to contest parliamentary elections, or found the financial wherewithal to do so, it tapped a welling of support for Labour candidates. To many Labour observers, at least, the three or four MPs it returned between 1906 and 1914 were simply the tip of the iceberg of Labour support, the vast majority of which remained unrevealed, due to the fact that the party could not afford to contest all parliamentary seats and, perhaps, due to the inequities of the parliamentary franchise. Yet, for a time, it appeared that the Labour movement nationally and locally might be faltering. There were political setbacks in 1908 and 1909, especially in parts of West Yorkshire where political truces were forged between Liberals and Tories. The national movement appeared to be convulsed with conflicts between the members of the ILP and Labour Party, and over the direction which the political movement was taking. For two or three years there even seemed to be the distinct possibility that internecine conflict or apathy might consume the movement and force Labour supporters back to Liberalism, pushed by Labour failures rather than won by the new Liberal ideology. This in-fighting within the Labour movement was more apparant in West Yorkshire than was new Liberalism.

The source of much of the temporarily rising frustration with the ILP and the Labour Party arose from the sense of irritation at the slow place of parliamentary reform. It is true that Fred Jowett, and other Labour members, had pushed the House of Commons into introducing municipal school feeding in December 1906, and that this was followed by other concessions to Labour. Yet progress appeared slow to some, and partly based upon Labour support for Liberalism. Indeed, by 1909 and 1910 some branches of the ILP, such as Farsley, were passing resolutions condemning any move towards establishing a Lib-Lab pact.[31]

It was Victor Grayson who most effectively amplified the suspicions of many Labour supporters that Labour might be becoming a mere adjunct to Liberalism. When he entered Parliament in 1907, Grayson remained aloof from his ILP and Labour colleagues. He harboured resentment over the ILP and the Labour Party's reluctance to endorse him for the Colne Valley by-election. As Groves suggests, he gained some revenge in his politely discourteous treatment of Keir Hardie at the great bazaar day in Huddersfield shortly before the ILP Annual Conference was held there in 1908. The ensuing conference saw some compromise arrangement by which the ILP agreed to pay his parliamentary salary, he was allowed to attend Labour Party meetings and have the Party Whips but was not forced to sign the constitution of the Labour Party. As he reiterated at the ILP Conference: 'I cannot sign the constitution of the Labour Party under any circumstances. I esteem it a pearl of great price that we should have independent socialism represented in the House of Commons, instructed by the conference. I cannot accept any other conditions'.[32]

In Parliament, Grayson refused to abide by the ILP and Labour Party decisions, and Fred Jowett later recalled that Grayson had always placed himself above party politics.[33] As is well known, Grayson protested when the debate concerning the King's visit to the Czar spluttered to a halt. The Labour group, and particularly Hardie, had protested against the Russian treatment of political prisoners and were concerned that secret treaty arrangements might have been forged between Britain and Russia.

155

But when Grayson was called Arthur Henderson moved the closure of the debate on the behalf of the Labour Party. The subsequent discussion in the pages of the Labour Leader presented Grayson's view that the whole affair had been contrived although the statements of Henderson and Hardie indicated that a decision to close the debate at that particular point had been made by prior agreement before the debate occurred.[34] More obviously, there was the unemployment debate, in which, on two consecutive days, Grayson was suspended from the House of Commons for cutting across the business of the House and demanding the discussion of unemployment, on one occasion shouting to the Labour members that 'You are traitors! Traitors to your class'.[35]

Throughout 1908 and 1909 the actions of Grayson in Parliament attracted the derision of the Liberal and Conservative press and the acclaim of some sections of the Socialist movement, particularly in Colne Valley and in other parts of West Yorkshire. As Reg Groves stresses, it is clear that he did garner considerable support for his views in some areas, though this must be qualified by the fact that Keir Hardie was extremely popular in West Yorkshire and that Fred Jowett, James Parker and Philip Snowden carried substantial local support throughout West Yorkshire.

Grayson's conflict with his Labour colleagues became even more pronounced when he joined the staff of the New Age towards the end of 1908. For three months he worked a joint editorship of the paper with Orage but left to join the staff of the Clarion in February 1909. From these newspaper platforms he mounted his campaign against the ILP and Labour Party leadership. He was involved in the famous Holborn Hall rally, or non-rally, where the refusal of Hyndman and himself to stand on the same platform as Hardie to address the Clarion Scouts led to Hardie's withdrawal from the meeting. Groves gives a graphic, if totally unbalanced account of these events, where the strident Grayson set himself against the 'hurt' and 'reproachful' Hardie.[36] However, if one examines the whole range of evidence presented in the Labour Leader then it quickly becomes clear that, whilst Grayson had touched a nerve amongst some of the younger members of the ILP, it was the established leadership which carried the weight of ILP support in the country and in West Yorkshire.

Grayson was just one of a number of ILP members who were at odds with the ILP leaders, parliamentary procedures, and the trade-union domination of the movement. Amongst his group of supporters was H. Russell Smart, who had been the ILP candidate for Huddersfield in the 1895 General Election. Smart had become increasingly critical of the leadership of Hardie, Snowden, MacDonald and Glasier - referring to them as the 'Junta'. He had written a number of articles in The Worker, the organ of the Huddersfield Labour movement, in 1907 and 1908, and repeated his accusations against the 'Junta' in the Labour Leader. The gist of his argument was that 'The I.L.P. is in Danger' of ceasing to be a democratic organisation:

> and is becoming, if it has not become, a mere machine for registering the desires of three or four men who for so many years have formed the inner circle of the N.A.C. I pointed out that this body had obtained control of the Party, all the wires are in their hands, one of them always occupies the chair at the annual Conference, one of them in on the Agenda Committee, and the powers that they have acquired enables them to impose their will upon the Conference and the Party even when the general sentiment of the Party is in opposition to them.37

Leonard Hall, once of Manchester but by now of Birmingham, was equally critical of what he saw as a challenge to the democracy of the party by its four main leaders. But whilst Smart and Hall hovered in the wings it was Grayson who took the centre stage.

The final showdown came at the ILP Annual Conference at Edinburgh in April 1909. The National Administrative Council of the ILP had sought to censure Grayson for his actions in Parliament, his refusal to sign the constitution of the Labour Party and his public insult of Hardie at Holborn Hall. The conference decided to refer the offending passage back to the NAC and Hardie, Snowden, MacDonald and Glasier resigned from the NAC. It was Hardie who explained the position of the 'Old Gang'. He objected to the notion that he, and the others, should be regarded as 'limpets clinging to the rock of office', and accused Grayson of being used 'by others who were even more unscrupulous than he was'. He made it clear that the resignations should be seen by the ILP as the opportunity to demonstrate whether it was to stand for consolidation of the working-class movement, or whether departing from the lines of sanity, they should follow some chimera called Socialism and unity, spoken of by men who did not understand Socialism and were alien to its very spirit'.[38]

Made a matter of confidence in the old leadership, the offending paragraph was reinstated by a vote of 249 to 110. But Hardie, and his three colleagues decided to adhere to their resignations and, although there was a move throughout the country to force them to stay in office, they were steadfast in their decision and only Glasier returned to the NAC at the 1910 Annual Conference.[39]

The reactions to the events at Edinburgh were fought out in the pages of the Labour Leader during subsequent weeks. Smart attacked the 'Old Gang' or 'Junta' for their mistakes and failure to push for Socialism and yet suggested to branches throughout the country that they should not let the four resign, as inconstitency of argument which was eagerly seized upon by W.C. Anderson, a supporter of Hardie, who became party chairman in 1910.[40]

A letter, signed by the 'Old Gang', demonstrated the depths to which this fissure extended into the ILP. It was clear to them that Grayson wished to form a new Socialist party which excluded trade unions and did not seek 'the advancement of Labour'. They particularly criticised the pamphlet The Problem of Parliament which had advocated the formation of Socialist Representation committees in the place of the Labour Party, and which stated that

> The basis of a Socialist Party must be the I.L.P., the S.D.P., the Clarion, and, if it can possibly be brought to the point of making up its political mind, the Fabian Society. There are also various local societies which are small but powerful in their neighbourhood[41]

Despite Groves's view that there was massive support for Grayson throughout the country, and particularly in Yorkshire, this is not borne out by the evidence of the conference nor by the evidence of branch opinion which appeared in the Labour Leader. Grayson did find support for his views and position in Colne Valley, but the Halifax ILP, the Batley ILP and the Manningham branch of the Bradford ILP signalled their support for the 'Old Gang'. Jowett was active in getting the Bradford movement behind Hardie; Robert Morley, James Parker and Henry Brockhouse did the same in Halifax, and Alderman Ben Turner was similarly active in Batley. Even the Huddersfield ILP, despite its close proximity to Colne Valley, was divided on the issue of who to support.[42] In the event the four members of the 'New Gang' who replaced the 'Old Gang' on the NAC, including Smart and Hall, resigned from the NAC after a year and eventually left the Party, having issued the 'Green Manifesto' Let us Reform the Labour Party, in 1910. Grayson's parliamentary defeat in the January 1910 General Election led to his further estrangement from the party.

By the early months of 1910 the main threat to the ILP, and the Labour Party, had passed and what is clear is that in West Yorkshire, as well as in the country as a whole, the dissident group's attempt to form a rival Socialist party was abortive, despite the publicity which Grayson, through the Clarion, and Hyndman, through Justice, gave to it. The attempt to form the British Socialist Party as an effective alternative to the ILP flickered briefly and failed miserably between 1911 and 1914.

It was Grayson who first announced the formation of the British Socialist Party in the Clarion during August 1911 with his opening sentence that 'The time for the formation of the BRITISH SOCIALIST PARTY has definitely come'.[43] He then called for others to follow his example and withdraw from the ILP, vowing never to join another Socialist organisation until the BSP, 'the one socialist party', had been formed. Grayson's example worked briefly. There was a period of ecstatic enthusiasm leading to the Socialist Unity Conference at Manchester in September 1911 where the clamour of support was evident. Within nine months the BSP had been formed and had held its first annual conference, but it was soon in difficulties. The vast majority of ILP members were not attracted to the BSP and it quickly became obvious that it was simply the Social Democratic Party (the old Social Democratic Federation) in a new form with H.M. Hyndman, Dan Irving and Harry Quelch pressing established policies on the new organisation.

As we have already noted, the idea of Socialist unity, based upon the ILP and the SDF, never attracted significant support in West Yorkshire during the 1890s. The preponderant Bradford and Halifax ILP branches saw no value to be gained in uniting with an organisation which could not muster a thirtieth of their combined strength. Also, whilst Grayson was a popular figure in Yorkshire and Lancashire, no Socialist Representation committee was formed in West Yorkshire. Despite the fact that Grayson was able to get the Colne Valley Socialist (ex-Labour) League to join the BSP, with its 600 members, it is clear, according to a letter from Albert Inkpin, Secretary of the BSP, that it paid infrequently after the first four months.44 Indeed the CVSL returned to the ILP in 1916.

Nevertheless, Grayson made determined efforts to win support for the BSP in West Yorkshire. Within a week of his pronouncement in favour of the BSP, he wrote that

> On Saturday I addressed a magnificent meeting in the Colne Valley, and at the close a resolution to the following effect was put to the meeting "That in the opinion of this meeting immediate steps should be taken towards the formation of a united British Socialist Party". The forest of hands that shot up in favour of the resolution was a beautiful sight to see, and there was not a single hand raised in opposition.45

On 24 September 1911, Grayson and H. Dawson Large opened their campaign on behalf of the BSP at St. George's Hall, Bradford. They filled the hall and Grayson made a determined appeal for the formation of a strong Bradford branch of the BSP. The following week some of the Yorkshire ILP branches were represented at the Socialist Unity Conference, held at Manchester, most notably the thirteen branches of the Colne Valley Socialist League.46 The first branch of the BSP in Bradford was opened in October and the first meeting of the Halifax BSP was held the same month in the SDP rooms at Mount Street, Cow Green.

There is no denying that Grayson did win support in West Yorkshire. Apart from the CVSL, the Wakefield ILP branch withdrew from the ILP, and a BSP branch of 70 members was formed.47 A large number of individual members of the ILP also appear to have joined the BSP. But Grayson's estimate that 30 per cent of ILP members had joined the BSP is excessive.48 If correct, that would have meant that at least 2,000 of the ILP's West Yorkshire members who had paid their fees to the ILP would have joined the BSP and that something in the region of 3,000 to 4,000 of the estimated membership would have left the ILP. The West Yorkshire district of the BSP,

Liberal Decline and Labour Growth 1906-14

whilst not including every branch of the BSP, claimed to represent 1,000 members in March 1912, when the local and national BSP movements were at their zenith.[49] Add to this the estimate of up to 800 members for the CVSL, and allow for some members who may have been overlooked, and a figure of 2,000 BSP members for West Yorkshire would not have been an unreasonable estimate. Yet perhaps 300 of these were members of the SDF/SDP, whose membership had increased in West Yorkshire since 1902, a large number of previously 'unattached' members were also admitted to, and much of the membership was short-lived and nominal.[50] Including Colne Valley's 800 members, soon to be reduced to 600, there were perhaps 1,000 to 1,300 ILP members who went over to the BSP. Most had drifted back to the ILP by the beginning of the First World War. Exclude Colne Valley from the totals and Grayson's influence was, of course, greatest there and the West Yorkshire ILP defections become relatively insignificant. Within four years, the ex-ILP members who remained within the West Yorkshire branches of the BSP did not number 200. J.B. Glasier's comment of October 1911 ultimately proved correct: 'The new party is merely the S.D.P. under a new name'.[51] Early incursions into ILP support only flattered to deceive.

This was obvious in Bradford, which saw Grayson begin his BSP campaign in the West Riding. Four Bradford branches of the BSP had emerged within a few months of Grayson's appeal. The first to be formed was the Bradford Central branch which quickly claimed 200 to 300 members, 'mostly unattached', and was eventually to claim 500 members.[52] Other branches were formed at Clayton, at Dudley Hill and Tong, and in the Bradford East parliamentary constituency. They all appear to have been energetic in 1911 and early 1912, but therafter faded badly. In the absence of E.R. Hartley, the Socialist candidate for East Bradford in 1906 and January 1910, who was touring New Zealand in 1911 and 1912, the only local BSP figure of any note was Dr. Dessin. No prominent Bradford ILP member, other than Hartley, joined the BSP and many, such as J.H. Palin, Fred Jowett and W. Leach were extremely critical of its presence in Bradford.[53] The Bradford BSP branches soon slimmed down to their SDP core and were prone to frequent bouts of inactivity. Indeed, only the East Bradford branch and the Central branch appear to have made any showing throughout 1912 and 1913. Even these two branches were prone to difficulties, particularly when national BSP imposed John Stokes, Secretary of the London Glass Blowers' Society and Secretary of the London Trades Council, upon East Bradford as the parliamentary candidate in place of E.R. Hartley.54 Local members were dissatisfied with the decisio- and a conference in February 1913 failed to heal the rift.55

Nevertheless, Harry Quelch, writing in *Justice*, gave the impression that matters were going well in Bradford and that in November 1913 there were three ILP and BSP candidates returned to Bradford City Council, after originally announcing that they were BSP candidates.56 In fact the three men they named - Thomas Grundy, Charlie Glyde and F. Lockwood Liles - were all long-established members of the ILP. Grundy was most certainly not a member of the BSP, though Glyde, who had joined the SDF in 1887, and Liles were. Glyde was most certainly returned for Tong because of his long-association with Labour politics in the town, and only Liles could be really described as a success for the BSP as such, being described as 'One of Mr. E.R. Hartley's band of Socialists. Member of the British Socialist Party, a trade unionist, and a member of the I.L.P.'57

Few other BSP centres in West Yorkshire reached even the minimal success of the Bradford branches. The 1912 BSP Conference report suggests that there were about 20 BSP branches in West Yorkshire, 13 of them connected with the CVSL.58 There was also a West Yorkshire District Council. Branches emerged and collapsed quickly and few BSP branches had claim to any successes. The Wakefield BSP soon became ineffective, despite its early success at winning the support of the local ILP branch. In Halifax, the BSP was largely based upon the old SDF/SDP, and won a little support in the Trades Council.59

The only other centre of BSP activity to rival Bradford in the West Yorkshire area was Leeds. Though there were no municipal successes, as in Bradford, there were five active branches of the BSP in Leeds - Leeds Central, the Clarion Scouts, Leeds North, Leeds West and Leeds West Ward. These branches produced a myriad of minor figures but the only one to emerge to national importance was Bert Killip, Secretary of the Leeds West branch. He became a member of the Executive of the BSP in 1913, and was a faithful supporter of H.M. Hyndman.60 He was largely responsible for organising many of the BSP propaganda meetings on Woodhouse Moor and appears to have been responsible for getting the local BSP organisation to affiliate with the Leeds Labour Party, well beforeof the national BSP adopted the same policy.61

The results of Grayson's campaign were not impressive. The BSP, even at its apogee, was unable to attract more than about 20 per cent of the membership of West Yorkshire ILP organisations, and many of those came from the Colne Valley Socialist League. Within a few months there was strong evidence of decay within the BSP branches in West Yorkshire, and they were never able to secure more than one or two municipal seats, and then only in conjunction with the ILP. Ranged against the membership and successes of the ILP, the BSP's impact was embarrassingly poor and failure generated failure. Most ILP members attracted to the BSP quickly drifted back to the ILP. Indeed, the impetus to the movement disappeared when Grayson quickly lost interest in the BSP, partly due to his i -health in 1911 and 1912 and partly due to the conflicts which occurred between himself and the Hyndman section of the BSP.62 As the Hyndmanites became predominant so Grayson withdrew from active work for the BSP. His short story 'The Lost Vision: A Spring Fantasy' which appeared in *Justice* during May 1912 reflected, in a vague and veiled way, his loss of hope and faith in the BSP.63 A grave illness in 1913 removed Grayson from the political scene and a biographical sketch of Grayson's life, which appeared in *Justice*, perhaps summarised the whole Graysonian episode when it said that his was 'A story of buried talents and wasted opportunities'.64

The Grayson challenge was, in West Yorkshire, merely an irritant to the ILP and the Labour Party. Nevertheless, it did tap some of the local frustrations which had developed as a result of the tendency of MacDonald and Hardie to thwart local ambitions of sponsoring parliamentary candidates. In West Yorkshire these tensions had become most apparent in two relatively unpromising constituencies for Labour - Pudsey and Keighley.

Before the First World War the Pudsey constituency surrounded the three Bradford constituencies. There were indeed some overlaps between Bradford and Pudsey for whilst the Tong and Dudley Hill areas returned councillors to Bradford City Council they were in the Pudsey parliamentary division. Prominent Bradfordians, such as E.R. Hartley and

Charlie Glyde, were also active in the Pudsey division because of this overlap with the City of Bradford. Yet whilst Bradford was the centre of the West Yorkshire Labour movement, and helped to establish a nucleus of Socialist support within the overlapping Pudsey division, the ILP and the Labour Party never became powerful in Pudsey. Glyde did much fine missionary work in Tong, Joe Walker did the same in Farsley, helping to produce the <u>Labour Herald</u> and Joseph Hazelip mounted a Socialist challenge in Horsforth. Yet these efforts were merely straws in the wind. There were a number of urban-district council and school board successes achieved by the ILP in the constituency but these were always fitful.[65] There were three major reasons for the weakness of Labour in Pudsey. The first was that the trade union movement was weak, although the Stanningley Trades Council was formed. The second was that there were a large number of outvoters, possibly about 5,000 out of an electorate of more than 15,000. This fact had dissuaded the ILP from contesting the seat in the 1906 Election. The third problem was that in the Horsforth area, in particular, there was a Ratepayers' Association, consisting of the Liberals and Conservatives, which had led to the defeat of Hazelip in the District Council elections of April 1908. In the same year, a Tory and Liberal combination at Farsley had resulted in the defeat of two ILP councillors, Walker and Allerton, in the Farsley District Council elections.[66]

Despite the difficulties which Pudsey posed for Labour candidates, Joe Walker, Secretary of the Pudsey ILP, kept up a barrage of letters to Hardie and MacDonald, insisting that there was a need to find a suitable candidate for Pudsey.[67] The National ILP's response was predictable. They rejected the demands on the grounds that the size of the ownership vote, the lack of funds and the weak commitment of trade unions meant that there was little prospect of success.[68]

Walker adopted a petulant tone in subsequent letters and the Pudsey ILP did warn the ILP not to make an alliance with the Liberal Party towards the end of 1909. But such irritant action failed to budge the NAC of the ILP. Pudsey was not officially contested by the ILP or the Labour Party before the First World War, though Hartley only withdrew from the 1900 General Election contest on the eve of the poll and though there was an Independent Labour candidate, J. Benson, in the June 1908 parliamentary

by-election.
    The situation in Keighley was even more protracted. W.T. Newlove had unsuccessfully contested the seat in the 1906 General Election. But the real problem was that despite the good Labour showing J. Brigg, a local wool manufacturer, was easily at the head of the poll and local as well as national, opinion appeared to be that whilst Brigg was contesting the seat for the Liberals there would be little prospect of success but that a Labour candidate ought to be selected in order that the seat could be contested if Brigg retired because of his advanced years. The NAC appears to have accepted the view of Tom Mackley, a leading local Labour leader, that the 'National I.L.P. cannot afford to throw away such a good constituency as Keighley', but were unsure whether or not Herbert Horner should be the candidate.[69] Horner was a founder member of the Keighley ILP, a teacher and Secretary of the West Riding Teachers' Association, a member of the National Union of Teachers, and had been returned as a County Councillor in April 1907.[70] A much respected local figure, he was nevertheless considered to be a rather weak character by many of the leaders of the National ILP. After some lengthy correspondence and selection arrangements he was selected to be the Labour candidate for Keighley and was to be supported in his election expenses to the tune of £100 by his union.[71] But it was clear that he felt that he had little chance of beating J. Brigg, the sitting Liberal MP, and he withdrew his candidature, in the hope that Brigg would retire and cause a parliamentary by-election, at the January 1910 General Election.[72] The death of J. Brigg, towards the end of 1911, forced a by-election but it was W.C. Anderson, chairman of the ILP, who was put forward, not Horner. In the 1913 parliamentary by-election W. Bland won the nomination instead of Horner.
    Apart from the fact that the NAC was evidently opposed to Horner's candidature it is clear that the period between 1909 and 1913 also saw a change in the political structure of the Keighley Labour movement. The Keighley LRC had joined the Trades Council by 1911 and the ILP, which had not advanced in membership from its position in the early 1890s, was divided between Horner, and some of the older established members, and W. Bland, and younger members. Indeed, by 1913 there were real fears that the local ILP would split. Horner threatened to form a second ILP branch in opposition to the Keighley ILP,

annoyed at the fact that Bland, and the 'Blandite' section of the Keighley ILP were excluding him from an active part in Keighley Labour politics. He obviously held grounds for resentment against Bland and the national leadership, particularly in the light of a Labour agent's report which was produced on Keighley, and correctly indicated that he had stood down in the January 1910 General Election on the advice of Philip Snowden. He had also stood down in favour of W.C. Anderson, the chairman of the party, in the Keighley by-election of 1911, 'although I had £100 guaranteed by the Executive of the National Union of Teachers'. He claimed that Anderson had assured him 'that I should lose nothing through my magnanimity'.[73]

The blunt tone of Hardie's reply, and the suggestion that Horner had no just cause for being aggrieved, hardly fitted the facts and was an indelicate response to a party faithful whose parliamentary ambitions had been thwarted by the misleading advice and promises of the leaders of the National ILP.[74]

Compared to the threat which Grayson posed, these local turbulences were mere pinpricks to the growth of the Labour movement in West Yorkshire and, as we have made abundantly clear, Labour's growth continued unabated from 1909 and 1910 onwards.

The West Yorkshire Liberal organisations were quite clearly losing control of municipal centres, such as Bradford and Leeds, in the face of the erosion of their working-class support by the Labour movement. In many areas, Labour was making inroads into the number of Liberal municipal representatives, even if the Liberals retained their predominance. But why did this occur? Why was it that Liberalism was unable to staunch the flow of support to Labour?

Part of the reason may well have been that the changes which P.F. Clarke detects for Lancashire did not occur in West Yorkshire. Clarke suggests that Lancashire Liberalism, particularly after 1910, was dominated by a new career-minded type of politician who replaced the local industrial, often textile, magnates as Liberal candidates and MPs. They were less steeped in Nonconformity, more interested in national rather than local issues, and in tune with the more progressive demands of some sections of the Liberal Party.[75] Even the most sanguine of historians of the Clarke school of thought could not suggest that

Liberal Decline and Labour Growth 1906-14

the Lancashire features pertained in West Yorkshire. The fact is that Liberalism in West Yorkshire continued to be dominated by the textile millocracy, Nonconformity still shaped the thinking of local Liberals, Liberal MPs rarely exhibited progressive policies and local politics remained important. What is blatently obvious is that the 1910 General Elections in no way represented a watershed for the West Yorkshire Liberal parties. West Yorkshire Liberalism continued along established lines and failed to respond to the rising identification of the working classes with the Labour Party. The development of class politics, insofar as there was a move by the working classes to attach themselves to the Labour Party, cut deeply into Liberal support well before the First World War and particularly, as we have noted, after 1910.

The evidence for these assertions in plentiful. In the first place, many of the Liberal MPs were still drawn from textile families and not from a career-minded type of politician. At the parliamentary level, which is the main location of Clarke's argument, many MPs were still drawn from the manufacturing classes. W.E.B. Priestley, Liberal MP for Bradford East between 1906 and 1918, was the son of Briggs Priestley - one of Bradford's leading industrialists, a Baptist, and Liberal MP for Pudsey between 1885 and 1900. Rowland Barran, MP for Leeds North between 1902 and 1918, owned a clothing firm in Leeds. Robert Armitage, MP for Leeds Central between 1906 and 1922, was a substantial ironmaster.[76] Percy Illingworth, who represented Shipley between 1906 and 1915, was the nephew of Alfred Illingworth and connected with the Illingworth firm, Whetley Mills, Bradford.[77] Many other MPs had business and textile connections. But even those who were not drawn directly from the local business community rarely exhibited what might be considered to be progressive Liberal ideas. A.J. Sherwell, returned as the Liberal MP for Huddersfield in the November 1906 parliamentary by-election, and represented Huddersfield until 1918, was a fairly traditional Liberal. He had been trained to enter the Wesleyan ministry and became involved in Wesleyan mission work. He worked with the Charity Organisation Society in the 1890s, produced a sociological study of the slums of Soho entitled <u>Life in West London</u>, and had become an international expert on drink and temperance. Although his views on temperance were less pedantic than those held by many Liberal Nonconformists, he tended to view poverty in terms of personal failing, and proposed self-help, not state intervention, as a solution. Sherwell's views, therefore, stopped short of the state intervention or collectivisation of the new Liberalism.

Those Liberal MPs who were not drawn from local business families or Nonconformity rarely showed evidence of new Liberal ideas. Sir George Scott Robertson, who was MP for Bradford Central between 1906 and 1916, and who might be regarded as a career politician, showed no inclination to offer progressive policies in his election campaigns.[79] In addition, there were comparatively few new Liberal MPs, contesting seats for the first time, appearing in the January and December general elections of 1910.[80]

Only two of the Liberal MPs could claim strong new-Liberal credentials. One was Walter Runciman who was returned as Liberal MP for Dewsbury in 1902. Although Martin Pugh's study of 'Yorkshire and the New Liberalism', largely about Dewsbury, stresses that he was a new Liberal it also points out that it was old Liberal Nonconformity, rather than new Liberal ideas, which ensured that Runciman was returned for Dewsbury. The other new Liberal was C.P. Trevelyan, Liberal MP for Elland from 1899 to 1918. Although Trevelyan's collectivist views eventually led him to join the Labour Party in 1918, it is clear that he barely pushed his new-Liberal views in the more traditional Liberal seat of Elland.[81] Whilst some new-Liberal MPs, and their supporters, were present in West Yorkshire before the First World War there is little to suggest that they exerted any marked influence upon the local Liberal parties, much less the working-class electorate.

The lack of support for Liberal progressivism in West Yorkshire is perhaps part of the explanation for the failures of Liberalism to prevent the haemorrhage of working-class support to Labour. Another factor must be that despite the Liberal reforms at the national level, local Liberalism, because it was unbending in its support for self-help and charity was reluctant to sanction local collectivist action by the town or city councils which it controlled.

In Bradford remarkably little was done to encourage collective responsibility for the ill and needy. We have already suggested that Bradford became a centre of the municipal school-feeding movement, largely in the face of Liberal opposition which fought a determined rearguard action against

what it saw as the 'municipalisation of poverty'.82
The provision of municipal housing in Bradford was
also only accomplished against a background of Liberal and Conservative opposition. Only after a
vigorous ILP campaign from the late 1890s, led by
Fred Jowett, was the trenchant opposition of Liberals and Conservatives overcome when the Council
agreed to press forward with the Longland scheme in
August 1901. A slum area was to be cleared, tenements were to be constructed to accommodate 432
people, and 'through' houses were to be built in
Faxfleet Street for the 925 displaced persons.83
Limited as this scheme was, compared to the total
slum problem of Bradford, it was strongly disapproved of by Tories, and some Liberals, who fought
to prevent any further extension of municipal housing. ILP leaders later argued that:

> The leaders of the Liberal party in Bradford,
> Alderman H.B. Priestman, has recently been
> claiming that his party is just as anxious to
> remove slums and remedy poverty as the Socialists. Whilst we do not doubt that in the main
> both Liberals and Tories have the kindliest
> feelings towards their poorer fellow citizens,
> yet we feel compelled to point out that when
> it comes to an actual conflict between the
> sacredness of human life and the sacredness
> of property, they are generally to be found on
> the side of property.84

A similar reluctance to consider progressive
measures occurred in Huddersfield. Ben Riley, a
Labour councillor and later Labour MP for Dewsbury,
reflected:

> How completely out of touch modern local
> official Liberalism ... is with the real progressive spirit of the time ... the leading
> dominant Liberals on the Council are either
> entirely opposed to enlarging the purpose of
> their politics or they are far too timid, too
> nervous, achieving no great aims.85

Riley's comment is in fact borne out by the
facts. The Huddersfield Liberal Association, and
its membership, placed its faith in the efficacy of
charity to deal with the social problems of the day.
The Charity Organisation Society was the main focus
of a charitable self-help approach which, in the
face of rapidly rising unemployment in the first

decade of the twentieth century, gave way to the more community-based and social casework approach of the Huddersfield Guild of Help. As with the Bradford Guild of Help, formed in 1904, many of the leading C.O.S. figures were to be found within the Guild and in essence the new organisation was merely a revamped version of the C.O.S. The Huddersfield Guild was also considered by Labour leaders to be a Liberal 'surrogate for municipal action'.[86] It was clearly the hope of the Guild that poverty could be dealt with without the need for additional legislation. It is true that the development of the Guild softened the traditional attitude of Liberal Nonconformists that much poverty was self-induced as a result of recourse to drink, but Samuel Bull, a Liberal manufacturer, still reflected the view of many Liberals that 'if the unemployed drank less it would raise their efficiency and give them employment'.[87] In the face of this lingering opposition to poverty being dealt with by the direct action of the state or the municipal authorities, it is not surprising that the Huddersfield Liberals dragged their heels in connection with social welfare. The Liberal-dominated town council did not commit itself to a housebuilding programme for the working classes until 1907 and did nothing on the matter until 1912.[88] Its only significant concession to district municipal action before 1914 was its decision to set up a Canteen Committee, financed from the rates, to provide school meals to necessitious children under the 1906 Eduction (Provision of Meals) Act.[89]

The exigent needs of working-class life were producing a demand for collectivisation which the Liberal parties of West Yorkshire were unwilling to meet. It was only the West Yorkshire Labour movement which was prepared to meet these needs with an advanced social programme, a programme which was attracting trade-union, and thus working-class, support.

Yet the rapid drift of working-class support to Labour, whilst it was encouraged by the rising level of industrial unrest which occurred in Britain and West Yorkshire in the years between 1909 and 1914, does not appear to have been influenced by the rise of syndicalist activity before the First World War. It is clear that there were a large number of industrial disputes in West Yorkshire between 1909 and 1914. It is equally evident that these disputes added to the support

Liberal Decline and Labour Growth 1906-14

for the Labour Party. But is must be remembered that the Manningham Mills strike of the early 1890s had encouraged the working-class drift towards Labour and that the trickle of disputes from the 1890s to 1909 re-enforced the message of Manningham - the need for the working classes to support an independent working-class political party. The militancy of the immediate pre-war years served to galvanise the Labour position, since so many of the leading West Yorkshire figures were in fact trade unionists. What is equally clear, however, is that syndicalism played a very limited role in the industrial unrest which occurred in West Yorkshire and that had it been more significant it might well have dampened the support for the Labour Party rather than have exposed the social and industrial failures of Liberal Britain.

The syndicalists were a group of activists, by and large led by Tom Mann, who hoped to capture the existing trade-union structure for the rank and file, to bring unity and militancy to trade unionism through the formation of industrial unions, which united all the unions of one industry into one union and to bring about the collapse of capitalist society by a General Strike which would pave the way for some type of workers' control. In essence, the syndicalist was an advocate of industrial as opposed to political action. Their policies were at odds with the Labour Party where, despite its close connection with trade unions, primacy lay with political rather than industrial, means of bringing about change. Labour leaders, such as Ramsay MacDonald and Philip Snowden, wrote pamphlets and books attacking syndicalism as an imported French movement which was alien to the British way of life. Indeed, it would appear that the vast majority of Labour leaders in West Yorkshire agreed with this view, though there was some sentimental support for Tom Mann and for the support which syndicalism gave to the emerging strategies of trade unions. But there is little evidence that syndicalism was ever prevalent in West Yorkshire. Several years ago, J.E. Williams, in an article on the Leeds Gas Strike of 1913, dismissed notions that syndicalists or syndicalism played a part in the dispute. When Bob Holton wrote his polemic on British Syndicalism, attempting to prove that it both achieved some degree of international success and that its influence did not expire after 1912 but continued up to the First World War, it is noticeable that he provided no hard evidence of the movement thriving in West Yorkshire.[90]

Indeed, the only real evidence of syndicalist activity in West Yorkshire emerges in the conflicts of the British Socialist Party. At the national level it was torn between the essentially political approach of Hyndman, who was opposed to strike activity, and Leonard Hall and H.R. Smart, both of whom believed in the need for industrial unionism. Hall wrote:

> The great defensive and destructive duties of Industrial Unionism must not be allowed to overshadow its essentially constructive function in the transition to Socialism ... Under Socialism itself the co-ordinating centres would be Parliaments of Industry not Parliaments of Politicians. No free and self-respecting community would have any need or room for partisan "Punch and Judy" politics.[91]

He was naturally opposed by Hyndman, and other SDF and BSP leaders, who had 'never known ... a successful strike'.[92]

The only serious support for Hall and Smart came from the Huddersfield branch of the BSP. A number of factors conflated to make the Huddersfield branch pro-syndicalist. In the first instance, Smart carried a little weight in the constituency, having been the ILP parliamentary candidate at the general election of 1895 and having retained his contacts in the area. In addition, E.J.B. Allen, one of the leading members of Tom Mann's Industrial Syndicalist Education League, had lived, worked and agitated for his views, in the Huddersfield area.[93] Also, leading members of the Huddersfield BSP, such as Arthur Gardiner, were trade unionists and committed to industrial action. It is hardly surprising then that the Huddersfield BSP resolved that its meeting

> realising the necessity of the return of Socialist members of Parliament, and on the local governing bodies, as well as the organisation of the workers industrially in their unions, both movements aiming at the abolition of the wages system of slavery, and the entire emancipation of the working class, pledges itself to secure Socialist representation where possible, and to assist in the building up of a powerful union movement.[94]

Liberal Decline and Labour Growth 1906-14

Yet even in Huddersfield there appears to have been little evidence of syndicalist presence in strike activity, no matter what the <u>Huddersfield Examiner</u> and the Liberal press might say.

The militant strike activity before 1914 did help to galvanise the links between the Labour Party and the trade union movement. Some of the Liberal legislation, such as the Unemployment section of the National Insurance Act of 1911 did engender some criticism from trade union ranks. But on the whole the militant period of industrial activity merely served to buttress the class alliances which had already been forged between trade unions and the Labour Party.

The West Yorkshire Liberal parties failed to meet the challenge of Labour between 1906 and 1914. Without needing to enter the involved and protracted debate about the inequalities of the parliamentary and local franchises which might, or might not, have helped the Liberals at the expense of Labour, it is evident that the Liberal voters were moving to Labour. Labour did well in both general elections and parliamentary by-elections and made deep inroads into the local position of the Liberal Party from 1910 onwards, after the setbacks of 1908 and 1909. There is no evidence that Labour's political growth was being checked in West Yorkshire between 1910 and 1914, and little evidence to suggest that local Liberalism was making the attempt to capture the working-class vote with its progressive social policies. On the whole West Yorkshire Liberalism was still dominated by the factory master and Nonconformity. The shibboliths of self-help and charity were offered by Liberals as an alternative to greater intervention and collectivisation. When these failed the Liberals often united with Tories as anti-Socialist combines. It was a ploy which both demonstrated the lack of Liberal progressivism and the seriousness of the Labour challenge. Labour was much stronger in West Yorkshire by 1914 than it had been in 1906 or 1910, and much of its growth was at Liberal expense. The First World War served to speed up the decline of the Liberal Party, of that there is no doubt. But it is clear that the signs of Liberal decay were already apparent before the war. Moreover, the identification of the working classes with the progressive policies of the Labour Party foreshadowed Liberal decline. There is also no reason to suppose that the Liberal Party should be more seriously affected by the war than was the Labour Party. The political turbulence created by the First World War was just as pronounced in the West Yorkshire Labour movement as it was within the Liberal Party. The fact that Labour survived and that Liberalism collapsed owes much to the class nature of political support which had accreted to the Labour cause before 1914.

NOTES

1. Clarke, *Lancashire and the New Liberalism*, p. 406.
2. Wilson, *The Downfall of the Liberal Party 1914-35*, p. 19.
3. *Labour Leader*, 30 Nov. 1906; *Independent Review*, Feb. 1907.
4. R. Perks argues this in his CNAA PhD study, at Huddersfield Polytechnic, on Huddersfield politics in the late nineteenth and early twentieth centuries.
5. *Independent Review*, Jan., Feb. 1907.
6. ILP Archive, Francis Johnson Collection, 1908/263, letter from Williams to Keir Hardie, 30 Jun. 1908.
7. Ibid., 1906/43.
8. *Daily Express*, 20 Jul. 1907.
9. Clark, *Colne Valley: Radicalism to Socialism*, pp. 5-6.
10. ILP Archive, Francis Johnson Collection, 1906/403.
11. Clark, *Colne Valley: Radicalism to Socialism*, pp. 129-61; R. Groves, *The Strange Case of Victor Grayson* (Pluto Press, London, 1975), pp. 20-42.
12. Colne Valley Labour League, Minutes, 13 Oct. 1906.
13. *Yorkshire Factory Times*, 22 Jun. 1906; Labour Party Archive, LP/CAN/06/2/65, circular issued by the Colne Valley Labour League in response to an ILP statement.
14. Clark, *Colne Valley: Radicalism to Socialism*, p. 131.
15. CVLL, Minutes, 13 Oct. 1906.
16. Ibid., 25 Feb. 1907.
17. Howell, *British Workers and the Independent Labour Party 1888-1906*, pp. 301-26.
18. Labour Party Archive, LP/CAN/06/2/40.
19. Ibid.
20. *ILP Report, 1907*.
21. Labour Party Archive, PL/CAN/06/2/42.

22. Yorkshire Factory Times, 12 Jul. 1907.
23. Labour Leader, throughout Jun. 1907.
24. E. Lockwood, Colne Valley Folk (Heath Cranton, London, 1936), p. 73.
25. Colne Valley Guardian, 26 Jul. 1907.
26. Sheppard and Halstead, 'Labour's Municipal Election Performance in Provincial England and Wales 1901-13', p. 42.
27. Woodhouse, 'The working class', p. 361.
28. Labour Leader, 9 Nov. 1908.
29. Ibid., 17 Apr. 1908.
30. Bradford West, Halifax, Leeds East and Huddersfield.
31. ILP Archive, Francis Johnson Collection, 1910/530.
32. Groves, The Strange Case of Victor Grayson, p. 59.
33. Ibid., p. 62.
34. Labour Leader, 20 Nov. 1908.
35. Groves, The Strange Case of Victor Grayson, p. 67.
36. Ibid., pp. 92-6.
37. Labour Leader, 15 May 1908.
38. Ibid., 16 Apr. 1909.
39. Ibid., 23, 30 Apr. 1909, 1 Apr. 1910.
40. Ibid., 30 Apr. 1909, 1 Apr. 1910.
41. Ibid., 16 Apr. 1909.
42. Ibid., 30 Apr, 1909 and subsequent issues.
43. Clarion, 4 Aug. 1911.
44. Letter from SBP to CVSL, 6 Jun. 1916 in the Colne Valley Labour Party records, The Polytechnic Library, Huddersfield.
45. Clarion, 11 Aug. 1911.
46. Ibid., 22 Sep., 6, 13 Oct. 1911.
47. Ibid., 8 Dec. 1911.
48. Ibid., 13 Oct. 1911.
49. Ibid., 2 Mar. 1912.
50. Ibid., 10 Nov. 1911.
51. L. Thompson, The Enthusiasts: A Biography of John and Katherine Bruce Glasier (Victor Gollancz, London, 1971), p. 169.
52. Clarion, 10 Nov., 7 Dec. 1911.
53. Bradford Pioneer, 7 Feb. 1913.
54. Justice, 30 Nov. 1912.
55. Clarion, 4 Nov. 1912, 14 Feb. 1913.
56. Justice, 18 Oct., 8 Nov. 1913.
57. Bradford Daily Telegraph, 4 Nov. 1913.
58. First Annual Conference of the British Socialist Party, 1912 (Communist Party of Great Britain, London, 1970 reprint), pp. 50-2.
59. Justice, 13 Oct. 1913, 26 Mar. 1914.

60. Ibid., 10 Sep. 1914.
61. Bradford Pioneer, 11 Apr. 1913.
62. W. Kendall, The Revolutionary Movement in Britain 1900-1921 (Weidenfeld & Nicolson, London, 1969); Clarion, 5 Jan. 1912; First Annual Conference of the British Socialist Party, 1912, pp. 9-10.
63. Justice, 4 May 1912.
64. Ibid., 21 Dec. 1912.
65. Labour Party Archive, LRC 17/534-6.
66. Footnote 29.
67. Labour Party Archive, LRC 17/534; ILP Archive, Francis Johnson Collection, 1907/70, 1908/156, 1908/159, 1908/199.
68. ILP Archive, Francis Johnson Collection, 1908/22.
69. Ibid., 1907/144.
70. Ibid., 1907/51, 1907/189. There was also a Labour Party agents' report which was critical of Herbert Horner 1909/500.
71. Ibid., 1909/549.
72. Ibid., 1909/549-50, 1909/568-9.
73. Ibid., 1913/306.
74. Ibid., 1913/307.
75. Clarke, Lancashire and the New Liberalism.
76. E.D. Steele, 'Imperialism and Leeds politics, c. 1850-1914', in D. Fraser (ed.), A History of Modern Leeds (Manchester University Press, Manchester, 1980), p. 328.
77. He replaced W.P. Byles as Liberal candidate for Shipley in 1897.
78. Huddersfield Examiner, 24 Nov. 1906.
79. W.D. Ross, 'Bradford Politics 1880-1906', unpublished PhD thesis, University of Bradford, 1977, particularly the biographical section.
80. Four in January 1910 and three in December 1910.
81. Morris, C.P. Trevelyan 1870-1958: Portrait of a Radical, p. 81.
82. Laybourn, 'The Issue of School Feeding in Bradford, 1904-1907', pp. 30-8.
83. Brockway, Socialism over Sixty Years, p. 52.
84. Forward, 18 Oct. 1907.
85. Huddersfield Examiner, 22 Oct. 1910.
86. M. Cahill and Tony Jowitt, 'The Bradford Guild of Help Papers', History Workshop, Issue 15, Spring 1983, p. 151; M. Cahill and Tony Jowitt, 'The New Philanthropy: the emergence of the Bradford City Guild of Help', Journal of Social Policy 9: 3 (July, 1980), pp. 359-82; Huddersfield Examiner, 22 Nov. 1913.

87. _Huddersfield Examiner_, 16 Dec. 1893.
88. Ibid., 19 Oct. 1907; Huddersfield Trades Council, Minutes, 28 May 1913.
89. Huddersfield Borough Council, Minutes, 24 Apr. 1907.
90. J.E. Williams, 'The Leeds Gas Strike, 1913', in A. Briggs and J. Saville, _Essays in Labour History_ (Macmillan, London, 1971).
Bob Holton, _British Syndicalism, 1900-1914_ (Pluto Press, London, 1976).
91. _Clarion_, 3 May 1912.
92. Kendall, _The Revolutionary Movement in Britain 1900-1921_, pp. 28-9.
93. _The Industrial Syndicalist, passim_.
94. Alfred Gardiner scrap book, p. 3, though the source of the newspaper cutting is not indicated. Photocopies of parts of the scrapbook are in the hands of Dr. K. Laybourn. Gardiner was a member of the Dyers' Union and a delegate to Huddersfield Trades Council.

Chapter Seven

THE FIRST WORLD WAR

Recent research on the First World War and domestic politics has divided historical opinion into two major schools of thought. The first, in which we include ourselves, maintains that the Labour Party had made deep inroads into Liberalism well before 1914. It has been our contention that the Labour Party was eroding the political support of the Liberal Party in West Yorkshire before 1914, and that the First World War merely speeded up the erosion of that support. The second school of thought, dominated by P.F. Clarke, Trevor Wilson and Roy Douglas, has emphasised the crucial impact of the War in dividing Liberalism and allowing a political vacuum to emerge which the Labour Party was able to fill. Wilson set the parameters of this particular school of thought when he wrote that

> The war not only inflicted such a disaster on the Liberals but provided Labour with the impetus to seize the opportunity. The impact of the war on the nation's economy so increased the importance of trade unions and so stimulated their political consciousness, that it correspondingly enhanced the position of the Labour Party, which had all along derived much of its limited importance from its association with organised labour.[1]

The problem with this second viewpoint is that it first of all ignores the substantial improvements made by Labour before the First World War and, secondly, it assumes that the war was more conducive to the growth of Labour opinion than it was to Liberal opinion. In West Yorkshire, Labour had made rapid inroads into the local political power of Liberalism, and it was also evident that the war

The First World War

posed just as many problems for the Labour movement as it did for Liberalism. There is no particular reason why the Liberal Party should have been any more inconvenienced by the war than was the Labour Party, which faced its own leadership crisis. Labour's political resilience, on the other hand, appears to have resulted from the inexorable growth of its working-class support. Conversely, Liberalism's loss of working-class support, rather than conflict amongst the leading Liberals, was the fundamental difficulty which it faced.

The 1914 ILP Conference, the 'Coming of Age Conference' as it was known, was the apogee of the ILP before the War. Apart from the fact that the meeting was held at the time of ILP growth and success, it was held in Bradford, the birthplace of the National ILP. Despite an excess of local pride, which coloured the speeches of many Bradford delegates, the conference did accurately reflect the local confidence of the movement. In his welcoming address to the 1914 Conference, J.H. Palin, reflecting upon the fact that the Bradford ILP had 1,600 members, 20 members on the City Council, three members on the Board of Guardians and one MP, asserted:

> they would see that the ILP was not only the political party of the future, but that, so far as Bradford was concerned, it was the political party of the present. ... and there was no danger of the Bradford branch going wrong and if they would follow its lead the party would go on, and would eventually become the dominant party in British politics.[2]

This confidence and sense of unity within the Bradford and West Yorkshire ILP organisations was to be quickly undermined by the First World War.

In the years immediately prior to the war, the Bradford and West Yorkshire Labour movements had committed themselves to oppose militarism. Both the Bradford ILP and the Bradford Trades Council responded to the increasingly threatening international situation by supporting international Socialist resolutions opposed to war. In 1912 the Bradford Trades Council resolved to express its approval 'of the proposal for a general stoppage of work in all countries about to engage in war, and further we urge upon all workers the necessity for making preparations for a simultaneous stoppage of work in those countries where war is threatened'.[3] Arthur Gardiner and the Huddersfield Socialist Party, which was briefly attached to the British Socialist Party, were also staunchly opposed to the war, despite the patriotic pressure applied by H.M. Hyndman.[4] On the eve of war numerous articles appeared in the <u>Bradford Pioneer</u> and the <u>Huddersfield Worker</u>, the local ILP newspapers, exposing the workings of secret diplomacy and the Armaments Trust, and advocating the fostering of unity across international boundaries.

The driving force behind such concern was the moral indignation of many ILPers who felt that the taking of human life was never justifiable. Underpinning this heartfelt rejection of violence was a traditional Nonconformist opposition to war which was galvanised within the ILP by the presence of a number of prominent Nonconformist ministers. One of the most frequent writers in the <u>Bradford Observer</u> was the Reverend R. Roberts, a Congregational minister who had had a somewhat stormy relationship with the ILP in the previous twenty years.[5] In early 1914, Roberts wrote:

> Alone amongst the parties of Britain the Labour Party is pledged against militarism... We must take up the Fiery Cross and carry it to the remotest hamlet in the country, call every man and woman to the colours. "Down with militarism". That is our cry - as it is also the cry of our comrades all over Europe. Blazon it on the banners. Write it on the pavements. Sing in the streets.[6]

The outbreak of the First World War came with startling suddenness. As late as 1 August 1914 Continental Socialist leaders were still not convinced that war was even a likely possibility. As Haupt suggests, they were captive of their own myths about their ability to prevent war and unaware of the depths of national chauvinism.[7] They were caught out by the events, pushed on to the defensive and literally became disoriented spectators, waiting to be submerged by the gathering wave of nationalism.

In Bradford, in the midst of the period of national ultimatums, the ILP called a mass meeting on 2 August which deplored the threatened war but did not advocate immediate working-class action to prevent it. Fred Jowett, the ILP MP for Bradford West, hoped that Britain would not be involved in

The First World War

the coming conflagration but, bowing to events, concluded: 'Let us who are Socialists keep our minds calm, our hearts free from hate, and one purpose always before us - to bring peace as soon as possible on a basis that will endure'.[8]

Such a unanimity of purpose evaporated with the declaration of war. Throughout West Yorkshire the ILP branch membership divided into pro-war and anti-war factions, divisions which rapidly became evident within cognate Labour organisations. In essence, there emerged three main strands of opinion. At one extreme there were pacifists who were opposed to war per se. At the other there were those who felt that the war had to be pursued to its successful conclusion for Prussianism to be defeated. Between these two groups were those, probably representing a majority of the movement, who were equivocal about the war. Whilst they supported the national and international peace movements they felt the need to protect Britain and to defend Belgium, some even going so far as to suggest that Socialist objectives had to be suspended for the duration of the war.

The National ILP had its fair share of pacifists whose ideas became more or less fully accepted by the ILP's National Conference in 1917. Bruce Glasier, Clifford Allen, Arthur Salter and Fenner Brockway, with Philip Snowden on the edge of this group though he was never a fully committed pacifist, set the pacifist tone of the national party which initially maintained the front that Socialists of all countries were solid against the war.[9] There was a professional, middle-class temper about this group, which was almost entirely composed of writers, journalists, academics and doctors. Though it included many prominent members of the ILP, it was never very numerous either at the national or the local level. In West Yorkshire there were few prominent individuals in its ranks. The pacifist strand in Huddersfield was led largely by Arthur Gardiner, although he was temporarily a member of the British Socialist Party rather than the ILP at this time. The leading ILP pacifists in Bradford were William Leach and Arthur Priestman, both of whom were employers who had joined the Bradford ILP in the mid 1890s. Arthur Priestman was a Quaker and a member of one of the largest business families in Bradford.[10] Leach, who was to become one of Bradford's MPs during the inter-war years, had originally been drawn into the ILP by Fred Jowett, whom he had once employed as an overlooker, and had

181

become a prolific writer within the Labour movement. He was a frequent contributor to the <u>Bradford Labour Echo</u>, the Bradford ILP paper of the late 1890s, became editor of <u>Forward</u>, the ILP's paper between 1904 and 1909 and, from October 1915, in the stead of the increasingly pro-war Joseph Burgess, became editor of the <u>Bradford Pioneer</u>. He articulated the paper's policy in the following manner:

> We hate all war, especially the present one. This is a pacifist or peace journal conducted among other purposes, with the object of stating as well as we can, the ILP position on the hideous tragedy now being enacted in Europe... Human life is the most sacred thing we know, and its preservation, its development, its best welfare, must therefore be our religion on this earth.[11]

Under Leach's editorship the <u>Bradford Pioneer</u> reported extensively on the activities of pacifists and opponents of war controls, such as the No-Conscription Fellowship and the Union of Democratic Control. When Bertrand Russell lectured at the ILP's New Picture House in Morley Street, Bradford in 1917, the <u>Bradford Pioneer</u> referred to him as 'a recent and very valuable acquisition to the I.L.P.'.[12] When E.D. Morel, of the Union of Democratic Control, lectured at the Picture House he was affectionately described as 'that distinguished jail bird... now a member of the I.L.P. and of the Bradford Branch'.[13]

Though Leach was badly defeated when he stood as the ILP/Labour Party candidate for Bradford Central in the 1918 General Election he still stuck firmly to his pacifist views, stating that 'I have never felt so pugnaciously right in my life. I still disbelieve in war. As long as I am in public life I will not support bloodshed for any cause, whether that cause appears right or does not. It looks as if this victory fervour has swept us out. But it will pass. Liberalism is defunct, Socialism is deferred, and the Coalition will be deflated'.[14]

Such passion of conviction was equally evident amongst those members of the ILP who did support the war effort. Jessie Cockerline, the regular trade union correspondent of the <u>Bradford Pioneer</u>, and a leading contributor to the <u>Yorkshire Factory Times</u>, the weekly paper of the Yorkshire textile workers, constantly argued that the cry must be 'My Country Right or Wrong', occasionally tempered with the thought that the War was not so much concerned with patriotism as the issues of right and wrong, might and right.[15] Cockerline wrote frequently on need to fight against Caesarism, one one occasion maintaining that 'The sword is drawn and it is drawn in the cause of democracy, in the cause of liberty and honour and we must, each one of us, realise that it can never again be sheathed whilst the terror of the Kaiser's dreams of universal domination have the most remote possibility of being realised'.[16]

There were certainly many other ILPers, often springing from a trade union background, who supported Cockerline's views. J.H. Palin, Hector Munro and Councillor A.W. Brown of Bradford, and James Parker of Halifax, were strongly pro-war.

Palin was a prominent trade unionist, had been chairman of the Amalgamated Society of Railway Servants at the time of Taff Vale, and a prominent public figure in Bradford, acting as an ILP councillor, and later alderman, up to and during the war. Until early 1917 he was the trade union correspondent of the <u>Bradford Pioneer</u>, having taken over from Cockerline, and prominently displayed his support for the War. At first his views were tolerated in the confusion of opinion over the War within the ILP ranks, but he became an increasing embarrassment to Leach and the anti-war <u>Bradford Pioneer</u> and was obviously out of step with resolutions passed by the Bradford ILP. This difference of opinion was sharply indicated at the 1916 ILP Conference when, despite being mandated to support a resolution advocating all Socialist parties of all nations to refuse to support every war entered into by any government, Palin cut across the comparative equanimity of the meeting and bluntly stated that

> We do not want the Germans here. Assume that the workers of this country had carried out this resolution at the beginning of the war, and the Socialists of other countries had not, and had rallied or been forced to join the Army, where at the moment would Great Britain have been? At any rate, it seems to me that more time is required to get a considered opinion to start afresh after the war.[17]

Although Palin was reprimanded by T.W. Stamford, President of the Bradford ILP, he remained unrepentant and subsequently went to France to help with war transportation.

Others campaigned strongly for the war effort and took themselves to France. Dr. Hector Munro, a prominent Bradford ILPer and sometime member of the Board of Guardians, went to France with an ambulance wagon at the beginning of the conflict.[18] Censuses of the Bradford ILP membership confirm that many young men volunteered to go to the front. A census in February 1916 indicated that of 461 young men in the local party membership of 1,473, 113 were in the trenches, four had been killed, one was missing, nine had been wounded, three were prisoners of war, 118 were in training in England, six were in the navy and 207 attested under the Derby Scheme were necessary home workers.[19] A similar survey in 1918 found that of the 492 members liable for service, 351 were serving in the forces whilst 48 were conscientious objectors or were on national war work.[20]

Such patriotism was to be found more broadly throughout the West Yorkshire Labour movement. Indeed, perhaps the most prominent of the ILP's pro-war contingent was James Parker, ILP/Labour MP for Halifax. From the outset, Parker identified himself with the war effort and the recruiting campaign. One critic, attacking the Keighley Labour Party for not supporting the war effort in early October 1914, noted that this neglect was being more than made up for by James Parker:

> Mr. James Parker, M.P., in pleading for more recruits in the Halifax district, declared that if Britain were defeated in the war, the working class would have everything to lose and nothing to gain. They would not be asked to serve in the army but would be bludgeoned into it not only in times of war but in times of peace. ... Parker is not a man to talk like this unless thoroughly convinced that the war is a joint one on our part.[21]

Parker's commitment to the war effort was amply demonstrated when he wrote to Francis Johnson, Secretary of the National ILP, in April 1915 responding to an ILP Conference resolution criticising his action: 'In reference to the Resolution re my recruiting campaign in Eccles Division and Bishop Auckland. I have nothing to add to my former letter beyond that I have been doing my duty'.[22]

Parker's influence appears to have told on the Halifax Trades Council, most of whose leading members were ILPers. When they discussed the recruiting campaign in September 1914 they supported it by 24 votes to 16. Alderman Arthur Taylor, a leading figure in the Amalgamated Society of Engineers and the doyen of the Halifax ILP, reflected that 'while he hated wars, there were times when it was absolutely necessary that people should recognise war was inevitable. England did not belong to the people, but neither did any other country. At any rate, England was the best country among "a blooming bad lot"'.23

Although not as forthright in his views as Parker and Palin, Ben Turner, the leader of the weavers and textile workers, who was re-elected as Mayor of Batley in November 1914, quickly accepted the need to fight and identified himself with the relief of the Belgian refugees.24 Elsewhere in West Yorkshire, ILPers were to be found putting forward similar arguments for the putative involvement of Socialists in the war effort.

The majority of ILP/Labour supporters in West Yorkshire do not appear to have accepted either the pacifist or patriotic line as such, but to have stood somewhere between the two positions, fluctuating in their emphasis as the mood of the nation altered. Generally they opposed the war but recognised the need for National Defence. Fred Jowett, Bradford West's Labour MP, reflected the opinion of this section. Throughout the war he articulated a viewpoint of what caused the war and how wars could be eradicated in the future. As he argued in his Chairman's speech to the 1915 ILP Conference at Norwich 'Now is the time to speak and ensure that never again shall the witches' cauldron of secret diplomacy brew the war broth of Hell for mankind'.25 He later wrote that 'I believe that the war would never have arisen if the government had carried out an open and honest foreign policy and disclosed to the people who had most to lose the relations between themselves and foreign governments with whom they were acting in collusion'.26 Jowett was a belligerent critic of the British Government which had arranged, though frequently denied the existence of, secret treaties. As the <u>Standard</u> said 'His fad is the democratic control of foreign affairs'. Given that there was a war, however, he demanded an end to the conflict as soon as possible and that the Government should specify its war aims to be forced to the negotiating table.

Although Jowett was clearly a stern critic of the Government he was equally adamant that a

British victory over 'Prussianism' had to be won and that he could not agree to a peace settlement which did not include the 'restoration of Belgium to complete sovereignty'.28 He maintained that a nation had a right to defend itself and frequently paid homage to those who had given their lives in the war.29 In many respects Jowett's policy closely resembled the views expressed by Keir Hardie in his famous article 'We must see the War Through, but denounce Secret Diplomacy'.30 Although Jowett's position on the war, as with the stance adopted by Hardie, often appeared ambiguous and at odds with the ILP's declared opposition to the war, he was categorical in his wish to see it speedily concluded in favour of the allies. This point is illuminated by his comment on the anti-war resolution passed at the 1916 ILP Conference, of which he was chairman, 'The I.L.P. resolution to which you refer only expressed the view that Socialist Parties as organised bodies should support no war. It did not attempt to lay down such a policy for individuals. If it did I should be opposed to it in principle'.31 Such semantics confused Jowett's critics and permitted him to both support and oppose the war by turns.

Such equivocation found widespread support throughout the West Yorkshire textile district. Many leading ILP figures who were formally committed to peace found the First World War to be the exception which proved the rule. The Rev. R. Roberts who, as already indicated, was taking up the 'Fiery Cross' against militarism in early 1914 was a converted man by the middle of August 1914, and argued that the legend of 'blood and iron' had to be shattered unless Socialism wished to be set back for generations.32 He later elaborated:

> Through 40 years of public life, I have preached peace ... I have never believed humanity would so far break down as to make it necessary to pay the extreme price of waging a war to preserve the peace. Yet, for my sins, I have lived to see that ... We are threatened with the ruin of civilized society. The success of Prussia in the awful tussle for life means that humanity will sink in smoking ruin.
> In the first what is our duty as a British people? We must fight the battle to a truimphant finish. At whatever cost of life and treasure we must fight (I cannot tell the

pain it cost me to write that sentence. I
never thought I should live to do it) ...
Better to die than be Prussianised. Better to
be wiped off the face of the earth than to
exist squealing and squirming under the
Prussian jack boots.[33]

Roberts's conversion reflects the difficulties
which the 'Anglo-German War' or 'European War'
imposed upon ILP and Labour Party organisations in
West Yorkshire. For instance, the Sowerby Division
Labour Representation Committee, which had been
formed in April 1908 as the Labour Party organisation for the division, does not appear to have
expressed a clear viewpoint on the war until May
1915 when it urged the Labour Party to oppose conscription 'unless it is accompanied by the conscription of all the material wealth of the country'.[34] For the rest of the war it protested against conscription and increasingly veered towards the
peace initiative of 1917. It declared its intention
to send representatives to the August 1917 Workers
and Soldiers' Council Conference in Leeds, organised in the wake of the earlier June conference,
although that conference was subsequently abandoned.[35]

It is hardly surprising that there was political fragmentation within the Labour movement and
some obfuscation about the ILP's precise position
on the war, given that Labour organisations were
not always unequivocal about the war and that many
ILPers did fight at the front. The claim to individual rights of opinion, as opposed to the collective will of the ILP, does appear to have led to
further confusion but this confusion does not
appear to have unduly damaged the ILP position in
West Yorkshire or to have weakened the bond with
the trade unions, and thus the working classes.

The trade union movement in West Yorkshire appears
to have been similarly divided over the war. We
have already stressed that the Halifax Trades Council co-operated in the war effort, goaded on by
James Parker and Arthur Taylor. The General Union
of Textile Workers, later to become the National
Union of Textile Workers, was led by Ben Turner,
Mayor of Batley and supporter of Belgium independence. There was also some ambivalance over the
fact that whilst the Socialist leaders of the Textile Workers' Union might deprecate the events
which led to war there were clear advantages in

terms of employment and wage rises for their
members.36 The <u>Yorkshire Factory Times</u> also remained neutral projecting both the pro-war views of
Jessie Cockerline and the anti-war sentiments of
'Sweeper Up'. The importation of national trade
union leaders to help in local recruiting campaigns,
as occurred when Jimmy Thomas, of the National
Union of Railwaymen, helped out in the Wakefield
Recruiting Campaign in October 1914 served to divide sympathies further.37

These problems are reflected in the difficulties faced by the Bradford trade union movement and
the Bradford Trades Council. The First World War
caught the Trades Council in a quandary. On the
one hand, in November 1912, it had passed a resolution calling for a general stoppage in the event
of an outbreak of war.38 On the other hand, it was
evident from the outset that many members of the
Trades Council were smitten by patriotic sentiments
when the war began. As a result of this imbroglio
the Trades Council permitted itself to drift with
events. Its commitments to international peace and
the International Socialist Bureau were forgotten.
It generally followed the Labour Party policy of
working with the Government and the authorities to
encourage recruitment; although there were occasional decorous statements from its officials and
delegates about the need to secure a peace as
quickly as possible. In general, the Trades Council
spent the early years of the war dealing with the
practical realities of living under war conditions.
In 1914 and 1915 the main activity of the Council
was to check upon famine prices and food stuff
shortages. This activity later gave way to Anti-
Rent Raising campaigns, the raising of money through
the Lord Mayor's Relief Fund, and to its involvement
in the activities of the Joint Food Vigilance Committee, alongside the ILP, BSP and WMF. Perhaps
the Council's most emotive campaign of the practical
type was its attempt to force the Government to
accept responsibility for providing pensions to war
widows and weekly relief and benefits to soldiers
and sailors injured in the fighting. All these
campaigns reflect the day to day functioning of the
Trades Council.39 But the Trades Council was also
a litmus-paper to the changing mood of the Bradford
working class to the war.

From the start there was a sizeable minority
of delegates on the Trades Council who opposed war.
The leaders of this group were George Licence,
Charlie Glyde and J.W. Ormanroyd. The anti-war

sentiments of Fred Jowett, expressed in the Year
Book for 1914, also tugged the heartstrings of many
delegates, although he was subsequently equivocal
about the war.[40] Yet the silent majority gave their
tacit approval to the war effort, and activists,
such as Alderman J.H. Palin, went to fight in France
alongside Bradford ILPers and trade unionists.[41]
By 1916 and 1917, however, the attitude of the
Council was beginning to change.

The threat of military and industrial conscription, first discussed in 1915, was pivotal in changing the attitude of the Trades Council, although several other issues conflated to compound the shift in thinking. In June 1915 the Trades Council passed a resolution opposing conscription 'in any form, military and industrial, and urged Parliament to offer their utmost opposition to any proposal to impose upon the British people a yoke which is one of the chief concerns of Prussian militarism'.[42] This was partly a reaction to the Munitions Act of 1915, which had suspended trade union rights and prevented vital workers from moving from job to job without a certificate of approval from their employer but also a response to the threat of military conscription. The Trades Council delegates began to drift away from supporting the TUC Parliamentary Committee's circular calling for trade union help in army recruitment and, in a series of votes and a ballot in 1915 and 1916, indicated its withdrawal from army recruitment campaigns. A vote of delegates towards the end of 1915 produced an equal number of votes for and against the recruiting campaign.[43] A Trades Council circular to affiliated trade unions in December 1915, requesting the opinions of societies to the recruiting campaign was voted upon by just over one-third of the societies and produced a result of 19 societies for and 11 against, though those unions in favour only represented 6,757 members compared to the 11,157 members of those unions opposing the recruitment campaign. Many small societies did not vote on the issue and three abstained.[44] Yet although the vote was inconclusive the introduction of conscription led to the Trades Council's withdrawal from direct involvement in helping army recruitment.

The anti-war section of the Trades Council drew strongly from the opposition to conscription, though this did not necessarily signify opposition to the war. The Trades Council pressured the Yorkshire Federation of Trades Councils to hold a No-Conscription Conference at the Textile Hall,

Bradford in December 1915 and January 1916. It also sent delegates to an ILP No-Conscription Conference at Leeds.45 As the 1916 Annual Report indicates, there were still 'differences of opinion on the war', but it is also clear that the anti-war position was burgeoning in the Council's meetings.

William Leach, editor of the <u>Bradford Pioneer</u>, was permitted to present the views of the Union of Democratic Control to the Trades Council, and in September 1915 the Council affiliated to the UDC.46 By 1916 it was possible to organise a Peace Conference under Trades Council auspices. That conference decisively condemned Labour MPs for joining the Government and pushed strongly for peace negotiations.47 The Trades Council also sent delegates to the Leeds Conference in June 1917, at which the Workers' and Soldiers' Council was formed, in the hope of forcing forward the demand for international peace negotiations.48

By 1917 the Trades Council was increasingly being dominated by, what Palin dubbed, 'militant pacifists'. The 'peace movement' was prevalent within the Trades Council, though there was still a substantial commitment to the war effort by some of the affiliated unions. Many of those Bradford trade unions who became committed to the Peace campaign of 1917 were not so much pacifists, or even opponents of the war, so much as opponents of the Government's military conscription policy. The imprisonment of Revis Barber, the son of Walter Barber who was the Secretary of the Trades Council, as a conscientious objector did much to win trade union support for the 'peace movement'.49 Thus by the end of the war, Bradford had become one of the centres of the anti-war movement.

The experiences of the Bradford Trades Council may not have been repeated in every West Yorkshire trades council, nor in all the major unions, but the general pattern of events was not unusual. In some areas, such as Huddersfield, the Trades Council appears to have established a much closer relationship with bodies which opposed conscription and aimed at protecting civil liberties than was the case in Bradford. After some early ambivalance over the war, the Huddersfield Trades and Labour Council was in the thick of the activities which led to the formation of the Huddersfield and District No-Conscription Council in January 1916. This new anti-war organisation was in fact formed at a meeting in the Friendly and Trades Societies Club, and Alfred Shaw, of the Trades Council, was in the

The First World War

chair.50 Moreover, the Trades Council had actually called the meeting. Along with the ILP and the BSP, the Huddersfield Trades Council campaigned against military conscription within the No-Conscription Council, sent a representative to the Workers and Soldiers' Council Conference of June 1917 and helped to form a local branch of the Workers and Soldiers' Council in Huddersfield.51 It also appears to have formed the Huddersfield and District Council for Civil Liberties, in place of the No-Conscription Council, towards the end of 1918 - the officers of both organisations being practically one and the same.52

Several points emerge about the attitude of trade unions towards the war. The first is that the attitude of the trade union movement was less delphic than that of the ILP. Trade unions, on the whole, appear to have supported the war effort in the first two years before giving way to the peace initiative during the last two years. This was the case in Halifax, Bradford and Huddersfield. Secondly, it is clear that whilst the national trade union leaders generally campaigned for the war effort their influence was to some extent countered by the strong local associations between the ILP and the trade union movement. The impact of the latter was not always immediate, and the attitude of ILP leaders towards the war was often ambivalent, but one must remember that many of the local ILP leaders, Fred Jowett for instance, were active trade unionists. Thirdly, the war does not appear to have unduly injured relations between the ILP and trade unions in West Yorkshire. There was no parting of the way as a result of the war. Rather, we would suggest that other factors led the Labour Party to replace the ILP as the vehicle of working-class aspirations in West Yorkshire. Indeed, by 1917 and 1918 the strong emphasis in favour of peace negotiations was being supported by the ILP and trade unions alike.

Anti-war sentiments reached their climax in West Yorkshire in the ill-fated Workers' and Soldiers' Council Conference which was held at Leeds in June 1917. Amongst the 1,150 delegates who attended the Conference on 3 June 1917 were many members of the West Yorkshire Labour movement.53 Most of the West Yorkshire trades council, ILP and Labour Party, organisations were represented. The Leeds Labour Party decided to attend by 75 votes to 15, the Leeds Trades Council by the much narrower margin of

191

37 votes to 30. The Bradford and Halifax trades councils and ILP organisations also attended.[54] Prominent West Yorkshire figures such as Fred Jowett MP and Fred Shaw were present, and Jowett and Joe Fineberg, both of Bradford, were appointed as members of the Central Committee of the Council of Workers' and Soldiers' Delegates.[55]

The conference was the confluence of a number of political tributaries. Its origins are to be found partly in the failure of the British Socialist Party to secure a mass following before the First World War. By 1913 the BSP, under the leadership of H.M. Hyndman, had decided to apply for affiliation to the Labour Party and to establish a United Socialist Council with the ILP and the Fabians.[56] Although the formation of the United Socialist Council had been announced with a fanfare of political demonstrations and meetings organised by the ILP and the BSP, it was quickly shelved as the pro-war stance of the Hyndman-dominated BSP clashed with the more anti-war attitudes of the ILP. It was only the defeat of the Hyndmanite section of the BSP, and the success of the international Socialist section, which permitted the Council to be resurrected as the basis of the Workers' and Soldiers' Council and the Leeds Conference. The immediate context of this resurrection was, of course, the Russian Revolution in March 1917, which symbolised the meeting of revolutionaries and reformists, and raised the prospect of moves towards an international peace settlement. But this event would have been of little significance had there not also been a general desire for peace, which the Spen Valley Trades Council delegate to the Leeds Conference, reflected when he reported that the working class was 'sick and tired of the war and thought it was time it ended'.[57]

The events, speeches and the resolutions of the Leeds Conference are legion. The four resolutions passed by the Conference - hailing the Russian Revolution, advocating moves towards establishing a general peace 'based on the rights of nations to decide their own affairs', demanding the establishment of a charter of liberties by the British Government and the establishment of Councils of Workmen and Soldiers' Delegates in every town, urban and rural district - were traducingly represented as threatening revolution in Britain by the majority of the national and local press. In reality, of course, this was not the view projected by the majority of those present at the conference.

The First World War

Indeed, the failure of the movement to establish Workers' and Soldiers' Councils throughout the country indicates this not to have been the case.

The Workers' and Soldiers' Council failed to sustain much interest in West Yorkshire. The reasons for this failure are fairly obvious. In the first place, the conference strongly supported the move towards democratic and civil rights which was occurring in Russia, only to find that commitment undermined by the Bolshevik Revolution in November 1917. But even before the Bolshevik Revolution the aims and objectives of the Leeds Conference had been challenged.

By mid-July 1917 the Labour Party had declared that none of its branches should have anything to do with Workers' and Soldiers' councils.[58] But even before this occurred doubts had been expressed at the efficacy of the putative organisation. Many of the delegates who attended as trade union and trades council representatives were immediately doubtful of the value of the conference. Even before the conference was held, the Leeds Labour Party had expressed its support for the first three resolutions but had refused to support the fourth resolution, setting up Workers' and Soldiers' councils throughout the country. These embryonic soviets were rejected by the Labour Party organisations before the Conference and by trade unionists after the Conference.

The main concern of trade unionists appears to have been that the Workers' and Soldiers' Council organisation might challenge their hegemony in organising workers. Returning from the Leeds Conference, the President of the Halifax Trades Council, G. Kaye, reported his disquiet:

> He was not at all satisfied with the Conference. ... personally, he did not support the resolution of a Workmens' and Soldiers' Council, taking the view that the place for these people was in the Labour and Socialist movement and that if multiple organisations were formed there was a great risk of wasting energy on side issues. The conference ought to be followed up by something on the lines of drastic and revolutionary action. His faith lay in the organised industrial workers, backed up by political action if they liked.[59]

When an attempt was made to set up a District Organisation of the Workers' and Soldiers' Council in West Yorkshire in the autumn of 1917, the Leeds Trades Council rejected the move for similar reasons to those referred to by Kaye. It was unanimously resolved that the propaganda work of the Soldiers' Council 'can and will be done best by the existing Labour organisations'.[60]

Most other trade unions and Labour organisations in West Yorkshire seem to have taken a similar view. Indeed, the Workers' and Soldiers' Council movement waned so quickly that the editor of the Yorkshire Factory Times reported at the end of 1917 that 'he had been 'wondering for a considerable time' what had occurred 'in connection with the great conference held in Leeds ... Somehow or other it does not seem to have gripped the public'.[61] The fact was that the Leeds Conference, and its resolutions, had been largely rejected by the organised Labour movement.

The failure of the Workers' and Soldiers' Council movement, both at the national and local level, had much to do with the internal struggles and demarcation disputes within the Labour movement. Yet there was some outside pressure upon events. The national and local press generally reported upon the Leeds Conference with undisguised hostility. In addition, there were attempts to undermine the peace campaign by bodies such as the British Workers' League, the Socialist National Defence Committee and the British Empire League.

The British Empire League had sent its representatives to Leeds to prevent the Conference being held in Albert Hall, and succeeded.[62] The Socialist National Defence Committee, a patriotic group of Socialists, threatened to put forward parliamentary candidates against ILP/Labour Party candidates who opposed the War. One of the notable figures in this organisation was Joseph Burgess, who had had a long association with the ILP since his newspaper, The Workman's Times, had been responsible for paving the way for the Bradford ILP Conference of 1893. Burgess had worked in Lancashire and London for many years before coming to live in Bradford prior to the First World War. He was editor of the Bradford Pioneer until the summer of 1915, and was elected as President of the Bradford ILP branch. Though Burgess had initially criticised British involvement in the war, proclaiming that 'We have no quarrel with Germany', he had radically altered his position by the summer of 1915 and had joined the Socialist National Defence Committee.[63] The Bradford ILP was very

The First World War

sensitive to the antics of a man who had so recently been at the centre of its activities. Not surprisingly, the pages of the <u>Bradford Pioneer</u> were filled with letters and articles in connection with what became known as the 'Burgess Comedy'.64

Yet it was the British Workers' League which posed the biggest threat to the peace campaign in West Yorkshire. Formed to unite patriotic trade unionists in the war effort, this organisation quickly found itself in vitriolic exchanges with the ILP. A. Howarth, of the BWL, said that 'Bradford had disgraced itself more than any other town in the country', whilst Victor Fisher, Secretary of the BWL, announced to a Bradford audience that 'Sinister pacifism is more rampant in your midst than in any other part of the United Kingdom with the exception of the Clyde and South Wales'.65 It is hardly surprising then that the League should form a Bradford branch towards the end of July 1917.66 This event in itself was probably not that significant and would have almost gone unnoticed had it not been for the fact that E.R. Hartley, a noted Bradford Socialist who, as we have already stressed was connected with the Dewsbury controversy of 1901 and 1902, was appointed as the organising secretary of the BWL in the Bradford area. Hartley was a powerful orator and a much-respected figure in the Bradford area but his death in early 1918 must have robbed the BWL of some of its impetus.67

Despite the efforts of the numerous organisations which proliferated in the attempt to arrest the development of the 'peace campaign', it is clear that the major reasons for the disintegration of the peace movement was more to do with the internal dissension within the Labour movement than outside pressure. What is equally evident is that the war as such does not appear to have distanced the working classes in West Yorkshire from the political Labour movement. Yet there were political changes occurring within the West Yorkshire Labour organisation.

Much attention has been focused upon the fact that the Liberal Party splintered during the war and that a section, sometimes known as the '1918 Liberals', joined the ILP and the Labour Party.68 The best example of such a defector in West Yorkshire is C.P. Trevelyan, Liberal MP for Elland between 1899 and 1918, who, through his work with the Union of Democratic Control moved into the Labour camp, en route to becoming a Labour Education Minister during the inter-war years. Yet whilst this drift from Liberalism to Labour was important it is also clear that, in West Yorkshire at least, there was a similar drift by trade unionists from the ILP to the Labour Party.

Such a switch was, of course not entirely new or totally unexpected. The Labour Party had effectively replaced the Liberal Party as the real fulcrum of Labour politics in Leeds before 1914. Yet in Bradford and Halifax, the main centres of ILP strength in West Yorkshire, there were no Labour Party organisations as such before the war. The ILP organisations ruled supreme in Labour politics.

What the war did was to undermine the established links between the ILP and trade unions. Whilst it is true that both the ILP and trade unions were divided on the issue of supporting the war effort, it is equally true that many pre-war ILP stalwarts, such as J.H. Palin and Michael Conway of the Bradford ILP, turned their attention to the Labour Party. In addition the ILP took in a significant number of anti-war Liberals who, by their very prominence, brought about an increasing divorce of the ILP and the working classes. Some of these ex-Liberals had more in common with the middle-class pacifist strand of the ILP than with the average working-class trade union member of the party.[69] This dichotomy was undoubtedly hardened with the return of many young male members of the ILP from the war.

Thus World War One had profound consequences for the Bradford ILP and served to disturb the long-established relationship between the ILP and the trade union movement. The war had had an unsettling effect upon the alliance. But it was other factors which led the trade union movement to sever its traditional links with the ILP in West Yorkshire.

Ross McKibbin has amply demonstrated that the new Labour Party Constitution of 1918, in enhancing the control of the trade union movement within the Executive at the expense of the more middle-class dominated Socialist societies, created tensions between the ILP, which was opposed to the new Constitution and the trade unions, who benefited most from it.[70] In addition it paved the way for the formation of new local Labour parties throughout the country to which local trades councils became affiliated. This transference of allegiance from the ILP to the local Labour parties did much to

The First World War

undermine the ILP in Bradford and Halifax.
   The ILP had run Labour politics in Bradford since the 1890s. During the 1890s it had dominated the political activities of the Labour movement in association with the Trades Council. From 1902 onwards it had shared the control of Bradford Labour politics with the Trades Council and the Workers' Municipal Federation, a body which had been formed to bring non-Socialist trade unionists more directly into Labour politics.[71] From 1907 the Joint Committee of the ILP and WMF made local political arrangements for the Bradford Labour movement.[72] But in 1918 the basis of that alliance was altered. Bradford was to be re-organised into four parliamentary divisions, instead of three, under the Representation of the People's Act, and a Local Labour Conference was held in November 1917 to discuss the changes.[73] At this Conference representatives of the ILP, trade unions and co-operative societies agreed to contest all four seats at the coming general election and formed a com ittee of twelve representatives to discuss the selection of candidates. However, also out of this committee, and its deliberations throughout 1918, sprang the decision to hold a Conference on the Formation of a Central Labour Party for Bradford in the September.[74] A further committee of eleven representatives was set up to draft a constitution and the Bradford Labour Party officially came into existence on 5 April 1919, formally uniting the ILP, the Trades Council and the WMF into one Labour organisation for the first time.[75] This move was to prove the undoing of the Bradford ILP whose importance within local politics began to diminish in the 1920s as the Bradford Labour Party increasingly became the focus of Labour politics.
   The Bradford ILP never fully recovered from the traumas imposed by the war and the developments within the wider Labour Movement during and after the war. It was already conscious that its prominence even within the national ILP organisations was under threat well before the end of the war. It launched the 'Bradford ILP Forward Movement' in 1918, pointing to the countrywide growth of the ILP and the tremendous steps forward which had been made in Leicester and Scotland.
   Halifax, the other ILP stronghold in West Yorkshire, experienced a similar fate. James Parker the ILP/Labour Party MP cut across many ILP members by actively participating in the recruiting campaigns during the war. This created dissension

within the Halifax ILP and the Trades Council, which whilst it intially supported recruiting, gradually drifted away from that stance, much as the Bradford Trades Council had done. The disorientation within Labour ranks appears to have been such that (in the general elections of 1918, 1922, 1923 and 1924) this once powerful Labour centre was unable to find a candidate to put forward for the single Halifax seat left by the 1918 Franchise Act. An unenterprising Labour Party took over from a declining ILP in 1918 and it was not until the 1928 parliamentary by-election that a Labour candidate, A.W. Longbottom, stood again and was swept into Parliament.[76] The war, the formation of the Halifax Labour Party, plus the fact that the Halifax MP, J.W. Whitley, became Speaker of the House of Commons in 1921, help to account for the decline of the Halifax ILP and the initial political hesitancy of the new Labour Party.

The War clearly had an impact upon West Yorkshire Labour politics. In 1914 the ILP, despite some competition for support from the Labour Party, still carried substantial political weight, particularly in its old-established centres such as Bradford and Halifax. But the Labour Party had made deep encroachments into working-class support in Leeds and many other parts of the West Yorkshire area which had only really experienced Labour stirrings with the formation of the LRCs and early local Labour parties. By 1918, however, the war had unhinged what had remained of ILP strength by creating confusion and some detachment between ILP organisations and their trade-union supporters. But the war was only one ingredient in the changing shape of Labour's political organisation in West Yorkshire. The emergence of a new Labour Constitution in 1918, and the proliferation of new constituency Labour Parties, gradually undermined the position of the ILP. It is perhaps no wonder that many ILPers, including Fred Jowett, began to question the need to continue with the ILP.[77] This anguish which both the national and West Yorkshire ILP organisations faced over whether or not to continue as separate organisations from the Labour Party is indicative of the fact that the ILPers had come to recognise the fundamental switch of allegiances that had occurred. The end product of this change is that, despite the fact that the Labour Constitution included a commitment to the ownership of the means of production, the trade unions and

The First World War

the working classes now attached themselves to an essentially Labour rather than Socialist organisation. R. McKibbin had it about right when he argued that the 1918 Labour Constitution plus the 1918 Franchise Act, which greatly increased the size of the electorate, led to the Labour Party truly becoming the party of the working classes and that class loyalty inhibited Socialist doctrine within the Labour Party.78

If West Yorkshire Labour politics became less overtly Socialist after 1918 than it was before 1914 that does not mean that it was any less successful. The 'coupon' election of December 1918 was extremely disappointing to Labour, with only one unopposed Labour candidate being returned for the 23 West Yorkshire constituencies which had just been reformed. Yet, despite its problems, the Labour Party had weathered the war rather better than the Liberals, had enhanced its working-class support, and was clearly to be seen as the liberating force for the working classes in the future. The ILP, which figured prominently in shaping Labour politics before 1914, was left to dwell upon the role of Socialists inside, and outside, the Labour Party.

NOTES

1. Trevor Wilson, The Downfall of the Liberal Party, p. 29.
2. Yorkshire Observer Budget, 13 Apr. 1914.
3. Bradford Trades and Labour Council, Minutes, 7 Nov. 1912.
4. Photocopies of newscuttings, normally without date or source, from A. Gardiner's scrapbook. Copies are held by Dr. K. Laybourn.
5. Roberts joined the ILP in the mid 1890s, was a member of the Bradford School Board, along with Margaret McMillan, between 1897 and 1903, but left the ILP in 1903 due to its unwillingness to co-operate with the Liberals. He drifted back to the Labour ranks on the eve of the First World War.
6. Bradford Pioneer, 9 Jan. 1914.
7. Georges Haupt, Socialism and the Great War: The Collapse of the Second International (Oxford University Press, London, 1972), pp. 195-215.
8. Bradford Pioneer, 9 Jan. 1914.
9. Cross, Philip Snowden, p. 129.
10. Bradford Labour Echo, 23 Nov. 1895; Bradford Daily Telegraph, 4 Oct. 1912; Bradford Pioneer,

The First World War

25 Jan. 1918; K. Laybourn, 'The Defence of Bottom Dog: The Independent Labour Party in Local Politics', pp. 234-5.
11. Bradford Pioneer, 22 Oct. 1915.
12. Ibid., 26 Oct. 1917.
13. Ibid., 19 Apr. 1918.
14. Bradford Daily Telegraph, 30 Dec. 1918.
15. Bradford Pioneer, 14 Aug. 1914.
16. Yorkshire Factory Times, 27 Aug. 1914.
17. Bradford Pioneer, 28 Apr. 1916.
18. Dr. Hector Munro took the first Volunteer Motor Ambulance Corps to the front and a Dr. Munro Fund was formed to provide financial help for this unit. See the Bradford Pioneer, 8, 15 Jan. 1915.
19. Bradford Pioneer, 25 Feb. 1916.
20. Ibid., 1 Mar. 1918.
21. Yorkshire Factory Times, 8 Oct. 1914.
22. ILP Archive, Francis Johnson Collection, 1915/72.
23. Yorkshire Factory Times, 3 Sep. 1914.
24. Ibid., 12 Nov. 1914.
25. Bradford Pioneer, 9 Apr. 1915.
26. Ibid., 2 Jun. 1916.
27. Brockway, Socialism over Sixty Years, p. 152.
28. Bradford Pioneer, 2 Jun. 1916.
29. Ibid., 2 Jun. 1916, 13 Apr. 1917.
30. Republished from the Merthyr Pioneer, in the Bradford Pioneer, 21 Apr. 1914.
31. Bradford Pioneer, 2 Jun. 1916.
32. Ibid., 14 Aug. 1914.
33. Ibid., 16 Oct. 1914.
34. Sowerby Division Labour Representation Association, Calderdale Archives Collection, TU 51/1, Minutes, 1 May 1915.
35. Ibid., 29 Jul. 1917.
36. Jowitt and Laybourn, 'The Wool Textile Dispute of 1925', pp. 11-12.
37. Yorkshire Factory Times, 29 Oct. 1914.
38. Bradford Trades and Labour Council, Minutes, 7 Nov. 1912.
39. Ibid., 15 Jan., 13 Feb., 8 Nov., 1915.
40. Bradford Trades and Labour Council, Year Book, 1914 (Bradford Trades Council, Bradford, 1915).
41. Bradford Trades and Labour Council. Minutes, 8 Feb. 1917. Palin took up his duties in France on 12 Feb. 1917.
42. Bradford Trades and Labour Council, Minutes, 17 Jun. 1915.
43. Ibid., 5 Nov. 1915.

44. Ibid., 10 Dec. 1915.
45. Ibid., 8 Nov., 9 Dec., 1915; 3 Jan. 1916.
46. Ibid., 9 Sep. 1915.
47. Ibid., 7, 30 Dec. 1916, 9 Jan. 1917.
48. Ibid., May and Jun. 1917.
49. Ibid., 29 Nov. 1917.
50. Huddersfield and District No-Conscription Council, Inaugural Meeting, 16 Jan. 1916. Deposited in the Polytechnic Library, Huddersfield.
51. Ibid., 2 Jul. 1917.
52. Huddersfield and District Council for Civil Liberties, 6 Aug. 1918. Deposited in the Polytechnic Library, Huddersfield.
53. British Labour and the Russian Revolution: The Leeds Convention: a report from the Daily Herald, with an Introduction by Ken Coates (Spokesman Books, no place or date of publication given), p. 18.
54. Yorkshire Factory Times, 7, 14 Jun. 1917.
55. British Labour and the Russian Revolution, p. 18.
56. Ibid., pp. 6-7.
57. Bradford Pioneer, 8 Jun. 1917.
58. Stephen White, 'Soviets in Britain: The Leeds Convention of 1917', International Review of Social History, vol. XIX (1974), Part 2, pp. 165-93.
59. Yorkshire Factory Times, 14 Jul. 1917.
60. White, 'Soviets in Britain', p. 191.
61. Yorkshire Factory Times, 13 Dec. 1917.
62. Ibid., 7 Jun. 1917.
63. Bradford Pioneer, 7 Aug. 1914, 30 Jul, 29 Dec. 1916; Cross, Philip Snowden, p. 166.
64. Bradford Pioneer, 8 Dec. 1916.
65. Bradford Weekly Telegraph, 9 Nov. 1917; Bradford Pioneer, 13 Jul. 1917.
66. Bradford Pioneer, 27 Jul. 1917.
67. Ibid., 25 Jan. 1918.
68. Bernard Barker, 'The Anatomy of Reform: The Social and Political Ideas of the Labour Leadership in Yorkshire', International Review of Social History, vol. xviii (1973), Part 1, pp. 1-27.
69. Ibid.,
70. McKibbin, The Evolution of the Labour Party 1910-1924, pp. 91-106.
71. Workers' Municipal Federation, Minute Books, 1902-16, in the Bradford Trades and Labour Council Collection, Archives, Bradford Central Library.
72. Ibid., 4 Mar. 1907.
73. Bradford Trades and Labour Council, Minutes, 15 Nov. 1917.

74. Ibid., 14 Sep. 1918.
75. *Bradford Pioneer*, 11 Apr. 1919.
76. Ibid., 29 Mar. 1918.
77. R.E. Dowse, *Left in the Centre* (Longman, London, 1966), pp. 35-48.
78. McKibbin, *The Evolution of the Labour Party 1910-1924*, pp. 236-47.

CONCLUSION

David Howell has noted, in his book British Workers and the Independent Labour Party 1888-1906, that the course of early Labour history was indirect and that each community varied in its response to the emergence of the ILP.[1] The varied industrial structures of communities, the role of individual trade union leaders, the extent to which the paternalism of industrial masters was prevalent, all helped to ensure different patterns of Labour development. This varied pattern was particularly evident in West Yorkshire where the variety of products manufactured by the woollen, worsted and engineering industries supported a variety of local industrial experiences. The Labour movement in Bradford, dominated by the production of worsted and fancy dress woollen goods, which gave rise to much female employment, was different in some respects from the experience of the Halifax Labour movement where the male-dominated engineering industry of Halifax was as important as the woollen industry in the local economy. The experiences of the industrial communities also differed widely from that of more rural communities such as Colne Valley, giving rise to a different type of Labour movement. But what gave this rather amorphous West Yorkshire Labour movement a recognisable form was the growing involvement of trade unionism and the increasing direction given by the national Labour leadership.

It was trade unionism which underpinned the burgeoning Labour movement in West Yorkshire. The ILP's capture of many trades councils in the early 1890s paved the way for the extension of its influence amongst trade unions. Even in areas where trade unionism was weak, as in Colne Valley, it is clear that many of the leading local Labour politicians were in fact trade unionists. The only

Conclusion

difference between many Labour strongholds and areas of patchy Labour support was the strength of the local trade union movement. In areas where trade unionism was firmly established and closely linked with the ILP, as was the case in Bradford and Halifax, powerful and effective political Labour organisations emerged. In other areas, where trade unionism was weak and ineffective, or where the ILP's trade-union links were not widely established, the ILP and Socialist organisations proved to be less resilient, prone to bouts of frenzied political activity followed by lengthy periods of inactivity in the wake of political adversity. This latter case was particularly evident in Keighley, and even Colne Valley, despite the return of Victor Grayson in the 1907 parliamentary by-election, before the First World War.

The intrusion of Keir Hardie, Ramsay MacDonald, Philip Snowden, and other members of the Labour leadership, into the affairs of the local Labour parties in West Yorkshire, whilst it was much resented, did help to temper the unrealistic political ambitions of some organisations and to harbour resources for more effective action in the future. These Labour leaders were able to direct the affairs of the ILP and the Labour Party by the control they exercised over the NAC of the ILP and the NEC of the Labour Party, and by their control over what was discussed at both ILP and Labour Party conferences. In addition their access to national funds to support parliamentary contests made their wishes insuperable to the majority of local Labour organisations. It is evident that in the conflicts associated with the candidatures for the Leeds seats, Keighley and Colne Valley, that the Labour leadership was attempting to exert its will, couched in terms of the needs of national responsibility, the desire to nurture trade-union support and, for MacDonald particularly, the need to establish and preserve some type of Progressive Alliance with Liberalism.

By allying itself with trade unionism, and by deferring Socialism for a later date, the ILP organisations in West Yorkshire secured increasing political success. From the 1890s to 1906 they made many local political gains. In 1906 they secured two parliamentary representatives, to which was added a third by the Colne Valley by-election of 1907. The euphoria of success was only briefly tempered by the improvement in some Liberal organisations after 1906 and the local political

Conclusion

alliances which Liberal organisations struck up with the Tories, and from 1910 onwards the ILP and the Labour Party swiftly eroded the local political power base of West Yorkshire Liberalism. By the First World War it was clear that the Liberal Party was incapable of arresting Labour's growth in West Yorkshire.

The continued domination of old Liberal ideas in West Yorkshire, based upon the views of a small number of industrial magnates, made it difficult for the Liberals to respond to the Labour challenge. Whilst an increasing proportion of the working class were demanding social reforms and collective action the Liberal Party remained firmly individualistic in its opinions, unwilling to contemplate the extension of the powers and responsibilities of the state and local authorities. They preferred, for instance, to recouch charity by the formation of guilds of help and proved to be hostile to reforms such as municipal school feeding. There is little evidence that their views were tempered by the more collectivist new-Liberal ideas which were emerging, though there were some new Liberals in West Yorkshire and though there is some evidence that a Progressive Alliance operating in Halifax to return James Parker as MP in 1906. Faced with the obdurate old-Liberal attitudes of most West Yorkshire Liberal organisations many working-class voters transferred their political allegiance to the ILP and the Labour Party.

By 1918 the Labour Party had effectively replaced the Liberal Party as the representative of the working classes, becoming the vehicle for the realisation of working-class aspirations. It is clear that the transferrence of the working-class vote from the Liberal Party to the Labour Party in West Yorkshire was only accomplished as a result of the alliance of trade unions with Labour's political organisations, and many ILP members would have concurred with W.H. Drew's image of the ILP and trade unionism as being two aspects of a single homogeneous Labour movement aimed at the emancipation of the working classes from poverty and exploitation.[2] That alliance ensured that the established two-party system would have been cracked in West Yorkshire even if there had been no First World War.

NOTES

1. Howell, British Workers and the Independent Labour Party 1888-1906, pp. 277-82.

Conclusion

2. *Bradford Labour Echo*, 1 Jun. 1895.

EPILOGUE

The inter-war years saw the continued decline of Liberalism in West Yorkshire. Whilst the Liberal Party was able to hold on to more than half the parliamentary seats in West Yorkshire at the 1918 General Election it had entered its fissiparous years, and its parliamentary performance was largely achieved as a result of the support of Conservative votes for Coalition Liberal candidates. Only one of the twelve Liberal MPs returned in 1918 was not a Lloyd George Liberal. Once shorn of the Coalition Alliance, the Liberal Party in West Yorkshire quickly disintegrated. By the late 1920s and early 1930s the Liberal Party was unable to make much of a parliamentary splash in the region, and its presence after the 1935 General Election was entirely confined to three National Liberals, including Sir John Simon, MP for Spen Valley, whose politics were almost undistinguishable from those of the Conservative-dominated National Government. The pre-1914 Liberal Party barely survived in West Yorkshire outside a few local, and isolated, pockets of support in areas such as Hunslet, Huddersfield, Bradford South, and Colne Valley. Even here, the return of Liberal councillors was more of interest as an historical curiosity than as an augury for the much vaunted Liberal revival.

The fact is that the old support of the Liberal Party was now divided between the Conservative and Labour parties. Much of the old middle-class and upper-working class vote had been captured by the Conservatives and the vast majority of the working-class votes had been secured by the Labour Party. Not surprisingly, it was these two parties which shared the major political honours of the inter-war years. In parliamentary and municipal contests it was they who dominated the two-party political

Epilogue

system and it is clear that, had it not been for the unusual circumstances of the 1931 General Election which returned the MacDonald National Government to power, West Yorkshire would have been regarded as a staunch Labour stronghold during the inter-war years.

Ironically, the ILP which had been responsible for the demise of West Yorkshire Liberalism was itself to become redundant. After the war many members had begun to question the need to continue with the party given that the Labour Party had acquired a Socialist programme. What kept many West Yorkshire members within the ILP was the sense of history and achievement which had surrounded its work. Their commitment was often more a symbolic gesture to the past than a demonstration of their faith that the ILP could continue to shape political events. The thinness of this commitment was demonstrated in the 'Disaffiliation Crisis' of 1932.

The immediate context of this crisis was the decision by the Parliamentary Labour Party to ensure that all Labour MPs pledged themselves to obey the Standing Orders of the party. This followed in the wake of MacDonald's defection to the National Government and could be seen as an attempt to ensure that there was party unity within Parliament. Jimmy Maxton and the ILP leadership saw the move in an entirely different light; regarding it as an attempt to restrict their freedom of expression. Since the political balance of the ILP had moved from Yorkshire and Lancashire to Scotland during the 1920s it is clear that Maxton, and his 'Clydeside' supporters were able to press for disaffiliation within the national movement. Their action was opposed throughout West Yorkshire.

The main critic of the campaign for disaffiliation was Willie Leach, a manufacturer and onetime employer of Fred Jowett, who found the whole idea of disaffiliation unacceptable and undesirable. In a powerful polemic he wrote that

> For some years the I.L.P. has been unhappily losing prestige and membership, due, I think, to two main causes. Firstly a disposition towards the belief that its work as a party was finished when the Labour Party adopted a Socialist programme and secondly because of the irreconcilable and foolish actions of some of its quarrelsome M.P.s. Vanities and disappointed ambitions have played their part. Besides all this the younger end have keenly

Epilogue

> desired quicker speed and spectacular action.
> Certain spectacular actions have, however,
> served to bring discredit. Leadership has a
> lot to answer for.
> ...
> I do not know the real will of the I.L.P.
> membership. I find it very difficult to be-
> lieve that a full party plebiscite on the
> issue of disaffiliation would endorse the
> views of Maxton and Co. I fear that branches
> may pass disaffiliation resolutions at tiny
> meetings where only the fiery element is in
> attendance and decisions will be taken which
> never would be taken on a proper plebiscite
> vote of the whole membership.
> ...
> MacDonald and Co. have gone East, the disaff-
> iliation would go West. All the fruits of ill-
> will, antagonism and open war are bound to
> follow in both cases. It would be the most
> melancholy situation that has ever yet arisen
> in British Labour politics.
> ... Suppose the disaffiliationists win.
> They will do so, as I think, on a minority
> vote of the members. They will march into
> the wilderness with less than half of the
> membership. It is all very sad and discon-
> certing.[1]

The precise details of Leach's attack were criticised by Fred Jowett, whose attitude towards disaffiliation had initially been to oppose the move but had become one of conditional affiliation.[2] Since the condition was that the Labour Party should drop its insistence upon imposing Standing Orders, this effectively meant that Jowett was in favour of disaffiliation. The conflict between the two protagonists was fought out in the press and at the meetings of the Bradford ILP in July 1932.[3] The Bradford ILP's Special Meeting favoured disaffiliation by the relatively narrow majority of 112 votes to 86, and the Bradford Pioneer published an 'Open Letter' to the delegates attending the ILP Special Conference at Jowett Hall, Bradford, advising them not to leave the Labour Party: 'The I.L.P. was born in Bradford. Have you come to bury it'.[4]

The decision of the National ILP to disaffiliate from the Labour Party was carried by Maxton, Brockway, Jowett and the 'Suicide Squad', despite the entreaties of Leach and the Bradford Pioneer.[5] The events which followed emphasised the prophetic

Epilogue

nature of Leach's polemical article. The Bradford ILP found difficulties in continuing to meet at Jowett Hall, lost much financial support, and found that only one of the 32 members of the Labour group on Bradford City Council were prepared to leave the Labour Party.6 Both the West Yorkshire and the national ILP organisations collapsed quickly in the wake of the disaffiliation decision.

It is interesting that Fred Jowett, standing as an ILP candidate, was unsuccessful in the Bradford East contest in the 1935 General Election, whilst Willie Leach was returned as Labour MP for Bradford Central. The fact is that the ILP collapsed as a result of the events of 1932. The <u>Bradford Pioneer</u> was correct, in commenting on the decision of the Special Conference, that

> The Independent Labour Party now joins the numerous small groups engaged in useless and obscure warfare against the organised Labour army. Along with the Communist Party, the Socialist Party of Great Britain and other eccentric groups quite unknown to the general public, the total sterility of a once great and influential party seems assured.7

After more than forty years in the political wilderness the ILP died as a political party in 1975.

NOTES

1. <u>Bradford Pioneer</u>, 8 Jul. 1932.
2. Ibid., 29 Jul. 1932.
3. Ibid., 8, 15, 22, 29 Jul. 1932.
4. Ibid., 29 Jul. 1932.
5. Ibid., 22 Jul. 1932.
6. Ibid., 5, 12 Aug. 1932.
7. Ibid., 5 Aug. 1932.

BIBLIOGRAPHY

Ashraf, M. Bradford Trades Council, 1872-1972 (Bradford Trades Council, Bradford, 1972)
Barker, B. 'The Anatomy of Reform: The Social and Political Ideas of the Labour Leadership in Yorkshire', International Review of Social History, vol. xviii (1973), Part 1, pp. 1-27
Bellamy, J. and Saville J. (eds) Dictionary of Labour Biography, vol. 3 (Macmillan, London, 1976) vol. 4 (Macmillan, London, 1977) vol. 6 (Macmillan, London, 1982)
Blewitt, N. 'The Franchise in the United Kingdom 1885-1918', Past and Present, 32 (1965), pp. 27-56
Board of Trade, Report on Trade Unions, 1896 (c.8644); Report on Trade Unions, 1900 (cd. 773)
Bradford Daily Telegraph
Bradford Labour Echo
Bradford Observer
Bradford Observer Budget
Bradford Pioneer
Bradford Review
Bradford Trades Council, Minutes, Archive Collection, Bradford Central Library
────── Year Book for 1914 (Bradford Trades Council, Bradford, 1915)
────── Workers' Municipal Federation, Minute Book, 1902-19, Archive Collection, Bradford Central Library
Bradford Typographical Society, Minutes and records, J.B. Priestley Library, University of Bradford
British Labour and the Russian Revolution: The Leeds Convention: a report from the Daily Herald: with an Introduction by Ken Coates (Spokesman Books, no place or date of publication given)
Brockway, A.F. Socialism over Sixty Years: The Life of Jowett of Bradford (Allen and Unwin, London, 1946)

Bibliography

Cahill, M. and Jowitt, J. 'The New Philanthropy: The Emergence of the Bradford City Guild of Help', Journal of Social Policy, vol. 9, Pt. 3 (Jul. 1980), pp. 359-82
―――― 'The Bradford Guild of Help Papers', History Workshop Journal, 15 (Spring, 1983), p. 152
Capital and Labour
Clarion
Clark, D. Colne Valley: Radicalism to Socialism (Longman, London, 1981)
Clarke, P.F. Lancashire and the New Liberalism (Cambridge University Press, London, 1971)
―――― 'The Electoral Position of the Liberal and Labour parties 1910-1914', English Historical Review, 1975, pp. 828-36
―――― 'Liberals, Labour and the franchise', English Historical Review, 1977, pp. 582-9
Colne Valley Labour League (Party/Union/Socialist League), Minutes, The Polytechnic Library, Huddersfield, also produced on microfilm by Microfilm Ltd, East Ardsley, West Yorkshire
Coneys, M. 'The Labour Movement and the Liberal Party in Rochdale 1890-1906', unpublished MA dissertation, The Polytechnic, Huddersfield, 1982
Craig, F.W.S. British Parliamentary Election Results 1885-1918 (Macmillan, London, 1974)
―――― British Parliamentary Election Results 1918-1949 (Macmillan, London, 1977)
Cross, C. Philip Snowden (Barrie & Rockliffe, London, 1966)
Dowse, R.E. Left in the Centre (Longman, London, 1966)
Drake, H.J.O. 'John Lister of Shibden Hall, 1847-1933', unpublished PhD thesis, University of Bradford, 1973
Emy, H.V. Liberals, Radicals and Social Politics 1892-1914 (Cambridge University Press, London, 1973)
First Annual Conference of the British Socialist Party (Communist Party of Great Britain, London, 1970 reprint)
Forward
Foster, J. Class Struggle and the Industrial Revolution (Weidenfeld and Nicolson, London, 1974)
Freeden, M. The New Liberalism: An Ideology of Social Reform (Clarendon, Oxford, 1978)
Groves, R. The Strange Case of Victor Grayson (Pluto Press, London, 1975)
Halifax Courier
Halifax Guardian
Haupt, G. Socialism and the Great War: The Collapse

Bibliography

of the Second International (Oxford University Press, London, 1972)
Hill, J. 'Manchester and Salford Politics and the Early Development of the Independent Labour Party', International Review of Social History, vol. xxvi (1981), Part 2, pp. 171-201
Holton, R. British Syndicalism 1900-1914 (Pluto Press, London, 1976)
Howell, D. The British Working Class and the Independent Labour Party 1888-1906 (Manchester University Press, Manchester, 1983)
Howkins, A. 'Edwardian Liberalism and Industrial Unrest: a class view of the decline of Liberalism', History Workshop Journal, 4 (Autumn, 1977), pp. 143-61
Huddersfield Borough Council, Minutes
Huddersfield and District No-Conscription Council, Minutes
Huddersfield and District Council for Civil Liberties, Minutes
Huddersfield Examiner
Huddersfield Trades Council, Minutes
Hyman, R. The Workers' Union (Clarendon Press, Oxford, 1971)
Illingworth, A. Fifty Years of Politics: Mr. Alfred Illingworth: Retrospect (Bradford Newspaper Co. Ltd, Bradford, 1905)
ILP Manifestoes, Deed Box 13, Case 64, Archive Department, Bradford Central Library
ILP National Archive, F. Johnson Collection, deposited in the British Library and microfilmed by Harvester Press, Brighton, 1981
ILP News
Independent Review
Inglis, K. Churches and the Working Classes in Victorian England (Routledge and Kegan Paul, London, 1963)
Interview with Mrs Ada Dalby, 1979, in possession of Dr. K. Laybourn
James, D. 'The Keighley ILP 1892-1900: Realising the Kingdom of Heaven' in J.A. Jowitt and R.K.S. Taylor (eds.), Bradford 1890-1914: The Cradle of the ILP (Bradford Occasional Papers, No. 2, University of Leeds Department of Adult Education & Extramural Studies, Bradford, 1980), pp. 56-72
——— 'The Emergence of the Keighley Independent Labour Party', unpublished MA dissertation, The Polytechnic, Huddersfield, 1980)
Jowitt, J.A. and Laybourn, K. 'The Wool Textile Dispute of 1925', The Journal of Local Studies, Vol. 2, No. 1 (Spring, 1982) pp. 10-27

Bibliography

Joyce, P. Work, Society and Politics: The Culture of the Factory in Later Victorian England (Harvester Press, Brighton, 1980)
Justice
Keighley Labour Journal
Keighley News
Kendall, W. The Revolutionary Movement in Britain 1900-1921 (Weidenfeld and Nicolson, London, 1969)
King, S.J. 'Bradford Politics and the Boer War' unpublished MA dissertation, The Polytechnic, Huddersfield, 1983
Labour Leader
Labour Party Archive, Labour Representation Committee Correspondence, 1900-7, also microfilmed by Harvester Press, Brighton, 1981
Labour Prophet
Labour Union Journal (Bradford, 1891)
Laybourn, K. 'The Attitude of Yorkshire Trade Unions to the Economic and Social Problems of the Great Depression, 1873-1896', unpublished PhD thesis, University of Lancaster, 1973
────── 'The Manningham Mills Strike: Its importance in Bradford History', Bradford Antiquary, New Series, Part xlvi, 1976
────── 'The Bradford Labour Movement and the Keir Hardie By-Election in East Bradford, November 1896' in J.A. Jowitt and R.K.S. Taylor (eds.), Nineteenth Century Bradford Elections (Bradford Centre Occasional Papers No. 1, University of Leeds Department of Adult & Extramural Studies, 1979), pp. 74-87
────── 'The Trade Unions and the I.L.P.: The Manningham Experience', in J.A. Jowitt and R.K.S. Taylor (eds.), Bradford 1890-1914: The Crade of the Independent Labour Party (University of Leeds Department of Adult Education & Extramural Studies, Bradford, 1980), pp. 24-44
────── '"The Defence of Bottom Dog": The Independent Labour Party in Local Politics', in D.G. Wright and J.A. Jowitt (eds.), Victorian Bradford (City of Bradford, Metropolitan Council, Libraries Division, Bradford, 1982), pp. 223-44
────── 'The Issue of School Feeding in Bradford, 1904-1907', Journal of Educational Administration and History, vol. xiv, No. 2. Jul. 1982, pp. 30-8
Leeds Trades Council, Minutes
Leeds Typographical Circular, Leeds Graphical Society
Lister, J. 'Early History of the ILP Movement in Halifax', MSS copy in Calderdale Archives Collection

Bibliography

Lichtheim, G. The Origins of Socialism (Weidenfeld and Nicolson, London, 1968)
Lockwood, E. Colne Valley Folk (Heath Cranton, London, 1936)
Mann, T. Memoirs (The Labour Publishing Co. Ltd., London, 1923)
Mattison, A. Collection, Brotherton Library, University of Leeds
McBriar, A.M. Fabian Socialism and English Politics, 1884-1918 (Cambridge University Press, London, 1966)
McKibbin, R. The Evolution of the Labour Party 1910-1924 (Oxford University Press, London, 1974)
McLellan, D. Karl Marx: His Life and Thought (Macmillan, London, 1978)
Morgan, K. 'The New Liberalism and the Challenge of Labour: The Welsh Experience', in Brown, K.D. (ed.) Essays in Anti-Labour History (Macmillan, London, 1974), pp. 159-82
Morris, A.J.A. C.P. Trevelyan, 1870-1958: Portrait of a Radical (Blackstaff Press, Belfast, 1977)
Parton, C. 'Liberal Individualism and Infant Mortality: The Infant Welfare Movement in Huddersfield 1900-1918', unpublished MA dissertation, Huddersfield Polytechnic, 1982
Pearce, C. The Manningham Mills Strike in Bradford, December 1890 - April 1891 (University of Hull Occasional Papers in Economic and Social History, No. 7, 1975)
Pelling, H. The Origins of the Labour Party 1880-1900 (Macmillan, London, 1974)
Perks, R.W. 'Trade Unionism and the Emergence of the Labour Party in Huddersfield', forthcoming article in J. Halstead and W. Lancaster (eds.) Socialist Studies (Harvester, Brighton, 1984)
―――― 'Liberalism and the Challenge of Labour in West Yorkshire 1885-1914, with special reference to Huddersfield', about to be submitted for a PhD, CNAA, The Polytechnic, Huddersfield at the time of preparation
Pugh, M. 'Yorkshire and the New Liberalism', Journal of Modern History, vol. 50, Pt. 3 (1978), D 1139- D1155
Purdue, A.W. 'The Liberal and Labour Parties in North-East Politics, 1900-1914: The Struggle for Supremacy', International Review of Social History, vol. xxvi, Pt. 1 (1981), pp. 1-24
Price, R. An Imperial War and the British Working Class (Routledge and Kegan Paul, London, 1972)
Reid, F. 'Socialist Sunday Schools in Britain, 1892-1939', International Review of Social History,

Bibliography

vol. xi (1966), pp. 18-47

Reynolds, J. and Laybourn, K. 'The Emergence of the Independent Labour Party in Bradford', <u>International Review of Social History</u>, xx, Pt. 3 (1975), pp. 313-46

Reynolds, J. <u>The Letter Press Printers of Bradford</u> (Bradford Graphical Society, Bradford, 1972)

────── <u>Saltaire: An Introduction to the Village of Sir Titus Salt</u> (Bradford Art Galleries and Museum, City Trail, No. 2, Bradford, 1976)

────── <u>The Great Paternalist, Titus Salt and the Growth of Nineteenth Century Bradford</u> (Temple Smith, London, 1983), chapter four

Roberts, A.W. 'Leeds Liberalism and Late Victorian Politics', <u>Northern History</u>, vol. v (1970), pp. 131-56

────── 'The Liberal Party in West Yorkshire, 1885-1895', unpublished PhD. thesis, University of Leeds, 1979

Ross, W.D. 'Bradford Politics 1880-1906', unpublished PhD thesis, University of Bradford, 1977

Ruskin, J. <u>The Crown of Wild Olives</u> (George Allen, London, 1886, 1906)

<u>Saltaire and Shipley Times</u>

Saville, J. 'Trade Unions and Free Labour: The Background to the Taff Vale Decision' in A. Briggs and J. Saville, (eds.), <u>Essays in Labour History</u> (Macmillan, London, 1960), pp. 317-50

Sheppard, M.G. and Halstead, J.L. 'Labour's Municipal Election Performance in Provincial England and Wales 1901-1913', <u>Bulletin of the Society for the Study of Labour History</u>, no. 39 (Autumn, 1979) pp. 39-62

Sheppard, M.G. 'The Effect of the Franchise Provisions on the Social and Sex Composition of the Municipal Electorate 1882 1914, <u>Bulletin of the Society for the Study of Labour History</u>, no. 45 (Autumn, 1982), pp. 19-25

Sowerby Division Labour Representation Association, Calderdale Archives Collection, TU 51/1, Minutes

Steele, E.D. 'Imperialism and Leeds Politics, c. 1850-1914', in D. Fraser (ed.), <u>A History of Modern Leeds</u> (Manchester University Press, Manchester, 1980)

Terrill, R. <u>R.H. Tawney and His Times: Socialism and Fellowship</u> (Andre Deutsch, London, 1973)

<u>The Industrial Syndicalist</u>

Thompson, E.P. <u>William Morris: Romantic to Revolutionary</u> (Merlin Press, London, 1955, 1977 edition)

────── 'Homage to Tom Maguire' in A. Briggs and J. Saville (eds.), <u>Essays in Labour History</u>

Bibliography

(Macmillan, London, 1960), pp. 276-316
Thompson, L. The Enthusiasts: A Biography of J & K Bruce Glasier (Victor Gollancz, London, 1971)
Thornton, W.T. On Labour: Its Wrongful Claims and Rightful Dues: Its Actual, Present and Possible Future (London, 1869, 1870 edition)
Todmorden Trades Council, TU 38. 1-11, Minutes and Records, Calderdale Archives Collection
Trade Union Commission, eleventh and final report, Cmnd 4123, xxi, 1868-9
Turner, B. A Short History of the General Union of Textile Workers (Yorkshire Factory Times, Heckmondwyke, 1920)
────── About Myself (Toulmin, London, 1930)
Wald, K.D. 'Class and the Vote Before the First World War', British Journal of Political Science, vol. 8 (1978) pp. 441-57
Watmough, P.A. 'The Membership of the Social Democratic Federation, 1885-1902', Bulletin of the Society for the Study of Labour History, no. 34, Spring 1977, pp. 35-40
Webb, S and Webb, B. The History of Trade Unionism (Longman, Green, London, 1894)
Williams, J.E. 'The Leeds Corporation Strike in 1913', in A. Briggs and J. Saville, Essays in Labour History, 1886-1923 (Macmillan, London, 1971), pp. 70-94
Wilson, T. The Downfall of the Liberal Party (Col (Collins, London, 1966, 1968)
────── The Political Diaries of C.P. Scott 1911-1928 (Collins, London, 1970)
White, S. 'Soviets in Britain: The Leeds Convention of 1917', International Review of Social History, vol. xix (1974), Part 2, pp. 165-93
Woodhouse, T. 'Trade Unions and Independent Labour Politics in Leeds, 1885-1914', unpublished paper produced in the mid 1970s
────── 'The working class' in D. Fraser (ed.), A History of Modern Leeds (Manchester University Press, Manchester, 1980), pp. 353-88
Wright, D.G. 'The Bradford Election of 1874' in J.A. Jowitt and R.K.S. Taylor (eds.), Nineteenth Century Bradford Elections (Bradford Centre Occasional Papers No. 1. University of Leeds Department of Adult Education & Extramural Studies, Bradford, 1980, pp. 50-73
Yeo, S. 'A New Life: The Religion of Socialism in Britain 1883-1896', History Workshop Journal, 4 (Autumn, 1977), p. 5-56
Yorkshire Factory Times
Young Socialist

INDEX

Amalgamated Society of
  Engineers 25-6, 48-9,
  60, 185
Anderson, W.C. 146, 158,
  165-6
Asquith, H. 1-2

Bartley, James 22, 32-3,
  42, 47-8, 60, 116,
  124,
Batley 185
  LRC 107
  Labour Union/ILP 22,
  24, 43, 158
  Trades Council 44-5,
  125
Beever, James 22, 35,
  51, 89-93
Belgium 15, 185-6
Bland, Paul 22, 30, 59
Bland, W. 165-6
Blatchford, Montague 34,
  90-2
Blatchford, Robert, 34
  90-3, 117
Boer War 110-12
Bradford
  Board of Guardians
  6, 123
  Cinderalla Club 123-4
  Conservative Working
  Men's Association 9,
  18
  Daily Telegraph 27,
  63
  East 30, 68

East by-election 95,
  104
Guild of Help 123-4
Labour Church 50, 61,
  95, 117
Labour Echo 63, 88,
  97, 182
Labour Electoral Asso-
  ciation 33, 47-50, 68,
  81, 83
Labour Union/ILP 4, 8,
  42-3, 48-50, 58-60,
  62, 64-5, 68-9, 96-7,
  108-9, 111-14, 130,
  158, 179-84, 192, 194-
  8, 204-5
  see also ILP Conferen-
  ces 1893 and 1914
Liberals 47, 49, 67,
  78, 166
Liberal-Conservative
  Pact 150-1, 154
municipal housing 169
Observer 6, 27-9, 32,
  42, 49-50, 65-6, 78,
  81-2, 85, 87-8, 97,
  109, 115, 147, 152,
  180
Printers 26-7
School Meals Issue
  122-4, 168, 205
SDF/SDP/BSP 98, 125
Socialist Sunday Scho-
  ols 117-19
Trades Council 9, 19,
  30-3, 44-51, 58, 105-6,

218

Index

113, 116, 179 188–90, 198
Typographical Society 30, 48
Unemployed Emergency Committee 66–7, 120–3
Workers' Municipal Federation 47, 103, 116, 197
Brighouse
  Labour Union/ILP/LRC 59
  Trades Council 45
British Socialist Party 159–163
Burgess, Joseph 119, 182, 193–4
Byles, William Pollard 6, 28, 81–9, 110–11

Chartists 16–17, 19, 105
Clark, David 10, 59, 61, 115, 130, 145
Clarke, P.F. 3, 134, 154, 166, 178
Clarion 91, 156, 159
Cockerline, Jessie 182–3, 188
Coit, Stanton 128, 131
Colne Valley 10, 22, 34, 80, 112, 115, 145, 148, 153, 156, 158–60
  Labour League/Union 10, 43, 59–62, 64, 71, 144–7, 154–5, 160–1
  see also Grayson, Victor
Connellan, O. 58, 87, 106, 108, 121
Cowgill, George 48, 50, 84

Dale, Rev. Bryan 34–5
Dewsbury 24, 153
  ILP 43, 59, 62, 64, 125–7, 130
  LRC 107
  Shoddy Cloth 45
  SDF 125–7
  Trades Council 45, 106, 125–7

Drew, W.H. 22, 42, 44, 50, 105, 116, 205

Elland 59, 62, 130, 195
Election Results
  local and municipal 64–6, 77–8, 108–9, 115, 148–52
  parliamentary 69, 77, 109, 153
Engels, F. 21, 30

Fabian Society 21, 35, 89
Fair Contracts 27, 124
First World War 4, 6, 10, 64, 142, 170, 178–99
Ford, Bessie 34
Ford, Isabella 34–5
Forward 120, 182
Franchise Acts
  1867 3, 15, 17–20, 29
  1884 3, 15, 29
  1918 4, 16
  1928 16–17
Friendly Society of Ironfounders 25–6

Gardiner, Arthur 172, 180–1
Garside, George 20, 60, 64
Gaskell, G.A. 30, 33
Gasworkers and General Labourers' Union 53–5, 187
Gee, Allan 22, 60, 105, 114
General Union of Textile Workers 135
George, Angus 22, 28
Gladstone, Herbert 21, 129–30, 132–3, 145–8
Glasier, J.B. 127, 143, 157, 161, 181
Glyde, Charlie 42, 98, 164, 188
Grayson, Victor 19, 59–60, 142, 144, 145–7, 155–61, 163, 166

219

Index

Halifax 21-2, 24-5, 34, 150, 191
  Boothtown Liberal Club 52
  Courier 65-6, 149-50
  Fabian Society 35, 89
  Guardian 65-6, 109, 149
  Labour Unions/ILP 35-6, 43-4, 58-60, 62, 64-5, 70, 89-94, 105, 109, 111-12, 114, 117, 130, 146, 158, 185, 192, 196-8, 204-5
  Liberal Four Hundred 52
  Tory-Liberal Alliance 150
  Trades Council 35, 45-6, 51-2, 58, 106, 184-5, 193, 198
  Workers Election Committee 116-17
Hall, Leonard 157, 159, 172
Hardaker, James 18-19, 34
Hardie, J.Keir 86, 91-3, 95-6, 110-5, 127-8, 144, 155-7, 186, 204
Hartley, Edward R. 34, 69, 98, 126-8, 133, 161, 163, 195
Hayhurst, Joseph 22, 50
Hill, James 9, 134
Hollings, John 30, 33
Horner, Herbert 165-6
Huddersfield 6, 9, 22, 24, 77, 169, 181
  by-election 1893 70
  by-election 1906 143-4
  B.S.P. 172, 181, 191
  Examiner 65, 78, 109, 115, 150, 152, 173
  Labour Churches 117
  LRC 107
  Labour Union/ILP 43, 59, 62, 64-5, 70, 89-94, 97, 99, 109, 135, 155, 191
  Liberal/Liberal Association 78, 119, 143-4
  Trades Council 44-5, 61, 106, 113-14, 187, 190
  Unemployed 66
  Worker 180
Hutton, E 82-85
Hyndman, H.M. 21, 156, 162, 172, 180, 192

Illingworth, Alfred 6, 19, 48, 68-9, 71, 76, 112, 123, 134, 169
Independent Labour Party
  Conference 1893 1, 9, 22, 30, 35, 43-50, 61, 69, 70
  Conference 1909 157-8
  Conference 1914 179
  Conference 1916 183, 186
  Conference 1917 181
  Conference 1918 185
  Conference 1932 (Special) 209
  membership 62-4, 89
  News 63, 65-66, 95-6, 109, 126, 150
  see also details of ILP under individual towns

Jarratt, J.W. 67, 88
Jowett, Frederick William 6, 22, 30, 33, 47-8, 88, 110-12, 127-8, 132-3, 143, 155-6, 161, 169, 180-1, 184-6, 189, 191-2, 198, 208-10
Judge, John 54-8
Justice 126, 163

Keighley 21, 25, 80, 104, 130, 153-4, 165-6
  business families 6
  engineering strike 51
  LRC 107, 165
  Labour Journal 79-80
  Labour Union/ILP 41, 43, 59, 62, 64, 80,

Index

118, 184, 185-6, 204
News 43, 65-6
Trades Council 9, 44-5, 51, 103, 106, 165-6
Kitson, James 21, 71, 112, 145, 147

Labour Church and related socialist activities 59-60, 117
see also relevant details for individual towns
Labour Leader 65-6, 93, 95-6, 109, 126, 147, 149-50, 156, 158
Labour Union Journal 63, 65-6
Leach, William 34, 161, 181-2, 208
Leeds 150, 153
  Labour Church 61, 95, 117, 133
  LRC 53, 58, 87, 103, 105-8, 129-30, 132
  Labour Union/ILP 43, 57, 62, 64, 70, 109, 112, 114, 191, 193, 198
  Liberal Party 20-22, 25, 34, 67, 114, 116-7
  Trades Council 30, 44-6, 53-8, 87, 106, 113-14, 121, 191, 194
  Unemployed 66, 120-1
New Liberalism 4, 10-11, 81, 85, 88-9, 114
Old Liberalism 6, 11, 40, 168
  working-class support 2
Lister, John 34-6, 58, 60-1, 69-70, 79, 89-94
Lister, Samuel Cunliffe 2, 20, 41-2
Littlewood, France 34, 43
Lloyd George, David 1-2

MacDonald, J. Ramsay 44, 87, 105-6, 108, 113, 125, 128-30, 132-3, 145, 147, 157, 171, 204
Macrae, J.D. 108, 129-130
Maguire, Tom 22, 30-2, 36, 54-5
Mahon, John Lincoln 22, 31-2, 36, 53, 56-8
Mann, Tom 54, 59, 61, 71, 92-3, 144, 172
Manningham Mills Strike 7, 40-2, 48, 87, 171-2
Marston, W. 54, 58
Marx, Karl 21, 30, 36
Mattison, Alfred 22, 30, 54
McKibbin, Ross 196, 199
Minty, George 22, 42
Morley Labour Union/ILP 63, 130, 135
  Trades Council 45
Morley, Robert 93, 131, 158
Munro, Dr. Hector 183-4
Myers, Tom 126-7

New Age 34, 156

O'Grady, James 108, 128-9, 132
Otley ILP 63, 130

Palin, J.H. 113, 161, 183, 185, 189-90, 196
Parker, James 105, 110-11, 128, 132-3, 136, 158, 183-5
Paylor, Tom 30, 53, 58
Priestman, Arthur 34, 60, 181
Pudsey 133, 163-4
  Labour Union/ILP 63, 128-30, 150, 163-5

Quelch, Harry 125-7

Radicalism 16-17
Riley, Ben 144-5, 169
Ripley, H.W. 20, 23

Index

Roberts, Rev. R. 34, 80, 180, 186-7
Robinson, Charles Leonard 22, 47, 65, 71
Royal Commission on Depression in Trade and Industry, 1886 23
Ruskin, John 21, 89

Salt, Titus 7, 16-17, 81
Saltaire 7-8, 16, 20, 22, 28, 81
Sanctuary, Jacob 22, 83, 85
Sewell, J. 47, 50
Shaftoe, Samuel 22, 29, 33-4, 47-50, 80-1
Shaw, Alfred 70, 190
Sherwall, A.J. 143, 167-8
Shipley
  ILP 43, 63, 85-6, 130
  Liberals 81-6
  Trades Council 45, 83, 106
  see also Byles, William Pollard
Smart, H. Russell 70, 157-8, 172
Snell, Harry 153, 159
Snowden, Philip 127, 131, 146, 156-7, 166, 171, 181, 204
Social Democratic Federation 21, 28, 96-98, 125-8
Socialist League 21-2, 31, 36
  Bradford 30, 32
  Leeds 30, 32, 53
Socialist Sunday schools 94-5, 117-19
Socialist Unity 91, 95-8, 158
Sowerby Bridge Labour Union/ILP 59, 63, 128-30, 187
Spen Valley 45, 130, 192
  Labour Church 117
  Labour Union/ILP 59, 63

Sugden, Walter 49, 81
Syndicalists 171-2

Taff Vale Decision 105, 110, 113-14
Tattersall, James 51-2, 89-94
Taylor, Arthur 185, 187
Thompson, E.P. 41, 46, 52, 53
Thompson, M.W. 18, 20
Tillett, Ben 48-9, 54, 61, 68-70, 79
Todmorden
  Labour Union/ILP 59
  Trades Council 45, 106, 128
Trevelyan, C.P. 88, 168, 195
Turner, Ben 22, 24, 60, 126-8, 159, 185, 187

Wakefield
  Echo 131
  LRC 103, 107, 131
  Labour Union/ILP 63-64, 160
  Trades Council 48, 106, 130-1
Walker, Joe 128, 164
West Riding Power Loom Weavers' Association 24, 41, 60, 113
  see also the General Union of Textile Workers
Wilkinson, James 128, 132, 144
Woodhouse, J.T. 112, 132, 143
Woodhouse, Tom 149-50, 152
Workers' and Soldiers' Council,
  Leeds Conference 1917 187-94
Workman's Times 194
Workers' Union 93

Yorkshire Factory Times 42-3, 121, 182, 188, 194